Fossils, Faith, and Farming

'The only true history of a country is to be found in its newspapers.'

Thomas Babington, Lord Macaulay
(1800–1859)

Edwin Sidney.
Courtesy Ipswich Borough Council Museums and Galleries.

Fossils, Faith, and Farming

Newspaper portraits of Little Cornard
in the Darwinian age
together with some account of
the Reverend Edwin Sidney, A.M.

P. H. M. COOPER

Little Cornard Conservation Society
Great Cornard, Sudbury, Suffolk
1999

Published 1999 by Little Cornard Conservation Society
23 Bures Road, Great Cornard, Sudbury, Suffolk CO10 0EJ

ISBN 0 9535463 0 6

© 1999 Peter Cooper

All rights reserved. No part of this publication may be reproduced, stored in a retrieval system, or transmitted in any form or by any means, electronic, mechanical, photocopying, recording or otherwise, without the prior permission of the author.

Cover design by Max Marschner, Ampersand Designs, Lincoln LN5 8PN
Typeset and produced for the publisher by Yard Publishing Services, Sudbury, Suffolk, CO10 2AG
Printed in Malta

British Library Cataloguing-in-publication data

A catalogue record for this publication is obtainable from the British Library

TO THE MEMORY OF MY MOTHER

who taught her children that
we are members one of another

CONTENTS

List of figures — 10
Preface and acknowledgments — 11
A note on editing and references — 15

REFLECTIONS — 17
INTRODUCTION — 22
  Little Cornard — 22
  Fires 1843, 1844 — 31
  Old-Fashioned Science — 37
    Darwin — 37
    Plato, Aristotle and St Paul — 42
    Factories and Poetry — 64
    Darwin again — 74
  Popular Science — 75
  Mudfog Years — 78
    Owen and Henslow — 86
  Edwin Sidney — 95
    Norfolk — 96
    Suffolk — 102

NEWSPAPER PORTRAITS — 135
  I   Auction 1843 — 135
  II Fire at Peacock Hall 1843 — 135
  III Fire at Caustons Hall 1844 — 136

IV	John Hum 1845	143
V	Enlarging a Sacred Edifice 1847, 1848	145
VI	Fossil Elephants 1849	147
VII	Handsome and Commodious Rectory House 1849	148
VIII	Lighting a Fire 1850	149
IX	Geology and Fertilisers 1850, 1852	149
X	Silver Salver 1851	164
XI	Late Lamented Duke 1852	166
XII	Seasonable Benevolence 1854	167
XIII	John Bell 1854	168
XIV	Ducal Visits 1856	168
XV	John Newman Sparrow 1857	169
XVI	*In Memoriam* 1857	170
XVII	Dissolving Views 1857	171
XVIII	Sapient Decision 1858	174
XIX	Sparrow's Loss 1859	175
XX	Brambles and Crinolines 1859	176
XXI	Unusual Proportion of Persons 1860	179
XXII	For The Church Missionary Society – Four Lectures:	180
	Japan 1861	180
	Islands of the Pacific 1862	182
	Madagascar 1863	184
	Arabia and the Arabs 1865	186
XXIII	Burglars? 1862	187
XXIV	Doctor of Medicine 1863	201
XXV	Wedding 1863	202

XXVI	Lecture To Juveniles 1863	204
XXVII	Henry Game 1864	205
XXVIII	Harvest Home 1860, 1864, 1865	207
XXIX	Valuable Pioneers and Coadjutors – A Letter from Dr Livingstone 1866	218
XXX	Isaac Mower 1866	219
XXXI	Brick Yard	220
	200,000 Superior White Drain Tiles 1851	220
	Henry Segers 1868	221
	Carrying on the Business 1868	221
XXXII	Michael Faraday 1868	223
XXXIII	Movements in Organic Life 1869	230
XXXIV	Unavoidably Prevented; or, Certain Crotchety People 1869	236
XXXV	Edwin Sidney 1872	240
XXXVI	John Sikes 1874	247
XXXVII	Eliza Sidney 1882	249
XXXVIII	*Terminat Hora Opus* 1891	249

Appendix I: Sermons and Offertories	253
Appendix II: Newspapers and the Reading Public	260
Further Reading	263
Index	270

FIGURES

Frontispiece: Edwin Sidney

Fig. 1	The graves of the Mumfords, Newman Sparrow and John Constable in Little Cornard churchyard	21
Fig. 2	*Farmer Giles & his Wife showing off their daughter Betty to their Neighbours on her return from School.* An etching by James Gillray from a watercolour by an amateur; published 1 January 1809	29
Fig. 3	The Great Chain of Being, as illustrated in Valdes's *Rhetorica Christiana*, of 1579	47
Fig. 4	William Cuningham's 'The Cosmological glasse' of 1559	49
Fig. 5	Henry Holiday's *Dante and Beatrice*, 1883	52
Fig. 6	Sir Richard Owen	88
Fig. 7	John Stevens Henslow	92
Fig. 8	Edwin Sidney's rectory	105
Fig. 9	Peacock Hall	134
Fig. 10	'Old' Caustons Hall, in its dilapidated state at the time of demolition in the 1960s	136
Fig. 11	Little Cornard Church	145
Fig. 12	The rectory barn	156
Fig. 13	Michael Faraday in 1857	222
Fig. 14	Michael Faraday lecturing at the Royal Institution	224
Fig. 15	John Langdon Haydon Down	231

PREFACE AND ACKNOWLEDGMENTS

This book is very gossipy. Perhaps it is more suitable for poking around in than for reading from cover to cover. It is offered to the people of Little Cornard, who have desired it more or less in the form in which it appears, though I have also had in mind history students in colleges and the newer universities who sometimes contemplate Victorian newspapers and wonder what to make of them and who, when taking courses upon programmes called 'The History of Ideas', sometimes find difficult the meandering but interwoven lineages of ideas about God and ideas in science. Mostly it is a hodgepodge of items from the early Victorian newspaper press of East Anglia, chiefly concerning a small rural community, Little Cornard, as tenacious now (1998) of its unique identity as when Edwin Sidney died, in 1872.

Edwin Sidney: busiest parson in an age of busy parsons; historian and biographer of lasting importance; humanitarian reformer internationally acclaimed; popular scientific, and Christian, lecturer second only, perhaps, in his day, to his friend Michael Faraday; and, in sum, characterful country clergyman deserving the kind of attention accorded to 'Parson' Woodforde or the Revd Francis Kilvert. Here was the problem at the root of my enterprise: how could one judge the import of *his* Little Cornard unless first one should know a good deal about *him*? Yet how in turn could one tell anything worthwhile about him unless it should be grounded in a view of his own wider world, a world of the Bible and science, of the *Prayer Book* and poetry, and of high-society friendships and continental travel, having little inevitably to do with work-a-day Victorians in Little Cornard? Instead of publishing newspaper items, therefore, should I perhaps attempt a short biography of Sidney? No, I could not: there were not enough materials, simply endless newspaper notices of his addresses, lectures and sermons delivered in East Anglia, and sometimes in London: and anyway, my friends in Little Cornard, ever supportive, reminded me always that what they desired were newspaper notices.

So I have complied. Recalling Lord Macaulay's dictum that 'the only true history of a country is to be found in its newspapers', I have adhered to my original conviction that what I had to offer should, on the whole, stand or fall by the characteristic eloquence and the intrinsic significance of Victorian newspaper notices when regarded *in extenso*. I have therefore brought together my more curious items concerning Little Cornard (the trial of young Micklefield, the death of Newman Sparrow, the quack medical practitioner who settled for two pullets, and so on); offered with them an assortment of items bearing upon the accomplishments of a good and remarkable man, who ministered to Little Cornard from 1847 till 1872; and subtitled the whole *Newspaper Portraits of Little Cornard in the Darwinian Age*, because Edwin Sidney's ministry in Little Cornard coincided so largely with the period which began with Charles Darwin's first sketching-out, in pencil, of his theory of evolution – 1842, and ended with the publication of his second major work, *The Descent of Man* – 1871; which events embraced a widespread revolution in men's understanding of the natural sciences against which Sidney's science teaching in Little Cornard and in Sudbury must inevitably be judged.

Though I have offered annotations for most items, often annotation has seemed needless. But sometimes I have thought it helpful to annotate at apparently undeserving length. This has been especially so with Sidney's lectures for the Church Missionary Society. Should any annotation seem a hindrance to enjoyment it may of course be ignored; likewise my Introduction, or any part of it.

Among my items I have inserted one from a national though obscure periodical – *The Churchman's Companion* (XVII). Once, in the matter of George Mumford's funeral, I have included for its particular eloquence an item from beyond 'the Darwinian age' (XXXVIII). And, for its vivid contextual significance, I have included also Dr Langdon Down's lecture on 'Movements in Organic Life' (XXXIII). My hodgepodge consequently has become enlarged, the brief Preface which I once intended has become an Introduction long and in sections, a different Preface and a sort of 'Preface part two' entitled 'Reflections' have appeared, and what I have to offer as a whole may perchance invite the comment that Sir John Boileau made upon one of Sidney's lectures – 'too much attempted to be crammed into it'. I trust even so that the whole will illumine an obscure Victorian community where a world of eclectic natural theology, and of pure and applied science, rubbed shoulders with a world of agricultural labour, and that, indeed, the reader will feel rather like that elderly native of the parish who, though spry in mind, and lettered, and opinionated, can no longer go about too much, and so has gone to live some miles away, with younger relatives, but keeps informed of parish matters – and will inform others of them, too – through what the papers say.

MANY HAVE contributed to the appearance of this book, some in ways hardly known to them. Robert Baker; Mrs Rosemarie Balls; Mrs Alison Bowden; Miss Betty Dickinson; Dr Robert Druce; Miss Susan Hackett; Michael Hills, Honorary Archivist, Sudbury Town; John Jackson; Noel and Mrs Eileen King; Dr Tom Plunkett, Keeper of Archaeology at Ipswich Museum; the Revd Peter and Mrs Sheena Thomas; Mrs Mimi Wheldon; and Mrs Betty Wyatt: all have helped with matters textual. Andrew Phillips (Lord Phillips of Sudbury, OBE) I must thank for special kindnesses. Mrs Elizabeth

Nurser, of Yard Publishing Services, has been generous with time, advice and the fruits of wide experience. For many years the Membership and the Committee of the Little Cornard Conservation Society have been patiently supportive.

Much fetching and carrying of papers, books and manuscripts was courteously undertaken by the staffs of the British Library Newspaper Library; the Cambridge University Library; the Ipswich Museum; the Suffolk Record Office, at Bury St Edmunds and Ipswich; and the Norfolk Record Office and Central Library, Norwich.

I am indebted also to those who have allowed the publication of certain of the illustrations: Ipswich Borough Council Museums and Galleries – Frontispiece (Edwin Sidney) and Fig. 7 (J. S. Henslow); the Walker Art Gallery, Liverpool – Fig. 5 (*Dante and Beatrice*); Mrs Jennifer de Pass – Figs. 8 (Edwin Sidney's rectory) and 12 (the rectory barn); Mrs Diana Simmonds – Fig. 9 (Peacock Hall); the Royal Commission on the Historical Monuments of England – Fig. 10 ('Old' Caustons Hall); National Portrait Gallery – Fig. 13 (Michael Faraday in 1857); and the Royal Institution of Great Britain – Fig. 14 (Michael Faraday lecturing at the Royal Institution). Paul Matthews took splendid photographs.

To all I am most grateful. Such errors and shortcomings as may appear are my responsibility entirely.

Peter Cooper
Michaelmas 1998

A NOTE ON EDITING AND REFERENCES

I have tried to keep footnotes to a respectable minimum. I have used superior numbers for them; the starred note of explanation in '"Harvest Cart" in Suffolk' (XXVIII) is in the original.

I have used upper cases for titles involving personal names, but not for titles involving place names only. Thus: 'Queen Victoria', but 'the queen of England', 'the prince of Wales'. 'Evangelical' with an upper case denotes 'the Evangelical party in the Church of England'; otherwise a lower case is used. 'Nature' with an upper case denotes 'nature to be regarded as having some kind of metaphysical or personal attribute or attributes'.

I have used ellipses in the ordinary way. In the case of every quotation and press item an ellipsis indicates an excision which I have made; it is not in the original.

Newspaper items are referred to throughout by their distinguishing Roman numerals.

REFLECTIONS

But most thro' midnight streets I hear
How the youthful Harlot's curse
Blasts the new born Infant's tear,
And blights with Plagues the Marriage hearse.

> William Blake (1757–1827), 'London'

The face of Mrs. Gamp – the nose in particular – was somewhat red and swollen, and it was difficult to enjoy her society without becoming conscious of a smell of spirits. Like most persons who have attained to great eminence in their profession, she took to hers very kindly; inasmuch that, setting aside her natural predilections as a woman, she went to a lying-in or a laying-out with equal zest and relish.

> Charles Dickens, *Martin Chuzzlewit*, 1843–44, chapter 19

Within the churchyard, side by side,
   Are many long low graves;
And some have stones set over them,
   On some the green grass waves.

Full many a little Christian child,
   Woman, and man, lies there;
And we pass near them every time
   When we go into prayer.

> Mrs C. F. Alexander, *Hymns Ancient and Modern*,
> Standard Edition, no. 575

In *Word from Wormingford* Ronald Blythe wonders how the two-year-olds of the Feast of the Holy Innocents can be dealt with by a century in which elected governments have bombed, gassed and burned millions of children. Indeed. It is thus tempting to be sentimental about Victorian rural England, especially when we contemplate its undoubted enchantment, and the life and witness of a country parson such as Edwin Sidney, who combined the highest standards of pastoral concern with a proper regard for the truths of *Prayer Book* religion and for the revelations, or most of the revelations, of advancing science. But temptation yields no increase: it must not be entered into; as this anthology shows, in Victorian rural England, despite its regard for Childermas Day (XVII), there was squalor, misery and ignorance, and much that was evil and grim.

Death, of people and of animals, is conspicuous in these pages, as are the robust rituals of Victorian mourning. Most Little Cornard people were probably healthier than most of their ancestors, despite their touching faith in quacks and quackery (XVIII). But death transfixed the Victorians, pervading their literature, their music and their visual art. Thus, Dickens anthropomorphizes death: death on the sweaty brow of Anthony Chuzzlewit is 'Death' with a capital 'D' as, in *Dombey and Son*, is 'the remorseless monster, Death', denizen of railway technology and travel. And Emily Brontë's poem 'Remembrance' batters our psyches – with Death uncompromising, terrifying, and with no promise of Redemption and Resurrection:

> Cold in the earth – and the deep snow piled above thee,
> Far, far, removed, cold in the dreary grave!
> Have I forgot, my only Love, to love thee,
> Severed at last by Time's all severing wave?

These are startling images; the Death occasioned by Dickens's railways was never remotely intimated in the local newspapers gaily celebrating the passing through Little Cornard of the Eastern Union Railway in 1849 (VI),[1] and the Redemption and Resurrection unpromised by Brontë was central to Christian teaching and commonplace in Edwin Sidney's sermons and scientific lectures. But often in the Sudbury area death seemed close to what a Dickens or a Brontë said of it, not to how, these days, it is commonly experienced. Though agrarian incendiarism had abated before Sidney came to Little Cornard, horror was still rife, and death was everywhere, not remote or clinical or sanitised. One Saturday in April 1847, festive thousands, some with their children, junketed to Bury St Edmunds to see that town's last public hanging of a woman, young and tragic Catherine Foster from Acton, near Sudbury. The occasion is still resonant; some years ago in Sudbury I met a man who as a boy had talked about it with a woman who as a girl had been there. Next day execution sermons had been preached in local churches. In Acton church the Revd Lawrence Ottley, vicar, and associate of Edwin Sidney in the humdrum concerns of local clerical life, preached for an hour and a half upon the text 'Be sure your sin will find you out' (Numbers xxxii 23). Long before the service the church was overflowing, and the churchyard so full it was difficult to reach the doors.

But most Victorians would not be hanged, so more than their descendants they might expect to die at home or in places familiar to them and, until it should be time for their funerals, to stay at home upon their beds or in their coffins, perhaps with the children peeping in. In a sombre but once famous hymn Mrs C. F. Alexander, wise Christian lady, wife of a bishop and a contemporary of Edwin Sidney, advised little children that death –

---

[1] The most detailed and vivid account of the opening of the Eastern Union Railway branch line from Colchester to Sudbury, through Little Cornard, appears in the *Chelmsford Chronicle* of 6 July 1849, p. 2. John Sikes, farmer in Little Cornard, seems to have been active in the Company's promotion,.

so stark in their midst and, in the newspapers, catching the eye as it looked for something else – was regenerative of life, and that therefore corpses must have their appointed places within the community of the living. She evoked the ancient Christian committal, found in the earliest English *Prayer Book*, of 1549 – 'I commend thy soul to God the Father Almighty, and thy body to the ground', as though in some sense the corpse were still a living person, and she captured thus the stasis of Victorian rural societies such as Little Cornard, their deep sense of the unity of past and present, and their needful regard to the rhythms of Nature's year in which to every thing there was a season, and a time to every purpose. In such societies, as the parish records of Little Cornard tend to show, many never travelled far from where they were born; all that existed by way of 'mass media' were the newspapers, which most could not afford even if they could read; and opposites – Blake was their poet, his Marriage hearse their horrid emblem – converged more evidently and often more poignantly than in our own modern experience: pleasure with pain, sickness with health, life with death, death with renewal and resurrection and, overall, the holy with the secular.

But Victorians coped; one does. Doubtless for them, as for us, life usually seemed as higgledy-piggledy as an urban roofscape, problematic to traverse, unless one should be good at bearing up – like tipsy Mrs Gamp, maybe, zestful converger of opposites in the matter of lyings-in and layings-out, and surveyor of a view from the top of a public house: 'I'm glad to see a parapidge, in case of fire, and lots of roofs and chimley-pots to walk upon'.

Because, then, Victorians read their newspapers in the usual way, as they were published, side by side from within their churchyards they themselves suggest that the items in this anthology should appear chronologically rather than by category, the trivial following the weighty, the weighty the trivial, the sententious mixed with the frivolous, all higgledy-piggledy as chimley-pots, affirming perhaps that randomness may define the moral community, as may Death, a teacher of science, or a writer of hymns.

Fig. 1 'Within the churchyard, side by side, / Are many long low graves.'
The graves of the Mumfords, Newman Sparrow, and John Constable
in Little Cornard churchyard.
Photo and © Paul Matthews.

INTRODUCTION

LITTLE CORNARD

> The old countryman is worth getting to know for his own sake: he is worth regarding against his natural background – the pre-tractor farming and the community which it nourished. So viewed he will appear as a living social document, and his true worth and dignity will emerge.
>
> George Ewart Evans, *The Horse in the Furrow*,
> London 1967, p. 17

Early in the reign of Queen Victoria the parish of Little Cornard, or Cornard Parva, some two miles and a half out of Sudbury, was a scattered community of around 1,600 rolling acres on the Suffolk side of the Stour river. Little that the eye perceived could have changed since the previous century; the people and the animals captured in the youthful Gainsborough's *Cornard Wood* must still have found it familiar. The parish church, dedicated to All Saints, was small, Perpendicular, unremarkable, yet in its setting attractive. The most comely parish residence, Peacock Hall, stood foursquare and prudent nearby, externally Georgian but occupying the site of earlier residences, and testifying perhaps to the Roast Beef of Old England and to systems of farming less intensive than those of a later and mechanised age.

The dozen or so farms were mainly arable and were the chief employers of labour. In 1869 Kelly's *Post Office Directory of Suffolk* listed the farmers' crops after the names of the principal landowners but before the name of the parish clerk (William

Rayner) – wheat, peas, barley, oats, beans and turnips. The fields producing the crops were described on the tithe map of 1841; they were mindful, one hopes, of Old Testament injunctions that fields should be joyful, for they had attractive names, suggestive of sturdy personalities craving admission to *The Post Office Directory* along with the crops and important parish persons: there was *Tiffens Field, Weedy Field, Button Piece, Nicklesons Field, Fish Pitts, Gosling Hill, The Spong, Pear Tree Field,* and a good many more. *Spong*, Old Norse in derivation, signified a driftway for cattle. *The Spong* today is the garden of *Long Meadow House*, on Kedington Hill, whilst *Pear Tree Field* comprises exactly the gardens of the dwellings between *Moss Cottage* and *Centuries*, on Upper Road.

At census time in 1841 the parish's population was 376, of whom 68 per cent were 'agricultural labourers' or their dependants. In 1871 the corresponding percentage was 58, of a total population of 429. But naturally, throughout the earlier Victorian period virtually all occupations in the parish were little removed from the needs of agrarian living. In 1841 the most notable occupations apart from 'rector' (1), 'farmer' (11) and 'agricultural labourer' (53) were 'haytrusser' (3), 'shoemaker' (2), and 'brickmaker', 'farmer's bailiff', 'carrier', 'broom-maker', 'mason', 'labourer', 'baker' (1 of each). In 1871 the only occupations less than wholly consonant with the immediate needs of an agrarian community were 'plate-layer' (2) and 'commercial traveller' (1; a young fellow called Walter Bane, husband and father of four).

There was family continuity. A faithful man shall abound with blessings – or so we are taught; well, if children be blessings Springetts were strenuous in faith, for Springetts abounded in the parish in 1841 – there were twenty of them. But a Springett had first appeared in the church register in 1575. Throughout the seventeenth century, and beyond, the baptisms, marriages and burials of successive Springetts were solemnised profusely in the church. So from time to time were those of Scotts, of whom there were seventeen in 1841. Again in 1841 there was a William Lorking with his family in the parish (III, XVIII). But Elizabeth, daughter of William Lorkin [*sic*], had been baptized in the church in June 1635, whilst in the 1650s and the 1660s baptisms had been solemnised for a galaxy of infant Lorkins, parented by William and Susan his wife. The church register in which these names appear is a parochially prized possession, for it records the marriage in April 1667 of Robert Gainsborough and Frances Mainard (Maynard), of Sudbury, grandparents of Gainsborough the painter,[2] and, in 1768, though in a different volume, the baptism in April and the burial in December of Amy, infant daughter of Nathan Constable, first cousin of the father of the painter Constable. Rayners, too, had probably inhabited the parish at least since the seventeenth century. In 1841, in Spout Lane, there was William Rayner, 'age 40', carrier and coal-carter, his wife and his eight children, including William Rayner, 'age 18', 'agricultural labourer': whilst on the road to Bures, opposite Stone Farm as tenant of Sarah Layzell, there was William Damon Rayner, 'age 45', blacksmith and long-serving church and parish clerk; William Rayner, 'age 15', his son; and William Rayner, 'age 75', probably his father. Such intimations of relative social immobility are confirmed more generally by the parish censuses. For instance, that of 1851 (the first to record places of birth) shows that 62 per cent of Little Cornard people were born within the parish, as were both partners to 20 per cent of parish marriages, and that most of the remainder were born in parishes not far away.

Little Cornard people in the earlier nineteenth century were mostly illiterate: of the 54 married in the church between the first

---

[2] The family tree of Robert and Frances Gainsborough and their descendants is reproduced in *A Short History of the Borough of Sudbury, in the County of Suffolk*, compiled from materials collected by W. W. Hodson, by C. F. D. Sperling, MA, Sudbury 1896, p. 196.

application of the Civil Registration Act in 1837 and the arrival of Edwin Sidney in 1847, 33 could not sign their names. Perhaps, too, they were vague or unknowing in matters of age; or perhaps they were shameless teasers of Public Authority in the persons of census enumerators; or perhaps Public Authority was lazy, not troubling to knock upon their doors to discover all that Public Authority should know. Whatever the case, William Rayner, for example, was 'age 75' at census time in 1841, but – according to the church's burial register – 'age 83' when he died in 1846; whilst William and Kezia Moss (husband and wife) were 45 and 50 respectively in 1841, but 62 and 64 respectively in 1851.

Yet despite such imperfections these labouring people could attain unlooked-for immortality. Take again the Moss family, and the family of young Benjamin Whyett, as they appear in 1851. Both families lived in 'Mosses Road', the road up which you went to visit Mosses. Eventually the upper part of 'Mosses Road' became Upper Road, but the cottage wherein Moss had lived (it belonged to Lord Walsingham; Moss had it as an employee of George Mumford) became *Moss Cottage*, which, much gentrified, it remains today. Conversely, the part of 'Mosses Road' where Whyett lived became Wyatt's Lane. Today Whyett's cottage, likewise gentrified, is *Tudor Cottage*. But in the 1970s the outbuildings of Pond Farm, near the top of Wyatt's Lane, became a private dwelling gracious and inviting. It was named, simply, *Wyatts*.

Until he died in 1998, Hugh Baker lived at *Wyatts*. This is handy for, with a little analogical thinking, the person of Mr Baker may transport us from the gentlefolk of Wyatt's Lane in the 1990s to the pubescent schoolgirls of Spout Lane in the 1850s, via Edwin Sidney's Sudbury and a smidgen glance at the Second Book of Chronicles. For Mr Baker is a descendant of the painter Henry Bridgman, who portrayed the townscape of Sudbury as it was when Little Cornard's rector (Sidney) lectured Sudbury's people upon the wonders of science. Bridgman's portrayal is serene, deceptively so because, *as we shall see*, whilst Edwin Sidney lectured, his friend the waspish vicar of All Saints, Sudbury, espying the parson of Sudbury's other benefice (St Gregory and St Peter) all decked out in folderols appropriate only (he felt) to popes of Rome, did battle with him, sending frissons galore through the townsfolk, rather as the Syrians, discovering King Jehoshaphat of Judah disguised as their enemy King Ahab of Israel, compassed about him to fight; as in the land of Gilead, so in the Sudbury of Bridgman and Sidney, and in Little Cornard too, appearances seemed to count: whether kingly robes or white scarves with violet bows or brambles and crinolines, one must be careful what one wore (XX).[3]

THE RECTOR of Little Cornard before Edwin Sidney was William Pochin, of the Pochin family still resident at Barkby Hall, in Leicestershire. Pochin became rector in 1815, though from 1806 to 1824 he was also vicar of nearby Edwardstone. He is a shadowy figure, typical perhaps of the indolent parsons to be found in many an English parish before the Church reformed itself in the 1830s and 1840s. During the last fifteen years or so of his life and incumbency, save for a spell between 1839 and 1842, services in the church seem to have been conducted by curates and deputies. One of the deputies was Thorpe William Fowke, vicar of All Saints, Sudbury, from 1811 to 1846. Of Fowke it was said that 'unaffected piety, meekness, charity, and every Christian virtue marked him for a man of God'.[4] Little Cornard may attest the charity, for, as if to disown credit for helpfulness, when Fowke came to deputise he

---

[3] Bridgman's painting, *View of Sudbury from the South East*, 1860, was acquired by Gainsborough's House, Sudbury, early in 1996; see the *East Anglian Daily Times*, 17 January 1996, p. 13, and the *Suffolk Free Press*, 18 January 1996, p. 18.

[4] Cited in Charles Badham, *The History and Antiquities of All Saints Church, Sudbury, and the parish generally*, London 1852, p. 66.

habitually signed himself 'William Pochin' in the church's register of services. In later years at least Pochin resided afar from his church, apparently on the Bures Road, near Blackhouse Lane, on a small property rented from Mrs Sarah Edwick, widow of a horse-dealer. In turn Mrs Edwick rented from him the old parsonage house and garden, on Kedington Hill. Pochin died in December 1846, a few weeks after Fowke. They put him in a gloomy mausoleum still there in the churchyard at Great Cornard, along with Mrs Pochin and Mrs Pochin's mother. (Fowke the meek and charitable went off with more panache, being the last person to be buried by torchlight in his family's vault at Walton-on-Thames.)

With clerical influence so weak, Little Cornard could have done with squires, caring and high-minded. But there were never squires in Little Cornard. Thus inevitably the parish was dominated by the farmers, the most significant of whom when Edwin Sidney came were George Mumford, John Newman Sparrow, and Henry Segers, whose families were all long-established in the parish. For years John Sikes (XVI, XXXVI) farmed within the parish, at Casefields Farm and Stocks Farm, but he lived in Sudbury, on the old Market Place. He is buried in the churchyard, with members of his family.

Mumford, by far the largest farmer, had the Caustons Hall estate, as tenant of Lord Walsingham. In 1871 he employed twenty-eight men and boys, to farm some 540 acres. His children were 'governess'-reared, if the 1841 census may be relied upon. The names of ten of them are in the church's register of baptisms. The youngest but one, Sidney Lugar Mumford, a solicitor who practised in London, in the Strand, was buried in the churchyard in 1937. For a quarter of a century Mumfords were Edwin Sidney's loyal supporters, within the parish and beyond. Mumford himself helped Sidney to form and then to sustain the Sudbury Agricultural Association, and Mumford's daughters did good works among the poor. Politically Mumford was a Protectionist Tory locally prominent in the 1850s. He became a J.P. The attainments of Mumford sons got noticed in the newspapers (XXIV), and in 1864 a Mumford daughter, Lucy Louisa, surely did well, by marrying a Bank of England clerk, of Bloomsbury, son of an attorney.

Mumfords, no doubt, were full of good counsels and just works. But to some, perhaps, they seemed hoity-toity and social pushers – 'Mumford is a d——d bad 'un,' said young and wretched Micklefield to Golding Gallant (III). Probably they had moved through and beyond that 'carpet and bell-pull' gentility ridiculed by William Cobbett in *Rural Rides* (1830), and, earlier, by James Gillray in a famous cartoon which has adorned many a text of agricultural history – *Farmer Giles & His Wife showing off their daughter Betty to their Neighbours on her return from School* (1809). (See Fig. 2.) Though they were never 'gazetted' (bankrupted, that is), they were caught, perhaps, in doggerel written in 1843 and quoted by G. M. Trevelyan in his *English Social History*, of 1944:

>OLD STYLE
>Man, to the plough;
>Wife, to the cow;
>Girl, to the yarn;
>Boy, to the barn,
>And your rent will be netted.

>NEW STYLE
>Man, Tally Ho;
>Miss, piano;
>Wife, silk and satin;
>Boy, Greek and Latin,
>And you'll all be Gazetted.

I wondered about the Mumfords. Was there a sliver of living testimony to what their aspirations might have been? There was. In September 1981, Miss Emma Jane Francis, J.P., was living in a

Fig. 2 Farmer Giles & his Wife showing off their daughter Betty to their Neighbours on her return from School. *An etching by James Gillray from a watercolour by an amateur; published 1 January 1809.*

retirement home in Bury St Edmunds. I went to see her. In 1913 George Mumford junior, eldest son and heir of George senior, had sold out in Little Cornard to her father, a farmer from the adjacent parish of Newton. The reason, Miss Francis confided, was that 'his wife thought the land not good enough, and wanted to take him off to London'. A year later Miss Francis died, aged 103.[5]

Sparrows and Segerses farmed fewer acres than did Mumfords, but they owned their land. Until he took Peacock Hall in hand in the 1850s John Newman Sparrow (XV) lived at Prospect House which, though in Great Cornard, was socially part of Little

---

[5] See also the *Suffolk Free Press*, 17 September 1981, p. 20. Old Caustons Hall was demolished in the 1960s.

Cornard. Henry Segers and his two sons, Henry John and Alfred, had Burnt House Farm. In 1817 Henry Segers had married Sarah, daughter of John Constable, namesake and kinsman of the painter; he could not sign his name upon his wedding-day. From Constable Segers inherited the farm. Segerses have their place in the history of Suffolk brickmaking, because Segers founded a brickworks (XXXI), which continued in the parish until the 1960s.[6]

Sparrows and Mumfords consort in death as doubtless they did in life, for they buried themselves compactly either side of a path near the church's vestry, prosperous tombstones finely inscribed, with fine iron railings for old George Mumford, removed in the Second World War. Aged John Constable joined them in 1844. So, two summers later, did Elizabeth Segers, twenty-two years old; she shares her grandfather's grave.

Here, then, is a community of the dead. They picket the community of the living, for we pass among them every time we go in to prayer from the direction of Mr Wheldon's orchard. Mrs Alexander would have thought them exemplary.

---

[6] See the *East Anglian Daily Times*, 27 August 1979, p. 6 – which, however, erroneously says that Elizabeth Segers was Constable's daughter.

FIRES 1843, 1844

> Therefore he said unto his servants, See, Joab's field is near mine, and he hath barley there; go and set it on fire. And Absalom's servants set the field on fire.
>
> 2 Samuel xiv 30

> Having been a tenant long to a rich Lord,
>   Not thriving, I resolved to be bold,
>   And make a suit unto him, to afford,
> A new small-rented lease, and cancell'd th'old.
>
> In heaven at his manour I him sought:
>   They told me there, that he was lately gone
>   About some land, which he had dearly bought
> Long since on earth, to take possession.
>
> I straight return'd, and knowing his great birth,
>   Sought him accordingly in great resorts;
>   In cities, theatres, gardens, parks, and courts:
> At length I heard a ragged noise and mirth
>
>   Of theeves and murderers: there I him espied,
>   Who straight, *Your suit is granted*, said, and died.
>
> George Herbert (1593–1632), 'Redemption'

To Mrs Alexander the dead were perhaps more pleasing than the living, for the dead were decently behaved in that, having no choice, they abided by the canons of conduct laid down for wherever they were sent, to heaven or to hell. But the living were a problem, especially in the 1840s when, *as we shall see*, their irregular behaviour obliged Mrs Alexander to produce 'All things bright and beautiful'. Not least were they a problem in East Anglia in 1843 and 1844, when some of them were agrarian incendiarists. One of the worst was a boy from Little Cornard.

Agrarian agitation and riots were endemic in much of England in the early nineteenth century and into the 1850s, particularly in the cereal-producing parts in the south and east. Accompanied by poaching and cattle-maiming, incendiarism was the characteristic form of this unrest after 1830.

There were several reasons. To begin with, the population of England and Wales rose impressively during the hundred years or so before 1850; it was around six and a half million in 1750, but by census time in 1851 it was nearly eighteen million. An increasing proportion of these extra people lived, of course, in towns and cities, sustaining the employment needs of trade and industry. More people meant more mouths for British farmers to feed. Consequently this hundred years was, on the whole, a period of prosperity in British agriculture, when spirited farmers responded ever more readily to the challenge of greater efficiency; the enclosure movement of the earlier part of the period was but one aspect of the process. Wheat farmers made particularly high profits in the years 1795–1815, when war with France prevented the importation of foreign wheat; in consequence these farmers aspired to be gentlemen, their wives to be ladies, and their households to acquire 'carpet and bell-pull' gentility.

In most of England there had not been a peasantry (that is, families of agricultural workers possessing their own small plots of land and cultivating them mostly with their own labour) since long before the later eighteenth century; instead, at the bottom of the rural social hierarchy, there were agricultural wage-earners, un-unionized until the 1870s, liable at any time to be exploited, and so to act irrationally, heedless of the savage consequences should they come to court. From the later eighteenth century they were increasingly exploited and proletarianised; for to work them hard and under-pay them was consistent with the farmer's need for greater efficiency, which, in turn, was consistent with his aspirations to gentility. After the end of the French wars in 1815 there seemed even better reason for bearing down upon agricultural labourers, because wheat prices were not now as high as farmers would have wished, even despite the Corn Laws which were intended to keep them high, whilst landlords pressed for ever higher rents, not least in the earlier 1840s in Suffolk where, largely in consequence, observed the great radical John Bright, tenant farmers were selling up, in keeping with the ninety-eight advertisements for the sale of farming stock which, he said, he had seen in one Suffolk newspaper during 1843.[7] And, of course, the Poor Law system did not help. Before 1834 it tended, on the whole haphazardly, to supplement wages where they were low, and thus to encourage underpayment; after 1834, through the brutal workhouse system, it stigmatised poverty, discouraged applications for relief, yet did nothing to encourage the raising of wages.

In the sixty or so years preceding 1850 the worst outbreak of agricultural protest occurred in 1830, in southern and in eastern England. But there was a later protest, as tragic though less known.[8] It was incendiary, and occurred in 1843 and 1844, chiefly in the Home Counties and in East Anglia, where at that time agricultural labourers formed the largest occupational group. Suffolk reaped the cruellest whirlwind and, said John Stevens Henslow, Hitcham's rector, stood disgraced, along with two or three other counties, 'in the eyes of England, Europe and the whole civilised world'.[9] But in

---

[7] *Parliamentary Debates,* 3rd Series, vol. 76, cc. 1106, 1107, 19 July 1844.

[8] The events of 1830 are dealt with by E. J. Hobsbawm and George Rudé, *Captain Swing,* London 1969; those of 1843 and 1844 by David Jones, 'Thomas Campbell Foster and the rural labourer; incendiarism in East Anglia in the 1840s', *Social History,* January 1976.

[9] *Bury and Norwich Post,* 31 July 1844, p. 3.

Suffolk, largely, the practice of agricultural 'improvement' had been pioneered. There, consequently, says Eric Hobsbawm, 'the labourer's status had been most completely transformed'. There, by the early 1840s, the manufacture together with the use of agricultural machinery was advanced the furthest; Ransomes of Ipswich, Garretts of Leiston, Wood of Stowmarket, Smyth of Peasenhall were all well established by 1845.[10] There, also by the early 1840s, the commercial manufacture of fertilisers was underway (IX). These were all significant circumstances. But significant too, no doubt, was the fact that farmers, troubled rent-wise though they were, talked about them, and engendered a climate of confidence about them, in public houses, market places, and corn exchanges, and at agricultural meetings, too often within earshot of labourers ill-paid (usually under ten shillings a week), ill-fed, ill-housed, and smouldering with resentment and despair.

Absalom smouldered with resentment, so he commanded his servants to set fire to the barley field of Joab. From the dry summer months, and the collapse of corn prices, of 1843, to the famous drought during the late spring and summer of 1844, the reports in East Anglian newspapers of madmen casting flames of fire and, often, of arrest, and convictions and punishments, were reminiscent of Old Testament calamities. Farmers in the Sudbury and Hadleigh areas of Suffolk were notably scathed. The fire at Peacock Hall (II), lately untenanted (I) (but why had Bird gone? had Sparrow screwed him for too high a rent?), was one of the earliest, though evidently not one of the worst; it may even have been an

---

[10] Hobsbawm and Rudé, *Captain Swing*, pp. 59–60. There is some disagreement, though, concerning the precise relationship between the advance of agricultural machinery on the one hand and, on the other, the supply and condition of agricultural labour; contrast, for example, the view of Hobsbawm and Rudé with that of G. E. Mingay, in G. E. Mingay, ed., *The Agricultural Revolution: changes in agriculture 1650–1880*, London 1977, pp. 38–46.

accident, caused by a smoking tramp, perhaps, or a child with matches – as was thought to have been the case in 1850 (VIII). In November, though, Mrs Stutter of Higham lost 140 coombs of barley in her barn at Stratford St Mary. The same night Baker, a farmer of Hitcham, a parish suffering heavily from unemployment, lost a haystack. Within days, and within forty-eight hours of each other, there were fires at Hawstead Lodge and Fakenham Hall, and also at Polstead, where the new barn was burnt, erected only in the summer to replace the old Red Barn, where Maria Marten had been murdered, which had been fired the previous Christmas. Before Christmas (1843) there was another fire at Hitcham, at the Hall, and one at Glemsford. 1844 was worse: before the end of March there were incidents among others at Polstead (again), Glemsford (again), Hengrave, Great Wenham, Mildenhall, Hadleigh, Aldham, Wrabness, Aldham (again), Hadleigh (again), Mildenhall (again), Naughton, Polstead rectory, Great Wenham (again), Bradfield, Gislingham, Tuddenham, Freston, Bacton, Stowmarket, Borley Hall (near Sudbury), Rickinghall, Gislingham (again; the property of Lord Henniker, MP), Chelsworth, Jackson's farm at Hitcham (the culprits, caught, were committed by Henslow as magistrate), Capel, and Tendring; before the end of June incidents among others at Pebmarsh (Essex, but near Sudbury), Buxhall, Little Cornard (III), Stoke-by-Nayland, Naughton (again), Mildenhall (yet again), Norden's farm at Assington (adjacent to Little Cornard; a fearful conflagration: high wind; all farm buildings, property in fact of farming co-operativist John Gurdon, destroyed; thirty shrieking swine rushed into the flames, fleeing attempts to drive them clear; cottages and *The Shoulder of Mutton* public house consumed), Stowmarket (again) and Kesgrave Heath. And so it continued.

Country and County were shaken. In 1841 Parliament had passed a bill substituting for death the punishments of imprisonment or transportation for agrarian incendiarism, and for certain other crimes; now, in 1843 and 1844, the Tory landed interest lamented that it had done so. In July 1844, T. M. Gibson, Liberal MP for Manchester as well as a magistrate in Suffolk sympathetic to the labourer's plight, instigated a debate in the House of Commons concerning troubled Suffolk. He noticed the kind of situation evident at Peacock Hall (II): 'Magistrates have stated', he said, 'that where labourers do not perpetrate the crimes themselves, they look on with a sort of satisfaction while the flames are destroying their neighbours' barns and stacks.' He cited Henslow as witness to the under-employment and hence the poverty of Suffolk labourers. At *The Angel Inn*, Bury St Edmunds, in September, frightened gentlemen and parsons created a 'West Suffolk Society for the Improvement of the Condition of the Labourers', having talked at length of allotments, benefit clubs, education and emigration. Next month at Bury the West Suffolk magistrates overcame their oft-proclaimed distaste for needless imposition upon county ratepayers, and invoked the 1839 County Police Act to follow East Suffolk in the creation of a rural police force for their half of the county; no longer were agrarian incendiarists to be apprehended chiefly by town and parish constables, or by the same agents of insurance companies.[11]

SO THE SHADOWY GRIEVANCE of James Micklefield concerning the potatoes (III) must be viewed with respect, though his tragedy was not unique. When redemption came to Little Cornard it came, in part at least, through Christian ministration charged with the precepts of old-fashioned science.

---

[11] *Bury and Norwich Post*, 9 October 1844, p. 2, 30 October 1844, p. 4.

OLD-FASHIONED SCIENCE

> How fresh, O Lord, how sweet and clean
> Are thy returns! ev'n as the flowers in spring;
> To which, besides their own demean,
> The late-past frosts tributes of pleasure bring.
>   Grief melts away
>   Like snow in May
> As if there were no such cold thing.
>
> Who would have thought my shrivel'd heart
> Could have recover'd greennesse? It was gone
>   Quite underground; as flowers depart
> To see their mother root, when they have blown;
>   Where they together
>   All the hard weather,
> Dead to the world, keep house unknown.
>
>   George Herbert, 'The Flower'

> All this surface world is only the medium in and through which we children of God work out our contact with the eternal and communicate our knowledge, our little knowledge, our glimpses of the eternal, and learn of citizenship which is not of the earth and does not pass away.
>
>   Charles Raven, Regius Professor of Divinity,
> University of Cambridge 1932–1950, and biographer of John
>   Ray, to a gathering of students, 1955

Darwin

IN 1996 A QUESTION was put to a teenage biology student in Chelmsford: 'Is Darwin given the recognition he deserves?' The student replied:

INTRODUCTION

It's hard to think back all those years and take stock of what Darwin's thought meant at the time. No, I really don't think he has been given enough credit when you consider the huge leap in human thought his ideas represent.[12]

Quite. But then neither could many of Charles Darwin's contemporaries think what was the meaning of Darwin's thought. Alice, for instance, in 1865, could not think what was the meaning of the Duchess's baby when it 'evolved' into a pig – "'If it had grown up,' she said to herself, 'it would have made a dreadfully ugly child: but it makes rather a handsome pig, I think.'"[13] Among the numerous extant newspaper synopses of his scientific lectures, Edwin Sidney left no trace of what he thought concerning Darwin's *The Origin of Species*, even though by 1850 he had reflected upon the principle of the mutability of species in the essentially true though limited form in which it had been proposed at the end of the eighteenth century by Erasmus Darwin, Charles Darwin's grandfather (IX).

Yet the date of the publication of *The Origin of Species*, 1859, became the best known date in Victorian science, the year when the natural sciences were suddenly topsy-turvy. For Darwin proclaimed not only the principle of biological evolution (which was dependent upon the principle of the mutability of species) but also, with magisterial originality, the principle of natural selection. The principle of natural selection was that varieties and species having attributes suited to their environment would be more likely to survive, and to propagate their kind, than those which had not, and that in the process of propagation the advantageous attributes would develop naturally in advantageousness. Take, for example, the family of squirrels. 'Here,' said Darwin,

---

[12] *Observer*, 8 September 1996, p. 9.
[13] Lewis Carroll, *Alice's Adventures in Wonderland*, 1865, chapter 6.

we have the finest gradation from animals with their tails only slightly flattened, and from others…with a posterior part of their bodies rather wide and with the skin on their flanks rather full, to the so-called flying squirrels; and flying squirrels have their limbs and even the base of the tail united by a broad expanse of skin, which serves as a parachute and allows them to glide through the air to an astonishing distance from tree to tree. We cannot doubt that such a structure is of use to each kind of squirrel in its own country, by enabling it to escape birds or beasts of prey, to collect food more quickly or, as there is reason to believe, to lessen the danger from occasional falls. But it does not follow from this fact that the structure of each squirrel is the best that it is possible to conceive under all possible conditions. Let the climate and vegetation change, let other competing rodents or new beasts of prey immigrate, or old ones become modified, and all analogy would lead us to believe that some at least of the squirrels would decrease in numbers or become exterminated, unless they also became modified and improved in structure in a corresponding manner. Therefore, I can see no difficulty, more especially under changing conditions of life, in the continued preservation of individuals with fuller and fuller flank-membranes, each modification being useful, each being propagated, until by the accumulated effects of this process of natural selection, a perfect so-called flying squirrel was produced.

Darwin considered necessarily the complex circumstances of ecological inter-relationships, an aspect of the circumstance of natural selection. For instance, he observed, the number of humble-bees in any district largely depends upon the number of field mice. For field mice destroy the combs and the nests of humble-bees. But field mice in their turn are destroyed by cats. And cats are more numerous around villages and small towns than around the open countryside. Therefore humble-bees are mostly to be found around villages and small towns. Such suggestions of randomness in the animal economy obviously called into question, implicitly, notions of the providential nature of class-structured human societies – such as prevailed, of course, in the contemporary Victorian countryside, including Little Cornard.

FOR SOME religious people, however, three features of *The Origin of Species* were especially disturbing. In the first place it subverted in general the principle of special creation by the God of Genesis. Secondly it subverted in particular the principle of the special creation of Man in the mould of God Incarnate. Thirdly – and this for truly intelligent churchmen was the most telling criticism – during Darwin's own lifetime it could not be satisfactorily explained, by Darwin or by anyone else, precisely *how* a changing environment could indefinitely stimulate random variations among living organisms to the point of producing not just new varieties but even new species, which could not inter-breed. In his final eloquent paragraphs Darwin addressed the matter of God, whose existence he went out of his way not to deny absolutely. Nevertheless his conclusion was unequivocal: 'Judging from the past,' he said, 'we may safely infer that not one living species will transmit its unaltered likeness to a distant futurity'. For the time being, therefore, the character of the obscure descent of Man was matter for the contemplation of morphologists and physiologists, and need not trouble clergymen.

Yet clergymen, notably the scriptural literalists among them, stayed troubled, because over and above those three specially disturbing features of Darwin's book, there was the fact that most of them had been educated in the ancient universities of Oxford and Cambridge, where they had experienced an intellectual tradition, 'natural theology', which made no absolute distinction between evidences that were physical and evidences that were metaphysical, and which therefore viewed as complementary the roles of naturalist and theologian. This was the tradition which

Shakespeare affirmed when he conceived a play, *King Lear*, about the moral condition of man and society, and erected it largely upon a naturalistic imagery which included 133 references to, variously, 64 animals. In recent times natural theology, to the extent that it has been thought about at all, has mostly been the preserve of theoretical physicists, geneticists, applied mathematicians, astronomers, physiologists, molecular biologists and microbiologists.[14] Clergymen have hardly seemed to care. But it was not so in Darwin's day; then, natural theology meant, precisely, 'teleology' – the notion that you may infer from the works of creation (the natural world, that is) the existence of a designing Creator.

Edwin Sidney, in Acle and in Little Cornard, always so inferred. His mind was not original, but he himself was an 'original' in that he propagated and popularised teleology with an imaginative vigour and energy probably unmatched by any other teleological parish parson in Victorian England. His mind is therefore worth exploring. But to understand it one must first consider two great traditions in Western thought, each deriving from an ancient Greek philosopher, the one Plato, the other Aristotle. Plato and Aristotle may at first seem remote from the world of early Victorian Little Cornard. They are, though, in various ways, central to it. In the following pages we shall see why.

---

[14] See, for example, a correspondence in *The Times*, December 1981.

INTRODUCTION

Plato, Aristotle and St Paul

> My face in thine eye, thine in mine appears,
> And true plain hearts do in the faces rest;
> Where can we find two better hemispheres
> Without sharp North, without declining West?
> What ever dies, was not mixt equally;
> If our two loves be one, or thou and I
> Love so alike that none do slacken, none can die.
>
> John Donne (1572–1631),
'The Good-morrow'

> The ring, so worn as you behold,
> So thin, so pale, is yet of gold:
> The passion such it was to prove –
> Worn with life's care, love yet was love.
>
> George Crabbe (born in Aldeburgh, 1754),
'A Marriage Ring'

PLATO (428/7–348/7 BC) said the things we think are real, dogs and cats and tables, say, are not real, they only appear so. When we see a dog, we say the word we have been taught, 'dog', because what we see corresponds with 'the idea of a dog', which is abstract, innate in our minds, and *truly* real, in that it is eternal, and will continue 'to be' even though particular dogs and we the particular people in whose minds the 'idea of the dog' is innate, will one day surely vanish. And the same is true of 'the idea of the cat' and the 'idea of the table'. Moreover, 'the Ultimate Idea', from which 'ideas' of dogs and cats and tables ultimately derive, is God.

Plato's doctrine of 'ideas' or 'forms' is to be found in his great dialogue, *The Republic*. Two facts especially made it seem convincing. First, the followers of Pythagoras (fl. 540–510 BC) had earlier discovered that if you took uniform strings, the lengths of which were simple numerical ratios, 1:3/4 : 2/3 : ½, you would produce harmonious sounds. In other words, 'symmetry' of number corresponded to 'symmetry' of sound; or, what was audible and pleasing emanated from something that was abstract and intellectually satisfying. In the second place, Plato himself invoked mathematics, for in respect of material things he argued that 'ideas' and 'forms' could be thought of in terms of geometrical shapes; it might of course be less easy to think geometrically of the 'ideas' of dogs and cats than of the 'idea' of a table, but it was not impossible. And anyway, the least mathematical among us has an innate apprehension of geometrical shapes: in another dialogue, *Menon*, Plato demonstrated that a boy plucked at random from a group of servants knew immediately what were the properties of squares, triangles and rectangles; he did not need to be taught. So, said Plato, take innate understanding as your starting point, build upon it, and you may aspire to a knowledge – a partial knowledge for most of us, no doubt – of 'the Ultimate Idea': God. Christians, later, agreed with what he said: the wonderful opening of St John's Gospel is clearly Platonic in its cast: 'In the beginning was the Word, and the Word was with God, and the Word was God. The same was in the beginning with God'. In August 1848 in Little Cornard Church, Lord Arthur Hervey preached upon 'the Ultimate Idea' – 'the Word', taking a text (1 Peter i 24, 25) which, as rendered in English, remarkably conflates 'the Word' with 'the word, or the message, of the Gospel' (V).

In a dialogue called *Timaeus* Plato said there is a Great Chain of Being. Aristotle (383–322 BC) developed what Plato said. Nobody today believes very much in the Great Chain of Being but, *as we shall see*, many of us have felt its resonance if we have heard our mothers or our grandmothers tell of how in days gone by they always wore their hats to church because the parson said they should.

The Great Chain of Being is a feature of the cosmology called Aristotelian, or Ptolemaic, after Ptolemy, a second-century astronomer. It is the name of the continuum thought to exist between basest matter and purist spirit, and associated with a universe of concentric spheres. Earth is at the centre of this universe (as Genesis agrees), and the planets in their spheres revolve around Earth in the following order: Moon, Mercury, Venus, Sun, Mars, Jupiter and Saturn. Beyond the planets in their spheres come, successively, the spheres of the Fixed Stars, the Crystalline Heavens, and the Empyrean Heaven, which is the sphere of God, origin of motion, but Himself unmoving. Basest matter is at the centre of Earth, and the Great Chain of Being is to be thought of as extending from that centre all the way to God Himself. Along the chain is located everything that is, in rank order from lowest to highest: minerals, plants, sponges, insects, fishes, serpents, birds, whales, viviparous quadrupeds, and man, and beyond man the celestial beings, located in the planetary spheres and in the spheres beyond them. Man is special, because part of him is matter (flesh) and part of him is spirit (understanding); part of him drifts down, towards the 'spheres' of animals, and part of him strives up, towards the sphere of God. Shakespeare understood; says Hamlet:

> ...What a piece of work is man! How noble in reason! How infinite in faculties! in form and moving, how express and admirable! in action, how like an angel! in apprehension, how like a god! the beauty of the world! the paragon of animals! And yet, to me, what is this quintessence of dust?
>
> *Hamlet* II ii 292–6

The Book of Common Prayer agrees absolutely, for upon Aristotelian teaching the beautiful office of matrimony erects St Paul's teaching concerning how the Christian spirit may triumph over the flesh. 'Matrimony,' it says,

> ...is commended of St Paul to be honourable among all men: and therefore is not by any to be enterprised, nor taken in hand, unadvisedly, lightly, or wantonly, to satisfy men's carnal lusts and appetites, like brute beasts that have no understanding; but reverently, discreetly, advisedly, soberly, and in the fear of God; duly considering the causes for which Matrimony was ordained.

Aristotle was much concerned with 'essence'; and the 'essence' of a thing as represented by the word we use to describe it is, to borrow the words of Bertrand Russell, 'those of its properties which it cannot change without losing its identity'. For example, the 'essence' of Aristotle himself, Russell would tell us, would be those properties in the absence of which we should not use the name 'Aristotle'. 'Essence' determined the place of a thing, as represented by its word, upon the Great Chain of Being; the 'thing' called 'Aristotle' would presumably be rather high upon the human section of the Chain, because of its – his! – magnificent intelligence.

Plato had been concerned not with 'essence' but with 'idea'; and 'idea' is 'form' is 'shape' is 'measurement' is 'number'. The teaching of Aristotle was in the ascendant through most of the middle ages; but towards the end of that period a significant change began in the intellectual climate of Western Europe: that is to say, many learned men began to consider that more concerning ultimate truth was to be found in the teaching of Plato than in that of Aristotle. Plato's *Menon*, so important for the development of mathematics and its philosophic implications, had been known in Europe since the thirteenth century. Much else produced by Plato was, however, unknown. But then, in the fifteenth century, the Byzantine empire, under threat from the Turks, sought to strengthen its contacts with the West, in the hope (forlorn!) that the West would come to its aid against the Turks. Some of these contacts were scholarly: scholars from Byzantium came to Italy and, through Italy, imparted to Europe generally a knowledge of Plato wider than Europe had previously had. In this way the teaching of Plato came to underpin the whole of the European Renaissance. Plato's mathematics informed the great astronomical discoveries of, for example, Copernicus, Galileo, Kepler, and Isaac Newton, sometimes to a degree of which they themselves were hardly aware; Galileo, for instance, though not a follower of mathematical Platonism, argued nevertheless that the 'book of the universe' was written in mathematical characters.[15]

Sometimes, however, it was a puzzle to determine what was chiefly Plato and what was chiefly Aristotle. For if I stand upon the sphere that is Aristotle's Earth, and look upwards to the sphere that God inhabits, I may perceive God's habitation (Heaven) in two ways: *either* I may think 'vertically', and perceive that God inhabits the upper end of the Great Chain of Being, *or* I may think 'horizontally', and contemplate the various activities that characterise whatever creatures are 'sign-posted' by this or that particular link in the Great Chain of Being.

All is made clear (or nearly so) in Fig. 3. Here we have a representation of the Great Chain of Being as it appeared in a book published in 1579. This representation is very incomplete and higgledy-piggledy and without a properly ascending order of significance – trees, quadrupeds, fishes, birds, people, celestial beings, and God: it is wholly inconsistent with the much better representation I have given in the fourth paragraph of this section of my Introduction. But this does not matter. The illustrator of

---

[15] Pietro Redondi, *Galileo Heretic*, London and Harmondsworth 1988, pp. 23, 63.

Fig. 3   The Great Chain of Being, as illustrated in Valdes's Rhetorica Christiana, *of 1579.*

1579, being in a helpful mood, has actually incorporated into his illustration a representation of a chain, so that we can 'think vertically' and better understand what this metaphorical Great Chain of Being is really all about. On the other hand, his representation of Aristotle's cosmos of concentric spheres is very crude: trees, quadrupeds, fishes, birds, and people should all inhabit the sphere called Earth – each category should *not* have a sphere to itself! (William Cuningham in 1559 – see Fig. 4 – had represented Aristotle's cosmos with fair accuracy but, alas, he had left himself no room to superimpose upon it the Great Chain of Being; and, being in a jokey mood, he allowed a cheeky Sun to escape from Sphere IV, where it belonged, to grin down upon everybody and everything from the top right-hand corner of the illustration.)

The crudeness of the 1579 illustration is, however, rather helpful, for it enables us to see that just as we have to think of our *own* sphere, Earth, as being flat or horizontal or a plain if we are to contemplate the things we have to do, such as shopping or setting the tea-table or playing cricket, so, if we are to contemplate the things that other beings have to do upon the spheres which *they* inhabit, we must think of those spheres too as being flat or horizontal: those celestial beings, for example, when they are not flying around must have a reliably flat or horizontal surface, or a plain, upon which to kneel if they are to say their prayers, and likewise God Himself must have a flat surface upon which to set His throne if He is to concentrate on wearing His Crown and juggling His orb and sceptre, and gravely to contemplate what the rest of us are up to.

So: once I have ceased to think, just for a moment, in terms of chains and concentric spheres, and have instead started to think in terms of horizontals, or plains, I may perhaps begin to find it comforting to hope that the more attractive or nobler features of life upon the plain that I inhabit (Earth), may in some way

Fig. 4   William Cuningham's 'The Cosmological glasse', of 1559.

'correspond' to, or bear a certain resemblance to, or be 'parallel' to, the plain that God inhabits (Heaven), very much in the way that the table in my kitchen 'corresponds' to, or is 'parallel' to, Plato's 'idea of the table'. And then, when I begin to regard myself as uniquely 'I', I may begin to hope that God and I may somehow 'correspond', that I, indeed, in my essential character and personality, am somehow an 'idea' that emanates from God. Likewise, as the marriage service would later point out, I may reflect that I am on a higher plain than the plains inhabited by 'brute beasts', including dogs and cats. But I may also reflect that between myself and animals there are 'correspondences' — physiological, certainly; mental possibly. Less easily I may discern 'correspondences' between myself and tables, though quite easily, perhaps, I may perceive a 'correspondence' between my living self and the once-living tree from which the tables were produced. Eventually, of course, in Bethlehem, God became Incarnate — became Man, that is. A Christian view of 'correspondence' then emerged, for Man was designed very evidently in the image of God the Designer.

Origen (?185–?254), a Greek and a giant among early Christian teachers, helped to widen the appeal of Christianity by arguing powerfully that Christian revelation was compatible with the teaching of the pagan Plato. Origen was shrewd, for Plato the philosopher was saying that 'Reality' — a 'real', objective and creating God, that is — determines both our more worthy day-to-day ideas and impressions *and* the language we use to express them. The importance for Christianity of Christianity's adoption of Platonism comes home to us if we consider the great twentieth-century philosopher Ludwig Wittgenstein (1889–1951). For Wittgenstein in his later work argued the other way round: that is, he argued that God emerges, or is created, *out of* our own more worthy ideas and impressions and the language we use to express them. If, though, God is thus created by Man then, clearly, God does not exist. Wittgenstein's ideas have been very influential; they have contributed much to undermining belief in the 'real' existence of the God of the Old and New Testaments. Since Wittgenstein, the Church has been ever more reluctant to argue that, because the 'reality' of the God in question can be attested by Plato's mathematics, the laws of Man and those of God must 'correspond'.

So in various ways theology in relation to cosmology was made to be important by Plato, Aristotle, the author of St John's Gospel, and St Paul. But not least among those who taught it to ordinary people upon the streets of Europe were the clockmakers. In the early fifteenth century Master Hanuš created the wonderful astronomical clock which modern tourists flock to see in the Old Town Square in Prague. Hanuš depicted not only Aristotle's sun, at the end of the hour-hand travelling around the Earth which was situated at the centre of the clock, but also the twelve Apostles and Jesus parading in two small windows above it. Likewise the late fifteenth-century clock set in the Clock Tower in St Mark's Square in Venice: the centre of the clock represents the Earth, Aristotle's sun travels around it at the end of the hour-hand, and during Epiphany and Ascensiontide figures of the Magi emerge on either side of it, and bow to a statue of the Madonna above it. But to the names of Plato, Aristotle, the author of St John's Gospel, St Paul, and late medieval clockmakers all over Europe must be added yet another: Dante Alighieri (1265–1321).

Did Edwin Sidney read Dante? We do not know. But Dante illuminates the lasting importance of what Sidney at his best, with his physico-theology, truly represented. For Dante's *The Divine Comedy* is one of the great poetic masterpieces of world literature. It was enormously influential down the centuries. In the nineteenth century it was known from illustrations produced by William Blake and especially Dante Gabriel Rossetti (1828–1882), as well as from the printed page; probably it was best known from Henry Holiday's

Dante and Beatrice of 1883, endlessly reproduced in Victorian history books and anthologies, and now to be seen in the Walker Art Gallery, in Liverpool. (See Fig. 5.)

Dante describes a Heaven and a Hell included within the Aristotelian cosmos, and presents to us Beatrice, whom he had loved during their childhoods in Florence and who, idealised in his poetry, is reflective always of the person of Jesus Christ – the Second Person of the Trinity – so that knowledge of, and love of, Beatrice is knowledge of, and love of, Christ (God). To put it differently: Dante shows love between man and woman to be cosmic in significance, because it corresponds to the love between God and Man; truly to apprehend the one, therefore, is truly to apprehend the other. Beatrice leads Dante onwards and upwards

Fig. 5   Henry Holiday's Dante and Beatrice, *1883.
The Walker Gallery, Liverpool.*

through the Aristotelian spheres to the tenth, Empyrean and unmoving sphere, where God resides. In a very beautiful poem in a work entitled *The New Life*,[16] produced in the years 1292–94, it is Dante's 'sigh' (alias his 'pilgrim spirit') which encounters Beatrice (alias Christ) beyond the Empyrean sphere, in a situation of love which no words can describe:

> Beyond the sphere that makes the widest round,
>   passes the sign which issues from my heart;
>   a strange, new understanding that sad Love
>   imparts to it keeps urging it on high.
>   When it has reached the place of its desiring,
>   it sees a lady held in reverence,
>   splendid in light, and through her radiance
>   the pilgrim spirit gazes at her being.
> But when it tries to tell me what it saw,
>   I cannot understand the subtle words
>   it speaks to the sad heart that makes it speak.
>   I know it talks of that most gracious one,
>   because it often mentions Beatrice;
>   this much is very clear to me, dear ladies.

This indescribable situation of love the office of matrimony in *The Book of Common Prayer* refers to as 'the mystical union that is betwixt Christ and his Church': 'Matrimony,' it says, '…is an honourable estate, instituted of God in the time of man's innocency, signifying unto us the mystical union that is betwixt Christ and his Church'. This teaching is derived from St Paul's Epistle to the Ephesians v 32. A Victorian bishop, Christopher Wordsworth, explained that the word 'mystical', here, 'signifies something kept *sacred* and *divine* which cannot be discovered by Natural Reason, but is unfolded by Divine Revelation'.

---

[16] Dante, *Vita Nuova*, translated with an introduction by Mark Musa, Oxford 1992.

This mystical union was made tangible and specific by the marriage ring, which is circular, not simply to fit upon a finger, but because a journey upon a circle is continuous and infinite, like a journey around a sphere of one of Aristotle's planets or of a celestial being. God, too, is continuous and infinite. The wafer that represents Him at the Holy Communion is circular; the ring that represents Him in the marriage service has a capital 'R': 'With this Ring I thee wed'; which is to say, 'I wed you, through the medium of God'.[17] Poets, of course, have greater licence than do compilers of prayer books; thus, in the last and characteristically Aristotelian verse of 'The Good-Morrow' the parson-poet John Donne can be taken to agree that if we wish to know what the carnal, the mental, and the spiritual fusion of a man and a woman in love can truly be, then we must think of the man and the woman each as being *precisely one half* of a particular unity – namely, *precisely one half* of a marriage ring (that ring – or that circularity – being recalled as, chiefly, an essential property of a sphere): 'Where can we find two better hemispheres…?'

Adam contemplating Eve made the point unmathematically: 'This,' he said, recalling that Eve was produced from one of his own ribs, 'is now bone of my bones, and flesh of my flesh: she shall be called Woman, because she was taken out of Man. Therefore shall a man leave his father and his mother, and shall cleave unto his wife: and they shall be one flesh.' St Paul, of course, took ahold of Adam's doctrine of Eve and welded it to Plato's doctrine of 'correspondences' and to Aristotle's doctrine of the Great Chain of Being (upon which ladies had a lower place than gentlemen), so to produce a doctrine of his very own – to wit, ladies must always wear their hats to church:

[17] This powerful intimation (six monosyllabic words) of God as medium is absent from *The Alternative Service Book 1980*, which has the bridegroom say, ' I give you this ring as a sign of our marriage' (twelve syllables). But a sign is not a medium.

> But I would have you know, that the head of every man is Christ; and the head of every woman is the man; and the head of Christ is God. Every man praying or prophesying, having his head covered, dishonoureth his head. But every woman that prayeth or prophesieth with her head uncovered dishonoureth her head. For a man indeed ought not to cover his head, forasmuch as he is the image and glory of God: but the woman is the glory of man. For the man is not of the woman; but the woman of the man. Neither was the man created for the woman; but the woman for the man.
>
> 1 Corinthians xi 3–5a, 7–9

Something 'mystical', then, precisely in the sense suggested by Bishop Wordsworth and Donne and the marriage ring was what Dante's sigh encountered when it contemplated Beatrice. All in all, therefore, for educated early Victorian Christians, reared in a culture as yet unruptured by Darwinian ways of thinking, extra-marital, carnal 'living together' meant 'living in sin'; for it meant non-acceptance of, or (even) a violation of, a set of interlocking circumstances central to cosmic Christian purpose.

But why should Little Cornard's history transport us so far into the matter of men and women and their love? Well, in Little Cornard Edwin Sidney always used the marriage service of *The Book of Common Prayer* (no alternative was available!); but Dante, Bishop Wordsworth, Donne and the marriage ring all testify that every time he did so he was rededicating himself to a way of thinking as characteristic of Aristotelianism as it was of St Paul. Though, however, the Aristotelian cosmos turned Dante's thoughts to love, part of it, as we have seen, was a Chain of Being: there was a hierarchy, in other words, and the God invoked in the marriage service was at its apex. This God, moreover, was very much an agricultural God; for when, in the second chapter of Hosea, we find one of the earliest biblical references to God's love for His people being synonymous with a husband's love for his wife, we find it grounded in allusions to the beasts of the field, the fowls of heaven, the creeping things of the ground, and corn and wine and oil; as God said, He would sow His people (His bride) unto Him 'in the earth'.

So, hierarchy – God's love – matrimony – the natural world and agriculture: four aspects of one thing – LOVE UNIVERSAL. For Sidney, agricultural parson pondering the marriage vow and, as Charles Badham said (XXXV), possessed of a mind 'powerful in its grasp, comprehensive in its range', what could have been more eloquent and more persuasive? When, therefore, we find him thinking hierarchically and instructing farm workers at harvest festivals or ploughing matches to keep to their stations in life, or when we find him classifying lunatics in Colchester, or if ever we should catch him admonishing girls and ladies always to wear their hats to church, then we should infer that his motivation is, profoundly, the motivation of love, not (as some historians would have us believe) that he desires to exercise some crude form of 'social control'.

In the sixteenth and seventeenth centuries the great astronomers, from Copernicus to Newton, demonstrated that the Aristotelian cosmos was nonsense: Earth, they said, was not at the centre of the universe, and the planets moved not in spheres but, more or less (said some), elliptically. But if you lived in Little Cornard it was less easy to dislodge the resonances of Dante and Beatrice, *The Book of Common Prayer*, and the celestial beings which, Dante agreed – contemplating them in an arrangement of three groups of three, which recalled the Holy Trinity – inhabited the lunary and supra-lunary part of the Great Chain of Being, each in its own sphere: namely, angels and archangels and thrones; dominations and virtues and principalities; and powers and cherubim and seraphim, some of whom you sang about in church on Sundays in the *Te Deum*. Moreover, the terrestrial section of the Chain, from Man down to minerals, remained more or less unscathed, simply because the great natural scientists of the eighteenth century (Linnaeus, for instance) loved to think of Aristotle when they allocated animals, birds, fishes and other living creatures to classes and categories, which they arranged hierarchically. It is easy to see, therefore, why the Great Chain of Being lurked within the scaffolding of educated minds until well into the nineteenth century, even to the extent that in 1849 a journalist reflecting upon a clothing charity in Little Cornard should have found it quite natural to write of the 'kindly chain' which (he felt) united rich and poor, the links in which were neither celestial nor terrestrial beings, but acts of benevolence and mutual service (VII).

PLATO WAS OF COURSE not forgotten. In the later seventeenth century his doctrine of 'ideas' was revived in England, in Cambridge, by a group of Church of England thinkers known as the Cambridge Platonists. In 1691 there appeared one of the most remarkable of the by-products of that group, the first edition of a work entitled *On the Power, Wisdom and Goodness of God, as manifested in the Works of Creation*, by John Ray (1627–1705).

Ray was a very great naturalist. He was born in Black Notley, near Braintree, in Essex. In Braintree there is a statue of him. His gaze across the street is quizzical, as though he questions whether scurriers-by needs must get their shopping done heedless of correspondences between the transient and the divine. He contemplated nature and thought it wonderful inherently, precisely in the way commended to us upon our television screens by such very 'modern' scientists as David Attenborough or Richard Dawkins. But, though his curiosity was 'scientific' and 'modern', Ray inferred from nature's miracles – as an Attenborough or a

Dawkins would not – that there was a grand Design, and that God was the Designer. This Design, of course, was not a Machine so, clearly, to say 'God the Designer' was not to say 'God the Engineer'. For engineering seemed scarcely numinous, and Ray perceived the numinous in nature, that nature had an ecstasy embracing oddities and incongruities. Like Plato, but unlike most 'modern' scientists, he delighted more to discern a mystery than to explain it; he therefore wished to know in a philosophical way what was 'behind' or 'beyond' the facts that he observed, much as in a later time he might have wished to know what was 'behind' or 'beyond' the melodies of a Mozart of a Schubert. Was it not wonderful, he mused,

- that a bird with young in the nest should know how to distribute morsels equitably among them, even though it could bring to the nest but one morsel at a time, and even though, presumably, it could not count;
- that chickens when left to themselves, but apparently not otherwise, would lay continuously only such number of eggs as they could conveniently cover and hatch;
- that a silkworm's eggs should hatch precisely when the mulberry tree began to bud;
- that a calf 'will so manage his head as though he would push with his horns even before they shoot';
- that 'another animal which hath no horns should not make a shew of pushing';
- that 'young animals as soon as they are brought forth should know their food';
- that young ducklings would naturally go into the water, though hatched and reared by a hen, provided that the hen should bring them there.

And so on. As George Herbert said, 'Who would have thought…'. For Ray, it seemed that nature existed for the delight of

God whose existence, very clearly, was prior to it.

Important eighteenth-century Christians admired *The Wisdom of God*. John Wesley did. So did Gilbert White, author of *The Natural History of Selborne* (1789). So did Joseph Butler (1692–1752), sometime bishop of Durham.

Butler wrote much about Design. In 1736 he published *The Analogy of Religion Natural and Revealed to the Constitution and Course of Nature*. He demonstrated that Nature constituted 'a scheme, a system, or constitution whose parts correspond to each other, and to a whole; as really as any work of art...' He argued that, *by analogy*, the 'moral government over the world', which we must suppose God to operate, must be a scheme or system too, even though 'quite beyond our comprehension'. By analogy also the life of man was preparation for the life hereafter, as the life of a child was preparation for the life of man. Perhaps more than anyone Butler furbished the ancient notion of 'correspondence' into the more serviceable notion of analogy, its task to jolt us into an understanding of one thing by comparing it to something else like it in one way but not in all ways.

Butler's *Analogy*, however, did not rely for its authority and impact simply upon the musings of John Ray, the speculations of the Cambridge Platonists and the revival of Platonism in the fifteenth century. The matter of its influence was, at once, simpler and more complex than that, for the *Analogy* emerged out of, and was presented to, a culture which took analogy for granted; that is to say, all kinds of people, the educated and the uneducated, were receptive to what it had to say, for three very notable reasons:

1. Both the Old Testament and the New, and *The Book of Common Prayer*, were steeped in analogy, often naturalistic. 'As the hart panteth after the water brooks,' says the biblical version of Psalm 42, 'so panteth my soul after thee, O God'. 'But some man will say,

INTRODUCTION

How are the dead raised up? And with what body do they come?' says St Paul, in the burial service, declaring that to understand the Christian doctrine of resurrection we must work step-by-step, analogically, 'upwards' from the earthy things we know from experience to the heavenly things we aspire to know:

> Thou fool, that which thou sowest is not quickened, except it die. And that which thou sowest, thou sowest not that body that shall be, but bare grain, it may chance of wheat, or of some other grain: But God giveth it a body, as it hath pleased him, and to every seed his own body. All flesh is not the same flesh; but there is one kind of flesh of men, another flesh of beasts, another of fishes, and another of birds. There are also celestial bodies, and bodies terrestrial....

2. The whole edifice of biblical prophecy and prefiguration, upon which Christian revelation depends is, often, analogical. 'Almighty and everlasting God,' says the opening prayer of the office of baptism,

> who of thy great mercy didst save Noah and his family in the ark from perishing by water; and also didst safely lead the children of Israel thy people through the Red Sea, figuring thereby thy holy Baptism; and by the Baptism of thy well-beloved Son Jesus Christ, in the river Jordan, didst sanctify water to the mystical washing away of sin; We beseech thee, for thine infinite mercies, that thou wilt mercifully look upon *this Child*; wash *him* and sanctify *him* with the Holy Ghost....

St Paul, moreover, going to the root of the matter (as always), observes the inverse analogy between the fallen Adam and the risen Christ, which underpins the Resurrection: 'For if through the offence of one many be dead, much more the grace of God, and the gift by grace, which is by one man, Jesus Christ, hath abounded unto many' (Romans v 15). Such a point would have been taken very seriously by Victorians, because in the margins of Victorian Bibles, against each verse, were references to other passages (different references in different Bibles, perhaps) that one ought to read in order to remind oneself of what was prefiguring what; for example, in my own Victorian Bible (inherited from a Great Cornard relative who had acquired it in 1888) from Romans v 15 I am directed to Genesis ii 17, Genesis iii 6, and also to 1 Corinthians xv 21 – 'For since by man came death, by man came also the resurrection of the dead'.

3. The finest English literature – in former times known to far more people than perhaps we imagine – was steeped in analogy. Shakespeare's Richard II comments thus upon his subjects:

> Did they not sometime cry 'All hail!' to me?
> So Judas did to Christ; but he, in twelve
> Found truth in all but one; I in twelve thousand, none.

Richard II IV i 169–71

In 'Redemption', George Herbert, parson as well as poet, brings the promise of redemption dramatically to earth by saying that the Old Testament covenant together with its supersession by the New is analogous to an agricultural tenancy which, unprofitable, might perchance be redevised upon a lower rent. In 'The Forerunners', intentionally or otherwise, he evokes (in its *Book of Common Prayer* version) the Collect for Ascension Day by invoking simultaneously Platonic 'correspondence' and an image of an Aristotelian 'essence', light, moving up the Chain of Being to its natural destination, the Light of God:

> True beautie dwells on high: ours is a flame
>   But borrow'd thence to light us thither.
> Beautie and beauteous words should go together.

So, Butler's *Analogy* was an important work of Christian apology, in its day an up-to-date Christian reformulation and consolidation of an ancient way of thinking. It was read by educated Victorians as well as by the parsons whose sermons they and their less educated neighbours listened to attentively. Twenty editions were published in the United Kingdom in the reign of Queen Victoria (1837–1901), ten of them by the year of the publication of *The Origin of Species* (1859). In 1896 an edition appeared which had been edited by the former prime minister, William Gladstone, who took the keenest interest in the education and training of Church of England clergymen. Gladstone described Aristotle, St Augustine, Dante and Butler as 'my four "doctors"'.[18]

Unsurprisingly, analogical thinking informed the best Victorian science. The examples below are very disparate; each was surely contemplated in the rectory at Little Cornard as Edwin Stanley prepared his scientific lectures. Of the first, one would like to know what was said between Stanley and Henslow, in Little Cornard's rectory or in Hitcham's, for the agnostic Darwin had once been Henslow's pupil:

(a) *Darwin*, in the first chapter of *The Origin of Species*, argued his proof of the principle of natural selection partly upon the analogy that he perceived between (on the one hand) the particular procedures of breeding used by a pigeon fancier to ensure ('unnaturally') the production of the particular breed he wants, and (on the other) the particular procedures of a particular situation in nature which ensure ('unnaturally') the survival of a particular species. 'The key,' said Darwin, 'is man's power of accumulative selection: nature gives successive variations; man adds them up in certain directions useful to him.'

---

[18] John Morley, *The Life of William Ewart Gladstone*, Macmillan, London ed. 1911, vol. i, p. 155, n. 1.

(b) *Michael Faraday*, the founder of electrical engineering and a friend of Edwin Stanley, erected whole programmes of physical and chemical research upon the bases of hypothetical analogies. Could he prove such-and-such a situation in *this* field, he would wonder, by exploring the implications of his hypothesis that it was analogous to such-and-such a situation in *that* field, especially if *that* field should be religious, or simply poetic? 'You can hardly imagine,' he wrote in 1845 to the Swiss chemist C. F. Schönbein, discoverer of ozone, 'how I am struggling to exert my poetical ideas now for the discovery of analogies and remote figures respecting the earth, sun, and all sorts of things – for I think that is the true way (corrected by judgement) to work out a discovery.'

(c) *Sir Roderick Impey Murchison* was a proud ex-soldier and the most acclaimed of Victorian geologists; his bustling professional energy puts one in mind of Edwin Sidney scrambling in the geology of the new railway cuttings between Colchester and Sudbury and Bury St Edmunds. Murchison internationalised a style of stratigraphical geology analogous to the style, beloved of his contemporaries, of putting social classes into strata. He discovered a fossiliferous succession in the Welsh borderland, and named it the 'Silurian system' because he thought that the British glory of the discovery of this key for unlocking the complexities of rocks of similar age throughout the rest of the world was analogous to the militaristic glory of the Silures, the Romano-British tribe which, he held, had once occupied the precise territory of his 'system'.[19]

---

[19] 'The analogy between artificial and natural selection is central to the *Origin*,' says James A. Secord ('Nature's Fancy: Charles Darwin and the breeding of pigeons', *Isis*, vol. lxxvii, 1981, pp. 183–6). Faraday to Schönbein is quoted in L. Pearce Williams, *Michael Faraday: a biography*, London 1965, p. 443. For Murchison see James A. Secord, 'King of Siluria: Roderick Murchison and the imperial theme in nineteenth-century British geology', *Victorian Studies*, vol. xxv, no. 4, Summer 1982.

So behind the homely analogies wedged in the ends of Edwin Sidney's lectures there was an awesome intellectual tradition. Hence the trekkings to hear him. 'My grandparents were Sudbury nonconformists,' Miss Francis said; 'but they would always *walk* from Sudbury to Little Cornard when he spoke, because they wanted to listen to something worth hearing'. Alas, even whilst Sidney lived, analogical reasoning was fading; in the Western world it had withered slowly between the 1870s and the end of the First World War. By the 1980s it had all but died, certainly in Little Cornard: on Easter Day, 1983, after the celebration of Holy Communion in the church, the officiating churchwarden proclaimed that 49 people had communicated, out of a congregation of 58, and that the offertory was £49.58p. The analogy was noted; everybody chuckled. But no one thought it providential.[20]

Factories and Poetry

ON THE WHOLE the naturalists who followed John Ray did not share his sense of the numinous. Had they done so the physico-theologians of Victorian England might better have coped with Darwin. For the questions that Ray put concerning chickens and silk-worms, calves and ducklings, were questions concerning 'wonder'. And the matter of 'wonder' is akin to the matter of 'wisdom', or the matter of 'morality', or the matter of 'giftedness', or the matter of 'responsibility', in that philosophically and scientifically it is dreadfully difficult to pin down. If, though, 'wonder', 'wisdom', 'morality', 'giftedness', or 'responsibility' were absent from our work-a-day vocabularies, then our lives would be impossible. Clergymen, therefore, should have kept ahold of John

---

[20] Sadly, after a recount the offertory was discovered to be £1 short of an analogy – that is, £48.58p.

Ray and George Herbert, who asked both the 'why' and the 'how' questions of science; they should have spotted that Darwin and the Darwinists were asking only the 'how' questions, and tending more and more to deny that the 'why' questions even existed.

BUT THE GRADUAL forgetting of Ray is hardly surprising, for two reasons: first, there was the influence of the French philosophers – the *philosophes* – of the eighteenth-century Age of Reason; second, there was the machinery, some of it in factories, of the Industrial Revolution.

Directly or indirectly the *philosophes* were admirers and disciples of Isaac Newton (1642–1727). Newton himself was a Christian, and a teleologist. 'A God without dominion, providence, and final causes,' he had said, 'is nothing but Fate and Nature.' But an apple fell upon his head; so, in *The Mathematical Principles of Natural Philosophy* (1687), he had explained the workings of God's universe according to the principles of a system that was mathematical. 'Principles', 'systems' – these were key words. Newton said that all things in the universe – celestial as well as terrestrial, angels (if they existed!) as well as apples – are governed by the same principles or laws of gravity; every particle in the universe, he said, attracts every other particle with a force that is directly proportional to the masses of the two particles and inversely proportional to the square of the distance between their centres.

Plato and the Athenian servant boy would have been amazed to learn that God's mathematics was much more complicated than they had supposed. They would have found it difficult to grasp Newton's concept of gravity. And they would have been worried to learn that Newton's rejection of the cosmos of concentric spheres was based upon observation and experiment, as well as mathematics, rather than upon aesthetics and faith, and reasoning supplemented by guesswork. Even so, they would have understood perfectly some of Newton's mathematical vocabulary; for instance, they would have understood 'directly proportional to', and 'inversely proportional to', and 'the square of the distance'. In other words, some of Newton's mathematical vocabulary was *their* mathematical vocabulary. And for Christians, of course, Plato's mathematical vocabulary seemed to underpin the Christian doctrine of the Incarnation. For this reason most eighteenth-century Christians found it perfectly possible, courtesy of Plato, to accept the teaching of Newton (the founder of modern physical science) as being compatible with traditional Christianity.

The trouble, however, was that to a great extent Newton was hijacked by the *philosophes* whose aims were mostly irreligious because, being men of Reason, they did not like the church – the church in France, that is. The father-figure of the *philosophes* was Voltaire (1694–1778), a major populariser of Newton's works, and not at all a Christian. The *philosophes* published encyclopaedias and other works containing the facts and information which, they held, underlay the 'principles' (Newton's word) and 'systems' and 'deductions' and 'progress' which incessantly concerned them. But as they did so they forgot that Newton had insisted that, despite God's mathematics, at the root of God's universe lay certain occult or mysterious principles, not amenable to discovery by men and women. In 1759, at the height of this Age of Reason, Jean le Rond d'Alembert, an editor of the French *Encyclopédie*, reflected upon the state of European learning in his day, as though European learning in his day – including natural science and 'the true system of the world' (whatever that might be!) – were a branch of business management or counting-house procedures, having little connection with the God of mystery in whom Newton himself very much believed. D'Alembert said:

If one considers without bias the present state of our knowledge, one cannot deny that philosophy among us has shown progress. Natural science from day to day accumulates new riches. Geometry, by extending its limits, has borne its torch into the regions of physical science which lay nearest at hand. The true system of the world has been recognised, developed and perfected... Thus from the principles of the secular sciences to the foundations of the religious revelation, from metaphysics to matters of taste, from music to morals, from the scholastic disputes of the theologians to matters of trade, from the laws of princes to those of peoples, from natural law to the arbitrary law of nations....everything has been discussed and analysed, or at least mentioned.[21]

The *philosophes* in France therefore found it quite natural to talk of 'First Cause' rather than of 'God'. In England not *all* clergymen copied them, but very many did: rather than of 'God' they talked of 'Deity', so attracting to themselves the name of 'deist'. Such clergymen did not worry very much about the fundamental doctrines of the Christian faith – 'rigmarole stories about the Trinity', as a pupil of the Cambridge teacher, William Paley, described them. They were apt to regard what they called the 'benevolence of the Deity' (a phrase that Paley used) as the sufficient basis of the Christian religion, and to take account of the mysteries and wonders of the Bible only when they thought them consistent with common sense. The religion of the deists was thus rather dreary; it did not move and shake. In opposition to it there arose the hot-blooded fervour of eighteenth-century Methodism, and Church of England Evangelicalism in which Edwin Sidney's family, the Hills of Shropshire, played so conspicuous a part.

In its broadest aspect this unexciting deism permeated much of English society through most of the eighteenth century. Wittingly

---

[21] Quoted in Stuart Andrews, 'Thomas Jefferson, American Encyclopaedist', *History Today*, August 1967, p. 502.

or otherwise many writers and thinkers promoted it. One was a great poet, Alexander Pope (1688–1774) who, though profoundly Christian, helped in poetry (as we shall see) to blunt that perception of the numinous in Nature characterising men such as Ray to the extent that such perception could only be revived, much later, by another major poet, William Wordsworth. Another promoter of deism was William Paley (1743–1805), archdeacon of Carlisle, but more famous as a naturalist and teacher than as a clergyman. Both contemplated the great tradition of teleology examined in these pages, and both diminished it, Pope by deflecting it to the 'taste' (or the preoccupations) of polite society which, later, d'Alembert would imply was on a par with 'the foundations of the religious revelation', and metaphysics; and Paley by making Nature seem like a machine.

In 1736 Butler published his *Analogy* and Pope his great poem, *An Essay on Man*. In his poem Pope said:

> See, through this air, this ocean, and this earth,
> All matter quick, and bursting into birth.
> Above, how high, progressive life may go!
> Around, how wide! How deep extend below!
> Vast chain of being! Which from God began,
> Natures ethereal, human, angel, man,
> Beast, bird, fish, insect, what no eye can see,
> No glass can reach; from infinite to thee,
> From thee to nothing. – On superior powers
> Were we to press, inferior might on ours;
> Or in the full creation leave a void,
> Where, one step broken, the great scale's destroyed;
> From Nature's chain whatever link you strike,
> Tenth, or ten thousandth, breaks the chain alike.

In the seventeenth century you took the Great Chain of Being very seriously from George Herbert; in the eighteenth you took it with a pinch of salt from Pope. But you thought it sensible to cling to it as a way of thinking. After all, was not Pope what today we would call a conservationist – or, one concerned with 'right order, as desired by God'? Did not Pope's 'one step broken' and his 'void in the full creation' remind you of Ecclesiastes – of the void that shall come when the silver chord be loosed and the golden chain be broken, and the dust and the spirit shall return whence they came? In Ipswich, too, in 1851, did you perhaps think of Pope and of Ecclesiastes, or even of Tennyson's whole round earth 'every way / Bound by gold chains about the feet of God',[22] when you applauded Edwin Sidney for saying, in the presence of the great geologist Sir Charles Lyell, that 'the more desirous we were to manifest a kind regard for those below us in station...the more would peace and prosperity, and order, and mutual respect, and kindness, be interwoven in a golden thread of light through every bond and link of the golden system'?[23] In all civilised societies, including the society of the biblical Hebrews and the society of Sidney's Little Cornard, there have been people wishing to conserve, and drawing analogies between the conserving of nature and the conserving of the social order, even when cruel abuse and cruel destruction of nature have seemed to testify to the contrary.

John Addison (1672–1719) was an earlier poet of Design. But his 'The spacious firmament on high' – a poem, or hymn, now rarely come across[24] – explicitly insists, in its third verse, that keeping hold

---

[22] 'Morte d'Arthur', published in 1842.

[23] *Ipswich Journal*, 20 December 1851, p. 3.

[24] ' Now rarely come across' was written on Saturday, 16 September 1995. The next day, Sunday, in Little Cornard church, a muddled rector gave out 'Hymn 170', in our books 'The spacious firmament on high', instead of 'Hymn 578', 'And did those feet in ancient time', which was what he had intended. He corrected himself. But after hurried consultation, upon our own perception that God had clearly intervened in favour of the preoccupations of the present author and upon Addison' s that putting in a word for Aristotle could hardly come amiss, we settled for 170.

of old and disproven ideas (those ideas proclaimed in the first six verses of the *Te Deum*) can be a reasonable thing to do, even when the scientists say 'no':

> What though in solemn silence all
> Move round the dark terrestrial ball;
> What though nor real voice nor sound
> Amid their radiant orbs be found;
> In reason's ear they all rejoice,
> And utter forth a glorious voice,
> For ever singing as they shine,
> 'The hand that made us is divine'.

So, there was the theology of Design and there were the poets of the theology of Design. Pope and Addison are important. For, at least from the earlier eighteenth century until around the time of the First World War, middle class people read poetry in their homes and recited it aloud. In Victorian times, indeed, love of poetry came second only to love of Bible and love of hymns – and many hymns, of course, were very fine poetry. The historian Noel Annan says that poetry then was music: 'It was an incantation to be chanted, as anyone who listens to the earliest gramophone records can tell'. In 1812 Francis Jeffrey, editor (1803–1829) of the prestigious *Edinburgh Review* praised Suffolk's most famous poet, George Crabbe (1754–1832), for addressing his poems to the 'middling classes of society'. The poetry of John Keats (1795–1821) went further than the 'middling classes', for it entered Victorian popular culture in cheap mass editions; perhaps educated people in Little Cornard read 'Ode to a Grecian Urn' which, though its final lines echoed Plato ('Beauty is truth, truth beauty'), turned Platonism on its head by suggesting not that we engage with the objects and impressions of everyday experience by referring them to representative 'ideas', but rather that we respond most fully to representations and abstractions by referring them to everyday experience: 'Heard melodies are sweet, but those unheard / Are sweeter' – no doubt, but we cannot judge the latter if we have never known the former.[25]

Keats's friend the poet Shelley (1785–1822) called poets 'unacknowledged legislators'. For scientists, most notably for geologists in Edwin Sidney's time, the greatest poetic legislator was William Wordsworth, poet laureate from 1843 till his death in 1850. Wordsworth, who knew John Ray's *The Wisdom of God*, reflected upon Ray's wonder at Nature and built upon it a testimony to the wholeness of Nature, and to Man, with his capacity both for good and for evil, as an integral part of that wholeness; for Nature and Man, said Wordsworth, in his great poem *The Excursion*, were imbued with the same '*active* Principle':[26]

> 'To every Form of being is assigned,'
> Thus calmly spake the venerable Sage,
> 'An *active* Principle: – howe'er removed
> From sense and observation, it subsists
> In all things, in all natures; in the stars
> Of azure heaven, the unenduring clouds,
> In flower and tree, in every pebbly stone
> That paves the brooks, the stationary rocks,
> The moving waters, and the invisible air.
> Whate'er exists hath properties that spread
> Beyond itself, communicating good,
> A simple blessing, or with evil mixed;
> Spirit that knows no insulated spot,
> No chasm, no solitude; from link to link
> It circulates, the Soul of all the worlds.'

---

[25] Noel Annan, *Leslie Stephen the Godless Victorian*, Chicago and London 1986, p. 330; Judith Chernaik, 'Season of shallow forgetfulness', *The Times*, 17 October 1995, p. 34; Keith Thomas, *Man and the Natural World: changing attitudes in England 1500–1800*, London 1983, p. 149. See also Appendix I.

The Excursion was especially important for Victorian geologists because, most of them being like Adam Sedgwick (1785–1873) – one of the greatest of their number – orthodox believers in the cardinal doctrines of the Christian faith, they were anxious always to be assured that, in the words of Sedgwick, 'All nature bears the imprint of one great Creative Mind and all parts of knowledge are, therefore, of one kindred and family'. Geology *seemed* to testify to one great Creative Mind; Wordsworth's poem *did* testify to one great Creative Mind. Wordsworth, that is, taught his friend Sedgwick to discern with confidence a Christian wonder in Nature which otherwise he might have discerned only with diffidence. Confidence supplanting diffidence: John Ray had needed no such support from George Herbert.

Small wonder, then, that quite often the scientific arguments of Edwin Sidney, who as we shall see was probably a pupil of Sedgwick, were anchored with poetry (IX), or that, more widely, even newspaper editors were sometimes poetical (XXVIII).

As 'The Flower' of George Herbert foreshadowed the science of Ray, so did *An Essay on Man* foreshadow the science of Paley.

From 1767 to 1776 Paley taught at Cambridge, at Christ's College, where Darwin later went. He said the will of God was happiness. So he was a very cheerful man, and thought all animal creation cheerful too. His scholarship though not profound was lucid, seemed full of common sense, and used words from factory workshops, such as 'lens', 'refraction', 'screw', 'lubricity', 'socket' and 'apparatus', to conjure up a God in overalls, benevolent, but contracted to the Industrial Revolution; precisely the God eschewed by Ray, and precisely the God of deadly terrors – of hammer and chain and furnace and anvil – challenged head-on by William Blake in his poem 'The Tyger'. Paley's publications were

[26] John Wyatt, *Wordsworth and the Geologists*, Cambridge 1995, pp. 122, 133, 207.

over-esteemed, but were prominent in Cambridge BA syllabuses in the early nineteenth century, and still there in the early twentieth. One of them was *Natural Theology: or evidences of the existence and attributes of the deity, collected from the appearances of nature.*

Paley grabbed the minds and souls of clergymen, rather as he grabbed me when, to write this paragraph, I requested at the Cambridge University Library a copy – *any* copy – of the first edition of *Natural Theology*, and which, in his own hand on the flyleaf, he had inscribed as a present to the Bishop of Ely. *Natural Theology* was a *tour de force* of teleology. It plagiarised extensively from Ray's *Wisdom of God*, was published in 1802, and had run into fifteen editions by 1815. Though, like Ray, Paley believed that God existed prior to nature, unlike Ray he thought he perceived a natural order created not for the delight and glory of God its Creator, but for the satisfaction and fulfilment of its own component parts, including Man:

> Were there no example in the world of contrivance except that of the *eye*, it would be alone sufficient to support the conclusion which we draw from it, as to the necessity of an intelligent Creator.... Its coats and humours, constructed, as the lenses of a telescope are constructed, for the refraction of rays of light to a point, which forms the proper action of the organ; the provision in its muscular tendons for turning its pupil to the object, similar to that which is given to the telescope by screws...; the further provision for its defence, for its constant lubricity and moisture, which we see in its socket and its lids, in its gland for the secretion of the matter of tears...; these provisions compose altogether an apparatus, a system of parts, a preparation of means, so manifest in their design, so exquisite in the contrivance, so successful in their issue, so precious and so infinitely beneficial in their use as, in my opinion, to bear down all doubt that can be raised on the subject.

Likewise, a designing God has given snouts to pigs that they may root in the ground, and has decreed that young deer shall have no horns, least they spike their mothers' udders. And likewise does a happy world of nature attest to God's design of happiness. 'The air, the earth, the water,' Paley says,

> teem with delighted existence. In a spring noon, or summer evening, on whichever side I turn my eyes, myriads of happy beings turn upon my view...a *bee* amongst the flowers in spring, is one of the cheerfullst objects that can be looked upon.... At this moment, in every given moment of time, how many myriads of animals are eating their food, gratifying their appetites, ruminating in their holes, accomplishing their wishes, pursuing their pleasure, taking their pastimes?

Darwin again

WHAT PALEY SAID about pigs, young deer, bees and myriads of happy beings would be rendered absurd by what Darwin would say about squirrels. For Victorian clergymen, however, that was only half the problem. The other half was that Paley, whom they had imbibed at University and whom in a muddled way they even managed to combine with an acceptance of evolution (though not natural selection), had encouraged them to view God's creation mechanistically, and seldom to perceive the numinous. So with Paley and Darwin in opposite ways triumphant over George Herbert, John Ray and the numinous, there was small chance in the longer term that Little Cornard or anywhere else physico-theology would effect social redemption, no matter the miles trudged by a centenarian's grandparents to learn all about it. For, on the whole, holiness had departed from science.

POPULAR SCIENCE

> The study of geology, in the narrow acceptation of the word, is confined to the investigation of the materials which compose this terrestrial globe; — in its more extended signification, it relates, also, to the examination of the different layers or strata of society, as they are to be met with in the world.
>
> 'The Geology of Society',
> *Punch and London Charivari*, I (1841), p. 157

> The little Gradrinds had cabinets in various departments of science .... They had a little conchological cabinet, and a little metallurgical cabinet, and a little mineralogical cabinet, and the specimens were all arranged and labelled, and the bits of stone and ore looked as though they might have been broken from the parent substances by those tremendously hard instruments their own names ....
>
> Charles Dickens, *Hard Times*, 1854, book i, chapter 3

HOLINESS HAD DEPARTED from science in that, by the earlier nineteenth century, Romantic poetry, when informed by natural science, had largely assumed the role of science itself as a vessel of holiness, or seemed to have done so to those with a knowledge of science and an interest in poetry; much of the poetry of Wordsworth, informed by the best geological science, was a vessel of holiness. Whereas the natural history of John Ray and – uniquely, perhaps, in the nineteenth century – the physics of Michael Faraday (XXXII) assumed that holiness, or the numinous, was 'real', that it actually existed, and should inspire scientific experiments, the geology of Sedgwick was conducted upon straightforwardly empirical and 'modern' principles, was absorbed by the poetry of Wordsworth *and then* sought assurance from the poetry of Wordsworth that it – geology – was characterised by holiness. Typically, the science of the nineteenth century was straightforwardly empirical; so, Sedgwick was much more typically a nineteenth-century scientist than was Faraday. To that extent, perhaps, the popularity of science in the nineteenth century was advanced; for, in an industrial age, men found it easier to be empirical than to be holy.

Popular science was a phenomenon in England from the years immediately after the Battle of Waterloo through to the middle years of Victoria's reign. It received its biggest impetus from the creation in 1831 of the British Association for the Advancement of Science. But earlier it had built upon a wavering tradition of popular scientific lecturing dating from the late seventeenth century, and upon a culture of 'self-improvement' (scientific, mathematical, literary and musical) characterising certain elements among the working classes since at least the eighteenth century,[27] and, subsequently, feeding not only upon the ever-increasing production of books and periodicals, and upon the profusion of literary and philosophical societies, but also upon the popular lecturing of Sir Humphry Davy, and more particularly – from 1825 onwards, in his Friday Evening Discourses – of Michael Faraday, at the Royal Institution. The essential feature of popular science was a widespread, obsessive interest in the 'ologies' of nature – geology, biology, palaeontology, ornithology, entomology, conchology, phrenology and so on. A minor feature was the deft confidence of its journalistic and its literary traces. For example, it was simply 'Mr Brown' (VI), 'Professor Henslow' (IX, XXXVIII), 'Professor

---

[27] Terry Parssinen, 'Mesmeric Performers', *Victorian Studies*, vol. xxi, no. 1, Autumn 1977, pp. 89, 90; E. P. Thompson, *The Making of the English Working Class*, Harmondsworth 1968, p. 322.

Owen' (XXXIII, XXXVIII). Your acquaintance was assumed, as was your acceptance of the waddling megalosaurus in the opening of *Bleak House*.

The times were propitious. In the first place, in the final years of the reign of George III (d. 1820) reflective, leisured persons, released from the worries of war, were troubled nevertheless by considerations of civic instability in a post-war society in which towns and cities grew and industries developed. Ordered worlds were much desired; Paley's world was ordered: his pigs, his deer, his bees, his myriads of other beings, were clearly very well behaved, else God would not have let them be so cheerful. So, minds attuned to public order were attuned to Paley too. Then, Paley was 'improving', for he suggested that the simplest scientific pursuits could lead to godliness. So, when you went for a walk you could discover the Design of God, if you collected rocks and shells and ferns and butterflies and spiders; so, eventually, if you poked around for fossils within the excavations made by railway navvies (VI), or by those who built in burgeoning towns and cities; so, if you went to Edwin Sidney's breathless lectures, and attended to the edifying bangs, pops, fizzles, fire-clouds and dissolving views that he frequently created, and that tallied very nicely with the 'mixed bills' and melodrama of the middle- and the low-brow theatres that you went to on other occasions.

Paley made you inquisitive. He impelled you to 'find out', and so to help yourself towards salvation. Thus, superficially, he suited Sidney's Evangelicalism. Materially, he was congenial to the ghastly world of Mr Gradgrind's children, to the self-help world of Samuel Smiles, acquisitive and energising, and, of course, to the clutter and curiosities of the Great Exhibition itself (1851), also 'designed', also 'improving'. Paley's *Natural Theology* shimmered through the mental world of half the nineteenth century. It was early Victorian by adoption.

MUDFOG YEARS

> I found Him not in world or sun
>   Or eagle's wing, or insect's eye;
>   Nor thro' the questions men may try,
> The petty cobwebs we have spun:
>
> If e'er when faith had fall'n asleep
>   I heard a voice 'believe no more'
>   And heard an ever-breaking shore
> That tumbled in the Godless deep;
>
> A warmth within the breast would melt
>   The freezing reason's colder part,
>   And like a man in wrath the heart
> Stood up and answer'd 'I have felt'.
>
> Alfred, Lord Tennyson
> In Memoriam, 1850, CXXIV

Between 1820 and 1840 geology became the science of the day. It captured popular imagination. In this age the names iguanadon, pterodactyl, dinosaur, gigantosaurus, megatherium, plesiosaurus became part of the English language; all inferred from evidence collected upon walks round countryside or sea-coasts, digging in caves, exploring in quarries. The geologists studded their pages with drawings of beasts hitherto confined to children's story books. A skilfully produced survey of geology sold more copies than a novel by Sir Walter Scott. They peered through a window into a fairyland with real ogres.

Owen Chadwick, The Victorian Church
part i, London 2nd ed. 1970, pp. 558, 559

IN THE EARLY VICTORIAN age the paramount sciences for those concerned with the security of biblical faith were biology and geology. Even before the publication of *The Origin of Species* these were the sciences which caused Victorian clergymen to peer nervously into successive journals and periodicals of learned institutions such as the Linnean Society and the Geological Society and the British Association for the Advancement of Science, for these were the sciences which bore most directly upon the matter of Creation as discerned in Genesis, and which, most evidently, might subvert the fundamentals of True Religion, and so of personal and social morality.

Edwin Sidney was a name-dropper; he simply could not help it, so eager was he to proclaim God's Whole Creation and her sister True Religion. You would take your seat for one of his lectures upon a particular scientific subject, and be treated to wonderful digressions into which names would be dropped concerning other scientific subjects. It was as though you came to Little Cornard Conservation Society upon a Thursday evening to hear about 'The Flowers of Suffolk' or 'Bats in Historic Buildings' and were required to grapple with Einstein or Heisenberg or Stephen Hawking. Ampère, perhaps, or Volta, say, would wriggle into lectures which you had not supposed would touch upon electricity; Faraday, too, might pop up when not particularly expected, because he was so religious. But rummagers among the newspapers will find three rather special names among those that Sidney noticed; two were French – the Chevalier de Lamarck (1744–1829), and Georges Cuvier (1769–1832); the third was British – Sir Charles Lyell (1798–1875). All were very important in the matter of biology in relation to geology in the years before 1859; they captured the attention of many English clergymen.

In respect of the animal world Lamarck believed in a rather complicated version of the Great Chain of Being. This was very important, for it was largely due to Lamarck that as a working concept the Great Chain of Being was carried forward into the nineteenth century to be adopted by clergymen such as Edwin Sidney.

According to Lamarck, God had designed the Great Chain of Being, at the top of which, on Earth, was the most complex 'animal' conceivable – man, representing organic perfection. At the bottom was the crudest – the mollusc, or some such creature. Lamarck also believed that organisms could be spontaneously generated and that subsequently they could work their way up the Chain, from microbe to man, so to say. Of course, as one went about the world this Chain, culminating in organic 'perfection', was not particularly what one noticed. Rather, what one noticed was the extent to which the animal world did not conform with it. But that, said Lamarck, was because living creatures were conditioned by their environments. Moreover, whatever characteristics they acquired in response to their environments would be inherited by their descendants – though Lamarck could offer no biological explanation as to how this could occur. There was evolution, therefore, and one of its major determinants was environment. Even so, these 'responses to environment' could not be seen as 'natural selection' or a 'struggle for existence', for they constituted simply a multitude of deviations from God's ordained plan, represented by the Great Chain of Being.

In geology Lamarck believed in uniformitarianism, an excellent definition of which was offered by Arthur Stanley, dean of Westminster, in his funeral sermon for Lyell (Westminster Abbey, 1875);[28] he said it was the idea 'that the frame of this earth was gradually brought into its present condition, not by violent or

---

[28] A. O. J. Cockshut, ed., *Religious Controveries of the Nineteenth Century: selected documents,* London 1966, p. 246.

sudden convulsions, but by slow and silent action, the same causes operating now, through a long succession of ages, stretching back beyond the memory or imagination of man'. Lamarck's uniformitarianism complemented his theory of evolution, for it provided the steadily changing environment which helped to determine steady evolutionary change. Lamarck was therefore useful to clergymen such as Edwin Sidney because he believed in God's Design, whilst offering a theory of evolution (complemented by a theory of uniformitarianism) which not only was totally subordinate to it, but which also explained away all evidence that Design did not exist.

Cuvier was a Christian, but he did not believe that in any way the Bible could be regarded as a scientific text-book. He created the science of comparative anatomy. At the end of the eighteenth century, long before the railway age (VI), he did important work on extinct animals of the elephant type. He said that animals and plants must be classified not simply with regard to their external characteristics, as Linnaeus in the eighteenth century had classified them, but much more particularly with regard to their internal characteristics, and with regard also to the correlation of those internal characteristics, which were usually to be discovered only with the scalpel of the anatomist. He pioneered the methodology which Owen was to apply to his examination of the Felixstowe phosphates (IX). He was also a geologist – a catastrophist, indeed: for he believed (the opposite of what Lamarck believed) that geological history comprised a series of great 'revolutions', or 'catastrophes', which had brought to a close each major stratigraphical sequence, killing off the creatures which had lived in the areas where they had occurred. Eventually stricken areas had settled down and been restocked with new kinds of living creatures, which had migrated from nearby areas unaffected by catastrophe.

Catastrophism was a notion which, both in Britain and on the

Continent, caused old-fashioned Christians greatly to approve of Cuvier, for it could be accommodated to the report of Noah and the Flood in Genesis. There was another fact, however, which for Christians was perhaps even more significant: it was that Cuvier was a functionalist. That is to say, on the basis of his renowned expertise in comparative anatomy, he argued that God must be regarded as God the Designer. He offered to Europe an up-to-date version of Paley's natural theology, for he insisted that (since the time of Paley) modern geology and its sister palaeontology had shown that throughout time each separate part of every living creature (a leg, a claw, an ear and so forth) had existed as a perfect co-ordinate of all other parts of the same creature, and that every living creature was designed *overall* to fulfil whatever function God had determined for it: in other words, a duck must have webbed feet, or it could not do the things that ducks must do, and so could not be a duck; a serpent could have no external limbs, or it could not address the business of serpents. Cuvier's harnessing of 'modern' geology and palaeontology to the 'ancient' doctrine of Design reminds one very much of the splendid reflections of St Paul in 1 Corinthians xii concerning the human body as a composite of various interdependent 'members' (eyes, hands, feet, a head, a nose and so forth), and as an analogue of the body of Christ's Church in which, through baptism, there are also interdependent 'members' – apostles, prophets, teachers, workers of miracles, healers, work-a-day Christians in Little Cornard, and so forth. No wonder, then, that Cuvier was especially attractive to clergymen such as Sidney, in a way that Lyell could never be.

As Cuvier refurbished Paley so Lyell prepared for Darwin. For Lyell, like Lamarck, was a uniformitarian; his teaching was contained in his *Principles of Geology* (1830–33). Lyell held a view which many of his contemporary geologists shared but which none before had so emphatically advanced. It was that, *on the evidence*, the age of the Earth should be calculated in millions of years, rather than thousands. This was very upsetting for those who gazed respectfully upon the margins of the King James Bible in its contemporary editions, which affirmed that God had created the universe in 4004 BC, and only a little less so for others, more cautious, who opted for around 6000 BC.

SO, WHAT WITH CUVIER and Lyell and a good many others, and with Lamarck in the background, the thirty or so years preceding the publication of *The Origin of Species* were years of argument and discomposure among many biologists and geologists and palaeontologists and physico-theologians. There was anguish, inevitably, among Christian people; Tennyson expressed it. But to the phlegmatic much of it seemed dotty. In 'The Mudfog Sketches' (contained in some editions of *Sketches by Boz*, 1836) young Charles Dickens merrily lampooned the British Association for the Advancement of Science – created largely by clergymen, in 1831 – and all it seemed to signify; Professors Snore, Doze, Wheezy, Woodensconce, Grime, Muff and Nogo, the Honourable and Reverend Mr Long Eers, and Mr Slug the celebrated statistician whose complexion was dark purple, were among the ornaments of the Mudfog Association for the Advancement of Everything, the sections of which were Zoology and Botany, Anatomy and Medicine, Statistics, and Mechanical Science – and also Umbugology and Ditchwateristics, to which a paper was read descriptive of a one–eyed bay pony seen standing in a butcher's cart at the corner of Newgate Market, winking its eye and whisking its tail simultaneously instead of sequentially, a thing hitherto unrecorded, where ponies were concerned, in all the annals of winking and whisking.

Three works defined those years of argument. The third, *In Memoriam* (1850), was truthful; the first, *The Bridgewater Treatises*, aspired to be so; but the second, *Vestiges of the Natural History of Creation*, was mostly nonsense.

The eccentric earl of Bridgewater died in 1829, leaving £8,000 to furnish a reward or rewards for a person or persons who should publish, in the style of a Ray or a Paley, a work entitled *On the Power, Wisdom and Goodness of God, as manifested in the Creation; illustrating such work by all reasonable arguments, as for instance the variety and formation of God's Creatures in the animal, vegetable, and mineral Kingdoms; the effect of digestion, and thereby of conversion; the construction of the hand of man, and an infinite variety of other arguments; as also by discoveries ancient and modern, in arts, sciences, and the whole extent of literature*. So, between 1833 and 1840, eight authors produced eight treatises, *The Bridgewater Treatises*. As the earl intended, the work was a consolidation of much that had preceded it; Owen Chadwick has called it 'the late flowering of the physico-theology of the previous century'.[29] Its effect was potent upon the minds of scientific clergymen. One of the *Treatises* was entitled *On the Power, Wisdom and Goodness of God, as manifested in the Creation of Animals and in their History, Habits and Instincts*. Its author was the celebrated entomologist William Kirby FRS, 1759–1850, vicar of Barham, near Ipswich, from 1797 till his death. Marginally the *Treatists* bore upon events in Little Cornard, to the extent that Kirby was a member of the clerico-scientific circle in East Anglia to which Sidney and Henslow also belonged.

Vestiges of the Natural History of Creation, by Robert Chambers, was published anonymously in 1844. It favoured the notion of God the Designer. It professed scientific seriousness but was cranky in detail. Andrew Crosse, of Somerset, and W. S. Weekes, of Sandwich, were two of the many 'electricians' who flourished in the wake of Michael Faraday. Crosse, said Chambers, had spontaneously generated little bristly insects by passing an electric

---

[29] Owen Chadwick, *The Victorian Church*, part i, 2nd.ed., London 1970, p. 561.

current through a saturated solution of silicate of potash. Weekes had later used ferro-cyanet to produce the same insects '*in increased numbers*'. The intellectual dogs of Monsieur Leonard could play a fine game of dominoes. Owls are musicianly, for they hoot in B flat. Patients in the Hanwell Lunatic Asylum showed signs of a particular abnormal cerebration which in lesser animals must be considered healthy. And so on. *Vestiges* embarrassed sober scientists (though not Richard Owen), but was proffered to the public as a worthy contribution to the advancement of natural theology, proclaiming in arresting, vivid detail the principle of evolution. Its sales were enormous; some read it as a work of science fiction. It helped to prepare the public for the topping-up of evolution with natural selection, in *The Origin of Species*.

Did Edwin Sidney like it? Probably he was sympathetic to parts of it at least, for in a splendid little textbook on electricity, which he published whilst he was at Little Conard, he disclosed that in the 1840s he had corresponded with Crosse and Weekes, and also with a third 'electrician', William Ladd, of London's Regent Street, who invented an 'improved magnetic coil', and manufactured an elegant device featuring a glass bulb and known as a 'good egg' for Faraday to demonstrate the relationship of electricity to gases at low pressure.[30] According to the newspapers Ladd sometimes turned up, with gadgets (including the 'good egg'?) on Sidney's Sudbury platforms (XXXII).

---

[30] For Crosse, Weekes, and Ladd see Edwin Sidney, *Electricity: its phenomena, laws, and results*, London ed. 1862, pp. 42–69, 131, 132. Ladd's 'good egg' is illustrated in Frank James, 'Time, Tide and Michael Faraday', *History Today,* September 1991.

INTRODUCTION

Owen and Henslow

THE CLASH CONCERNING *The Origin of Species* between Bishop Samuel Wilberforce of Oxford and Thomas Huxley (XXXIII) at the annual meeting of the British Association held in Oxford in 1860 is a famous episode in Victorian history. Richard Owen, it is said, primed Wilberforce with arguments. Robert Chambers, it is said, prompted Huxley to defend Darwin. Henslow, up from Suffolk, chaired the occasion.

Like Henslow, Owen (1804–1892) was a friend of Edwin Sidney and came to Little Cornard and possibly to Sudbury (XXXIII, XXXVIII). He was the best-known scientist in early Victorian England; indeed he was internationally renowned. Despite the fun poked at him largely on account of his disconcerting physical appearance, his achievements were important. In 1846 he became the first Hunterian professor of comparative anatomy and physiology at the Royal College of Surgeons of England, and in 1856 superintendent of the natural history department of the British Museum. He lectured far and wide, mingled with the great, was feted by learned societies, and sat on committees. He invented the word 'dinosaur', and inspired the creation of the Natural History Museum in South Kensington, that fine temple to the glory of God the Designer. He was called 'the British Cuvier', for he had studied with Cuvier in Paris, had agreed with Cuvier's functionalism, and had continued Cuvier's work in comparative anatomy. He was the leading authority on all matters concerning zoological and palaeontological classification. His particular skill was in deducing the appearance of a whole animal from a small fragment of bone; this was the skill he employed in the matter of the Felixstowe phosphates (IX).

The frequent scientific quarrels between the reactionary Owen and the radical Thomas Huxley – twenty-one years younger than

Owen, and one of the 'Young Turks' of Victorian natural science – were well known to Victorian people, who often laughed about them. Charles Kingsley made a joke of Owen, and of Huxley, in his children's novel, *The Water Babies*, of 1863; the artist Linley Sambourne liked the joke, and for the 1885 edition drew a little picture:

> ....no one has a right to say that no water-babies exist, till they have seen no water-babies existing; which is quite a different thing, mind, from not seeing water-babies; and a thing which nobody ever did, or perhaps ever will do.
>
> "But surely if there were water-babies, somebody would have caught one at least?"
>
> Well. How do you know that somebody has not?
>
> "But they would have put it into spirits, or into the *Illustrated News*, or perhaps cut it into two halves, poor dear little thing, and sent one to Professor Owen, and one to Professor Huxley, to see what they would each say about it."

TWO THINGS MAY perhaps be said about Owen's lecturing visits to Little Cornard and, possibly at some point, to Sudbury, at the invitation of the Revd Edwin Sidney:

INTRODUCTION

PROFESSOR OWEN AND THE SKELETON OF *DINORNIS MAXIMUS*.
Taken about 1877.

Fig. 6   Sir Richard Owen. From Richard Owen, Memoirs on the Extinct Wingless Birds of New Zealand, *vol. ii, London 1879, pl. 97.*

1. One of Owen's special interests was the world of vertebrates. On the basis of his anatomical researches Owen believed that in the mind of God there had been a pre-existent vertebra from which through the millennia all particular forms of vertebrae had evolved; so, for example, the skeleton of the fish, or the skeleton of the dog, or the skeleton of man, were all modified descendants, each more complex than the original, of a pre-existent blueprint which Owen himself called 'the Archetype, or primal pattern'. Owen supported his belief with his notions of 'homology' and 'analogy', thereby revealing a cast of mind immediately intelligible and satisfying to educated people of his day, those people, that is, so preoccupied with 'correspondences'. A homologue, he said, was 'The same organ in different animals under every variety of form and function'; an analogue was 'A part or organ in one animal which has the same function as another part or organ in a different animal'. The difference is clarified by Owen's most recent biographer, paraphrasing Owen himself:[31]

> Owen often cited the example of a little lizard, the 'flying' reptile *Draco volans*, in which five pairs of ribs are significantly elongated to support a membrane which can be spread out to form a flitting organ. The little dragon's front legs are homologous with the wings of a bird, whereas its 'parachute' is analogous to these, but homologous with ribs. Conversely, the pectoral fin of the flying fish is not only analogous to the wing of a bird, but, unlike the flying dragon's flitting organ, also homologous with it.

Legs and wings and 'parachutes' and ribs and pectoral fins, and indeed the creatures themselves which bore them, had all 'evolved', thought Owen, but not from a single biological cell, aeons ago; rather, they had evolved from – or 'advanced' from – a single, archetypal vertebra, each one of them independently of all the

---

[31] Nicolaas A. Rupke, *Richard Owen: Victorian naturalist*, New Haven and London 1994, p. 164.

others. So, Owen's evolution was not Darwin's evolution, for Owen's evolution could find little place for natural selection, and none at all for the transmutation of species.

From this matter of 'the Archetype' a question thus arose: Was Owen a Platonist? Owen thought he was not because, as he rightly observed, the Platonic 'idea' is transcendent and perfect (the dogs and cats and tables which we have about us in our homes are *imperfect* realisations of the 'ideas' from which they arise), whereas the archetypal vertebra which he envisaged had millions of years earlier become *immanent* (in fact he ventured to draw a picture of it – it looked rather like the skeleton of a fish) and was *less* complex than the various vertebrae which had evolved from it. But although Owen argued that 'the archetype in the Mind of God' had 'become immanent', he did not argue that the archetype had ever in fact existed, in flesh and bone; indeed he could not, for no geologist or palaeontologist had ever discovered an example of it. Perhaps for this reason it was not easy for many of his contemporaries to grasp the subtle distinction which he himself made between what could properly be regarded as Platonic and what could not. Owenism, such people reasoned, equals Platonism, and Platonism equals the Word of God (as in St John's Gospel); so, if we *must* have evolution, let us invite Owen to such places as Edwin Sidney's rectory barn in Little Cornard, or to his Sudbury Literary and Mechanics Institution, then widespread in society we may have a doctrine of evolution Christian and scriptural, in that it eschews natural selection and the transmutation of species.

2. In his day many people disliked Owen because, they thought, he was an obsequious tory snob who kowtowed to the ruling classes; that, they suspected, was why he held forth about the archetypal vertebra, for the archetypal vertebra smacked of Platonism, and Platonism appealed strongly to bossy, conservative-minded

Christians wanting to keep other people in order. But again there is a question: Why should an obsequious tory snob, busy kowtowing to the ruling classes, waste time coming to Little Cornard – or even to Sudbury? Little Cornard was obscure; no social acclaim was to be had from lecturing to the farmers or those other, rather ordinary people who lived round about and would have flocked to hear him. All in all, even when allowance is made for such incidents as his gallivanting with the prince and princess of Wales when otherwise he might have been in Sudbury (XXXIII), Owen was perhaps a rather nicer person than we have been led to believe.

The Darwinists, especially Thomas Huxley, and to a lesser extent Darwin himself, denigrated Owen because, they thought, his scientific theories were mystical mumbo jumbo. And the Darwinist view of science and the world was the view that triumphed, universally. Consequently Owen was written out of the history books. Nowadays, however, thanks mostly to a splendid biography published in 1994,[32] the worth of Owen's fundamental researches in the natural sciences, and his originality are properly recognised; Owen has re-emerged as a notable scientist of the nineteenth century.

John Stevens Henslow (b. 1796) had entered St John's College, Cambridge, in 1814, and graduated in 1818. In 1822 he had become professor of mineralogy in the University, and in 1825 professor of botany. He made botany popular in the University, created the University Botanic Garden in the 1840s, and later became one of the great pioneers of scientific education in elementary schools. Darwin, who entered Christ's College in 1828, was his favourite pupil, and became known as 'the man who walks with Henslow'. In 1831 Henslow procured for Darwin the place of gentleman companion to Captain Robert Fitzroy, Commander of HMS *Beagle*,

---

[32] Rupke, *Richard Owen*.

Fig. 7   John Stevens Henslow.
Courtesy Ipswich Borough Council Museums and Galleries.

a situation which in practice enabled him to be unpaid naturalist aboard the *Beagle*, then about the commence a five-year voyage to survey the South American waters and to circumnavigate the globe. During the voyage Darwin read the first volume of Lyell's *Principles of Geology*, which, just before he left England, Henslow – impressed by Lyell's uniformitarianism – had advised him to read. Fitzroy had presented him with a copy, a fact which Darwin acknowledged in pencil upon the flyleaf; this volume, somewhat dilapidated, is now in the University Library at Cambridge, a near-neighbour, upon the shelves, of the autographed *Natural Theology*, presented by Paley to the bishop of Ely. When Darwin returned to England he spent some time in Cambridge with Henslow, who helped him arrange the specimens he had procured upon the voyage, and to prepare for publication his *Journal of Researches into the Geology and Natural History of the Various Countries visited by HMS Beagle*. The fruits of these researches contributed to the making of *The Origin of Species*. Soon after the publication of the latter work Henslow visited Darwin, in Kent. 'Henslow will go a very little way with me and is not shocked at me,' Darwin told a friend.

In 1837 Henslow was presented to the rich crown living of Hitcham, in Suffolk. Hitcham in 1837 was a large, miserable, run-down parish, and so by 1839 Henslow the professor was spending only the minimum of time in Cambridge. Otherwise he was in Hitcham, creating one of the great Anglican pastorates of Victorian England: to elevate the poor he founded schools, benefit and cricket and athletic clubs, allotments, horticultural shows, and parish excursions; to help the farmers, who were usually at odds with the poor, he gave unsparingly of his knowledge as the foremost agrarian scientist resident in East Anglia.

He was one of the founders of the Ipswich Museum, which opened in 1847. Thenceforth he was its guiding light, until he died at Hitcham in 1861. From 1850 he was its president. Edwin Sidney was a vice-president. John Glyde – hairdresser, bookseller and local historian of Ipswich – reveals that Sidney lectured there along with some of the most notable scientists of early Victorian England: George Airy, astronomer royal, on 'Astronomy'; David Ansted, geologist, on 'Coal and Iron'; William Carpenter, physiologist and naturalist, on the 'Instinct and Reasoning Powers of Animals'; Richard Owen on the 'Gigantic Birds of New Zealand'; Adam Sedgwick on 'Geology'; and, of course, Henslow himself on 'Botany and Geology'. Sidney lectured on 'Electricity and Galvanism'.[33]

The Ipswich Museum was a glorious Suffolk monument to the aspirations of Victorian popular science. It still is. Perhaps, though, at the time of its opening it seemed to its founders to presage a new era, when the slightly dated sciences of Paley and of Bridgewater and of Kirby the entomologist should make way for sciences more modern, such as the evolution taught by Richard Owen (not by Darwin), or electricity as taught by Faraday and Sidney.

But Kirby was not dead. In December 1847, frail, ancient and weak-eyed, he tottered into the Museum's opening meeting from his vicarage in Barham. He rose to second a resolution which did not need his seconding because it had been seconded already, by Sir John Boileau, of Norfolk. 'I beg to second the resolution,' Kirby said. 'I am sure it will be of great advantage in all classes to study the works of God. He is the maker of all, and He is the promoter of...' He trailed off and sank into his chair. 'We regret to state,' said a newspaper, 'that the venerable and esteemed gentleman, from age and his consequent infirmities, was unable to proceed.' Someone nudged Edward Stanley, bishop of Norwich, and chairman for the occasion, advising him that Kirby should be thanked for his work

---

[33] John Glyde, *The Moral, Social and Religious Condition of Ipswich in the Middle of the Nineteenth Century*, Ipswich and London 1850, pp. 177, 178.

as president of the Museum. Stanley dropped a funereal hint: 'You are sinking in the Vale of Years,' he said, 'and may God grant that as your life has been useful to those around you, so may you sink to the grave, happy in having done your duty.' But Kirby did not die. So, late in 1848, when F. H. Bischoff painted his portrait (it hangs today in the stairwell of the Museum) he showed Kirby, with a beetle and a book about insects on a table close by, seated near a window through which, in the distance, could be seen Barham church, tinged with the rays of the setting sun – 'indicative,' it was said, 'of the decline of life'. Kirby lingered. Eventually he died, in July 1850. He was nearly 91. Stanley the moderniser predeceased him, in 1849. He was 70.[34]

EDWIN SIDNEY

For the invisible things of him from the creation of the world are clearly seen, being understood by the things that are made, even his eternal power and Godhead.

St Paul's Epistle to the Romans i 20

I consider, then, that intrinsically interesting and noble as are scientific pursuits, and worthy of a place in liberal education, and fruitful in temporal benefits to the community, still they are not, and cannot be, the instrument of an ethical training; that physics do not supply a basis, but only materials for religious sentiment; that knowledge does not occupy, does not form the mind; that apprehension of the unseen is the only known principle capable of subduing moral evil, educating the multitude, and organising

---

[34] R. A. A. Markham, *A Rhino in High Street: Ipswich Museum – the early years*, Ipswich 1990, pp. 17, 18; *Ipswich Journal*, 18 December 1847, pp. 2, 3.

society; and that, whereas man is born for action, action flows not from inference, but from impressions – not from responses, but from Faith.

> John Henry Newman, *The Tamworth Reading Room*, 1841

Lessons of piety are not only written in the gospel, but those lessons we find there, are enforced by a right knowledge of nature. The natural and moral perfections of God are in perfect unison; and we may be certain, that as science advances in Christian lands, its discoveries will help to close the lips of the sceptic, and the true light brightening at the same time, "wisdom and knowledge" will indeed become both the "stability of our times, and the strength of our salvation."

In order, however, that this happy result may accrue, it is necessary not merely that we should view nature in the great and the small, with the admiration of the power and wisdom of the Creator, but that we should see physical truth through a spiritual medium.

> Edwin Sidney, *Blights of the Wheat and their Remedies*, 1846

Norfolk

EDWIN SIDNEY was countryman complete, unsuited to cities and their ways. He and his great contemporaries John Henry Newman and Thomas Henry Huxley together reveal what, for different people, seemed possible or impossible or only partly possible to believe about religion and the natural world by the middle of the nineteenth century. *Newman*, future cardinal, discerned that evidences of Design for a St Paul or a John Ray were not quite the same as those for a Butler or a Paley, and that these in turn would not be quite the same as those for, say, a Christian particle physicist of the late twentieth century. So, concluding that organic evidences are apt to let one down, he emphasised another part of the teaching of St Paul, the part which said that Faith is the substance of things hoped for, the evidence of things not seen; Faith and Prayer alone, therefore, must anchor one even though, as Newman observed in 'Lead, kindly Light', Faith can prove more difficult with one's advancing years. But Newman was a very learned man, and his teachings, except those proclaimed in two or three of his well-loved hymns, were less accessible to ordinary people than were those of Edwin Sidney. *Huxley*, agnostic and greatest of the popular scientific lecturers of the nineteenth century, contemplated the teaching of such clergymen as Sidney and Henslow, and raged against 'Theology & Parsondom...the natural & irreconcilable enemies of Science'. Inconsolable upon the death of his infant son (1860), he observed that apes grieve for their dead offspring as men and women grieve for theirs: therefore he revered the laws of Nature, red in tooth and claw, and declined the comfort of Faith and Prayer and evidences of Design; he declined, that is, to draw a religious conclusion from the fact that though he could think and write about the grief of apes, no ape could think and write about the grief of him.[35] *Sidney*, sentinel for evidences of Design, as well as man of Faith, was not credulous (as Huxley would have thought him), though he pitched against credulity. He celebrated Life; in the process he persuaded obscure people in obscure places that they were players upon an intellectual stage extending from Plato and St Paul to Butler, to Paley, to Faraday, and to Owen (though never quite to Darwin), and that being so meant being called to Christ. This was his achievement. It was biblical: he sowed Light for the righteous, and gladdened the upright in heart.

Sidney is elusive. He left no papers, diaries or journals. Samples of his handwriting are hard to find. He is mentioned insignificantly

[35] Adrian Desmond, *Huxley: the devil's disciple*, London 1994, pp. 253, 287, 288.

in Arthur Stanley's *Life* of Edward Stanley, bishop of Norwich, but not at all in the biographies of other eminent contemporaries whose attention he attracted. He is revealed but dimly through his own published writings, and through fleeting references in some of the papers of Henslow and in the unpublished journals of Sir John Boileau. Chiefly, then, he must be discovered in the newspapers.

He was born in the village of Cam, in Gloucestershire, and died, in his seventy-fifth year, on 22 October 1872. They buried him in Little Cornard churchyard. He lived his term, for in the previous April there had been a strike, for higher wages, of agricultural workers in the parish of Newton, adjacent to Little Cornard: this strike was the advent in Suffolk of agricultural trade unionism, which challenged fundamentally, *and* largely on evangelical religious grounds, the rural social order that Sidney had been so concerned to sustain.[36]

Sidney was related to the famous Hill family of Shropshire. He was brought up by the Revd Rowland Hill (1744–1833) (XXII), *protégé* of the great George Whitefield. Hill himself was a significant figure in the Evangelical movement of the eighteenth and early nineteenth centuries. He composed a sacred song beginning 'When Jesus first at Heaven's command' for which he hijacked the tune for 'Rule Britannia', and coined a famous question – 'Why should the Devil have all the best tunes?'[37] Sidney's relationship with the Hill family was life-long and intimate. Eventually he would write biographies of Rowland Hill, of his brother Sir Richard Hill, Bart., and of the Revd Samuel Walker, curate of Truro in the early eighteenth century. These three works (the first ran to five editions) are still important; they are regularly consulted by modern historians writing about Evangelical and Methodist history. In a

---

[36] Nigel Scotland, *Methodism and the Revolt of the Field: a study of the Methodist contribution to agricultural trade unionism in East Anglia*, Gloucester 1981, pp. 13, 72.

[37] Ian Bradley, *Abide with me: the world of Victorian hymns*, London 1997, p. 185.

minor way he would contribute also to the historiography of the Napoleonic wars, by producing the only biography of the first Viscount Hill of Hawkstone and Almarez, the Peninsular war general, nephew of Richard and Rowland, and a corps commander at Waterloo. Through Lord Hill, undoubtedly, he came to know the dukes of Wellington.

He graduated BA at St John's College, Cambridge, in 1821, having arrived in 1817. As was the case with the great majority of Cambridge graduands of his day, he graduated with an unclassified degree. Had he graduated with high honours – 'had his early training been less imperfect,' as Charles Badham put it (XXXV) – he might well have become a fellow of his college, pursued an academic career, and been as well known to posterity as Henslow or Sedgwick.

Henslow in 1817 was a third-year undergraduate at St John's. Possibly, therefore, Sidney, like Darwin later, was one who 'walked with Henslow', and had his interest in science nurtured by him. Certainly in later years he learned from Henslow in matters botanical and mycological (IX). And certainly he knew, and was influenced by, Henslow's close associate, the Revd Adam Sedgwick (IX), a fellow of Cambridge's Trinity College, a founding father of modern geological science, an exciting teacher, and the University's professor of geology from 1818. Sometimes, in the Lake District, Sedgwick was accompanied on his geological excursions by the poet Wordsworth, who learned geology from him. Sedgwick agreed with Joseph Butler that the constitution of Nature was analogous to the constitution of God's moral government, and with Paley's theology of Design, though not with his doctrine of cheerfulness. But what he learned from Butler and Paley he expressed in his own special way; and Edwin Sidney copied him: my epigraph from *Blights of the Wheat and their Remedies* was written by Sidney but wholly reflects the teaching of Sedgwick, by whom equally it could have

INTRODUCTION

been written.

From 1821 to 1847 Sidney was the curate-in-charge of Acle, in Norfolk. He was much regarded for his talents, especially his lecturing, which was copied by clergymen in Norwich.[38] By the late 1840s he was a renowned figure in Norfolk county society. Sir John Boileau, Baronet – cultivated, high-minded, friend of statesmen, squire of Ketteringham, near Norwich – admired him, and sat attentively through many of his lectures, in Norfolk and in London. Sometimes he played schoolmaster – 'not interesting as it might have been and familiar,' he wrote on one occasion, 'but too much attempted to be crammed into it'.[39] At Boileau's seat, Ketteringham Hall, Sidney was always a welcome visitor, even in his Little Cornard days; indeed it is possible that his fitting-out of the so-called rectory barn in Little Cornard (VII) was inspired by the hall which Boileau had built in the grounds at Ketteringham, and in which Sidney was wont to lecture.[40] He was much esteemed by the bishop of Norwich, Edward Stanley, a friend of Boileau, and the father of Owen Stanley, the commander of H.M.S. *Rattlesnake* upon her voyage into the Southern Pacific (1846–1850) to secure northern Australia for British settlers and the surrounding seas for British merchantmen; *Rattlesnake's* assistant surgeon was young Thomas Henry Huxley, whose researches as a marine biologist upon this epic voyage were the foundation of his later career as one of the great natural scientists of the nineteenth century. Edward Stanley himself was a keen amateur scientist, whose speciality was ornithology, in which he was accomplished. A splendid portrait of him, by T. H. Maguire, hangs in the Suffolk Geology Gallery at the

---

[38] According to Bishop Stanley (*Norwich Mercury*, 13 December 1845, p. 3).

[39] Journal 1846–1850, 21 May 1847. Sidney had been lecturing at the Royal Institution, 'on Parasitic Fungi appearing in inhabited houses'. Boileau would have liked more 'general information of Dry Rot, etc.'

[40] Owen Chadwick, *Victorian Miniature,* London 1960, pp. 44, 97.

Ipswich Museum. In Norfolk Stanley would descend upon Sidney's lectures, intervening affably as he was inspired.

One has a dreamy vision: for an Edwin Sidney lecture of a helter skelter kind tickets are procured not only by trudging Nonconformists but also by a bottled water-baby and a one-eyed pony and a waddling megalosaurus. Does it seem a wonder? To the audience, perhaps; but not to Edwin Sidney, who thinks it opportune and apt.

One wet December night in 1845, at Acle, there was – with help from the bishop – a lecture rather of that kind. Before an audience of gentlemen and ladies, clergymen, farmers and yeomen, who had crowded about the entrance long before the time of opening ('Nothing,' the *Norwich Mercury* disclosed, 'could exceed the anxiety to get admission to this Lecture' – so desirous were they of obtaining information), but who, once admitted, were seated as comfortably as might be, after Sidney had spoken breathlessly concerning 'the structure and functions of leaves', and had explained 'ramina', 'petioles', 'stipules', and their connections and 'cuticle', 'stomata', 'evaporation', 'exhalation' and 'absorption', and had likened forcibly the light that nurtures leaves to the Light that nurtures Truth, and had shown respiration in plants to be the exact converse of the same function in animals, and had considered also the properties of lime, and had used a 'Scientific Lantern', and an 'oxy-hydrogen microscope' (to explore the structure of leaves 'in the most distinct and brilliant outline': great astonishment) and an 'oxy-hydrogen blowpipe' (to perform 'beautiful experiments' upon lime – including, of course, the production of limelight: more astonishment), the bishop rose and produced some aged beans – from Sicily, he said. Peculiar beetles crawled out. The farmers, looking thoughtful, wondered what to say. The bishop requested that if ever they themselves should discover a thing so curious, they should let him know. The audience applauded. They sang the

Doxology. Their bishop blessed them. Then they went home.[41]

In 1823 Sidney had married Eliza Vaughan, of Shrewsbury, who was older than he, yet survived him (XXXVII). She was lively. When they came to Ketteringham to stay with Boileau she got on well with another guest, Amelia Opie – skittish, Quaker, novelist and poetess, widow of a famous painter and friend of Byron, Scott, and Wordsworth. Mrs Opie was a cousin of Baron Alderson who in 1844 passed vicious sentences at the Suffolk Summer Assizes (III), and she had met Cuvier. Boileau suffered much from haemorrhoids, and other things. Eliza and Mrs Opie once tried to cheer him up, but their doing so seemed to make him gloomier still.[42] Upon the presentation of Bishop Stanley, who had inherited the patronage from William Pochin, Sidney brought Eliza out of Norfolk to testify to Truth in Little Cornard; it was his first and only benefice. With them came their housemaid Phillis Manthorpe, their cook Louisa Bussey, and their manservant Charles Nightingale. It was 1847. That same year, by happy correspondence, out of a parsonage house in bleakest Yorkshire came *Jane Eyre*, to reaffirm for Victoria's England what Dante's Beatrice had testified to Europe, that woman's truest love was Christ-like and redemptive.

Suffolk

> Study to shew thyself approved unto God, a workman that needeth not to be ashamed, rightly dividing the word of truth.
>
> 2 Timothy ii 15 (XXXV)

---

[41] *Norwich Mercury*, 13 December 1845, p. 3.

[42] 'Mrs. Opie & Mrs. Sidney setting to cheer me up – I almost fear what the thing will come to.' Journal 1846–1850, 28 December 1847.

With the exception of the staircase, and his lodger's private apartment, Poll Sweedlepipe's house was one great bird's nest. Gamecocks resided in the kitchen; pheasants wasted the brightness of their golden plumage on the garret; bantams roosted in the cellar; owls had possession of the bedroom; and specimens of all the smaller fry of birds chirruped and twittered in the shop. The staircase was sacred to rabbits. There in hutches of all shapes and kinds, made from old packing-cases, boxes, drawers, and tea-chests, they increased in a prodigious degree, and contributed their share towards that complicated whiff which, quite impartially, and without distinction of persons, saluted every nose that was put into Sweedlepipe's easy shaving-shop.

> Dickens, *Martin Chuzzlewit*, chapter 26 (XXIII)

> The rich man in his castle,
> The poor man at his gate,
> God made them, high or lowly,
> And order'd their estate.
>
> Mrs C. F. Alexander

HOW SHOULD a workman approved unto God apportion truth in Little Cornard in 1847? The parish was wretched (VII). But God had said to Moses, 'Be circumspect'. If, then, too soon and too stridently, Little Cornard's new rector should hold forth about the bondage of the labouring poor he would antagonise the farmers, their souls scorched by the criminality of Micklefield (III) but whose good will he needed. So Sidney was circumspect; he never had to struggle with his farmers as Henslow did with his; he attended first to the conduct of church services, to furnishings, and to matters of bricks and mortar. Quickly dispensing with curates, he became the regular officiant at services in the church, and remained so till he died, despite his travels and excursions. He attended to the improvement of the church itself (V, VII). The organ and the west gallery[43] he installed lasted till beyond the First World War, whilst his 'modern' pews – neat, narrow, angular, unkind to the elderly – are still in use. Before the end of 1849 the splendid new rectory was near completion, on the site of the old one, on Keddington Hill, and the rectory barn had been equipped. Part of the barn still stands, near the rectory gate. It is used as an art studio. In 1854, at the bottom of Spout Lane, a small school was built, which is now the village hall. Its opening was not reported in the newspapers; perhaps because Sidney had long attended to the education of the parish children anyway (VII), probably in the rectory barn, its appearance occasioned no special excitement.

These, then, were Sidney's early material achievements in his parish. But he was active also in the wider world of Suffolk.

FREDERICK AUGUSTUS HERVEY (1730–1803), fourth earl of Bristol, bishop of Derry in Ireland and keen amateur geologist, lived long enough to know that age which viewed museums as 'improving' institutions. He planned Ickworth House partly as a repository for the works of art he had collected, envisaging a house

---

[43] Parish memories are now dim concerning precisely what went on in Sidney's west gallery. It seems certain, though, either that the gallery was allocated to children, or that it was occupied by a choir which sometimes – perhaps in the absence of anyone with the accomplishment of Mr Ambrose? (V) – was accompanied by a barrel organ, the meagre remains of which mysteriously disappeared from the vestry in the 1980s. Perhaps most of the choir and most of the barrel organ faded away altogether. For the present writer recalls a Sunday in the 1970s when Morning Prayer had been conducted by Mr Leonard Moore, an elderly and rather deaf lay reader, better known locally as a retired vendor of tobacco in Sudbury's North Street. After the service Mr Moore struck up a conversation with Mrs Violet Cutmore, steadfast to the church, sole and elderly occupant of the choir stalls in the chancel, and witness triumphant to the mortality of other choral people: 'Are you the choir?' 'Yes, I am the choir. But I was one of 29.' 'Ah, one of 29.... Well, where are the other 28? Are they on holiday?' 'No, no, no! I *was* one of 29 – *was* one of 29. The other 28 are dead. Ho! ho!'

Fig. 8 '*A handsome and commodious rectory house*': *Edwin Sidney's rectory.*
Photo and © Paul Matthews.

'combining the uses of the National Gallery with those of the British Museum'; the oval rotunda would supply the living quarters, the wings would contain galleries for pictures and sculptures. Alas, his schemes came to nothing.[44]

On sunny days, within its park near Bury St Edmunds, Ickworth House can entrance. But in the late afternoons of late autumn, when shades lengthen, sightseers depart, nature's worlds seem hushed, and work for guides and attendants and ticket-vendors is for a while done, this folly of a house for noblemen can impart a troublous resonance even to the countryside through which one travels home. One broods upon this house, upon the enormous rentals which produced and then supported it, upon the fevered life

[44] Gervase Jackson-Stops, *Ickworth, Suffolk*, The National Trust 1978, pp. 6, 7, 31.

of Micklefield some twenty miles away, and then upon the hell of Norfolk Island where Micklefield was sent (III), and one finds them of a piece.

Within the house, in a corridor close by major works of European art, are three watercolour portraits. Contemplation of them only slightly reassures. To the left are four delightful children, captured with a sharpness more typical of modern colour photography than of most schools of painting. Seated between two children in the portrait to the right is a woman somewhat resembling that other client of the artist (Sir William Ross) who portrayed her, the younger Queen Victoria. The centre portrait is of a clergyman in early middle life. Though he is handsome in a fleshy kind of way, and his pose and his churchy surroundings — he contemplates ascension into a pulpit — imply his meetness more for a stained-glass window than for a watercolour portrait, there is good sense about him; one imagines a churchman alert to his own limitations in certain spheres, fain to go forth as a vessel of usefulness, or of 'improvement', as others may request. The clergyman is Lord Arthur Hervey (V, IX), the woman is his wife, the children are their children.

The Revd Lord Arthur Hervey was a grandson of the earl-bishop. Perhaps his portrait belied his substance, for he was a fine classicist, modern linguist and tennis player. When small he had hobnobbed with the tsar of Russia and, like Edwin Sidney, had known the duke of Wellington. In 1817 Wellington had come to open Waterloo Bridge, bringing with him a bag of medals to distribute to those present, among them the fledgling Hervey. Hervey dived into the bag and grabbed as many medals as he could. 'Oh,' cried the duke, 'you must only take one!' But Hervey took two, and kept them. Later, in Bury St Edmunds, he established the Athenaeum as a literary and scientific institution, which included a reading-room, lecture-hall, museum and observatory. He kept it going subsequently, procuring Lyell, Sedgwick, Owen, Airy, Henslow, Charles Kingsley and others to lecture there.[45] In the cultural life of Bury St Edmunds Hervey the clergyman held the place which Sidney the clergyman held in that of Sudbury.

Hervey's progress as a churchman complemented his social station, for he had an eye for clerical preferments much as he had had for medals. He became rector of Ickworth in 1832, rector of Ickworth-with-Horringer in 1852, archdeacon of Sudbury in 1862, and bishop of Bath and Wells in 1869. In the 1850s he joined Sidney and Henslow to constitute a kind of missionary troika of 'improving' popular lecturers, co-ordinating their efforts, standing in for each other, and rising on each other's platforms to present and then to thank each other. In this partnership Sidney supplied the flair, Henslow the originality, and Hervey the social distinction, for though as well as classics and tennis and modern languages he knew some history and rather more theology he did not know much science, so could contribute little of real substance to the primary lecturing concern of Henslow and Sidney. A hurly-burly letter from Henslow to the curator of the Ipswich Museum shows what they were up to:[46]

Hitcham, Bildeston, Suffolk
1 Aug 1857

My dear Knights,

Sidney has become President of the Sudbury Institution – & writes for *immediate* information as to capabilities on my part of exchanging a lecture with him – Another he exchanges with Ld. A. H. – I have suggested the great convenience of Ipswich Bury, & Sudbury having lectures on different days of the week, to

---

[45] J. F. A. Hervey, *A Memoir of Lord Arthur Hervey, DD, Bishop of Bath and Wells*, [London] 1896, pp. 2, 7, 15, 16, 36.

[46] Henslow letters 1850–1858, Ipswich Borough Council Museums and Galleries, High Street, Ipswich.

effect these exchanges – Bury (I think) occupies Tuesday – I suggest Friday for Sudbury, & as I believe many at Ipswich wish … the Market day (Tuesday) not to be the Lecture day, perhaps you can consult the proper Authorities and see whether we can't get some other day – (not Monday as it wd. be inconvenient on several accounts) Wednesday is Hadleigh Market & Thursday Stowmarket – but I don't think these considerations need interfere – At all events let me know as soon as you can what days are open *to me* for 2 lectures or 2 exchanges, & I will arrange accordingly. I hardly know what subject – but I think Botanical Geography will do for 2 or at least one – if I can get it ready. If I can't I will fall back upon some old subject which I have not given at Ipswich ….

So, for many years, like one of Paley's cheerfullest bees, Sidney buzzed around the eastern counties, and up and down to London, to Michael Faraday's Royal Institution, and to other places, 'getting up' his subjects skilfully and quickly, and making sure the substance of his lectures was published in the papers, for the benefit of those who had not come.[47] Sometimes he would attract audiences of over a thousand. As needed, loyal Nightingale would buzz as well, with gadgets and equipment. And when country nights were dark, and parties came in carriages from far away, then Sidney would arrange a course of lectures irregularly, to suit the disposition of the season's moonlight. By the early 1860s he was giving travel talks, full of geological information, and based on lengthy journeys he had made. In 1861 he addressed the Sudbury Literary and Mechanics Institution on 'A Visit to the Alps in 1860'. In 1862 his subject was 'A Visit to the Hebrides in the autumn of 1861'; twelve months later, 'A Visit to the Bernese Oberland in the Autumn of 1862'; and twelve months after that, 'A Visit to the Tyrol, in the autumn of 1863'. During the 1863 excursion he passed through

---

[47] 'All his notes he afterwards gave to Mr [?] who was here to make an article about [it],' Boileau observed, after one of Sidney's lectures (Journal 1846–1850, 29 October 1847).

Heidelberg and called on Gustav Kirchhoff, eminent physicist, the first part of whose *Researches on the Solar Spectrum and the Spectra of the Chemical Elements* had recently appeared in England.

*   *   *

DICKENS, as one might expect, had a thing or two to say about preachers. 'My friends,' says Mr Chadband, vessel 'in the ministry' of no particular denomination, and Mrs Snagsby's guest for tea,

> "Peace be on this house! On the master thereof, on the mistress thereof, on the young maidens, and on the young men! My friends, why do I wish for peace? What is peace? Is it war? No. Is it strife? No. Is it lovely, and gentle, and beautiful, and pleasant, and joyful? O yes! Therefore, my friends, I wish for peace, upon you and yours."
>
> In consequence of Mrs. Snagsby looking deeply edified, Mr. Snagsby thinks it expedient on the whole to say Amen, which is well received.[48]

Preachers were everywhere in Edwin Sidney's day. Chadbands were charlatans, others were sublime. Sidney himself was much better than average. His sermons were expository and exhortatory, usually constructed upon a three- or four-part basis, wary always of mere oratorical contrivance, and grounded in an evangelicalism redolent at once of St Augustine and of Faraday's science, in that 'the *positive* sinfulness of man' which it proclaimed was defined uncompromisingly as the 'privation of light'.[49] His favourite

---

[48] Charles Dickens, *Bleak House*, 1852–1853, chapter 19.

[49] Sidney cited John i 5, Acts xxvi 18, 1 Peter ii 9, and Colossians i 13. See his *Select Notes of the Preaching of the late Rev. Rowland Hill, A.M.*, London 1837, pp. xxii, xxiii. St Augustine said: 'This then is the original evil: man regards himself as his own light, and turns away from that light which would make man himself a light if he would set his heart on it' (*De Civitate Dei*, trans. and ed. by Henry Bettenson, London 1972, book xiv 13, p. 573).

sermon causes were the Society for the Propagation of the Gospel, the (Evangelical) Church Missionary Society, and efforts made by anyone to convert to decent protestantism the Jews, and also Roman Catholics, particularly the Irish. But not all causes were exalted. Regularly, for instance, he was sent for by innumerable neighbouring clergymen, to be star turn at the dedication of innumerable small organs in small churches, and at the opening of innumerable village school-rooms, when innumerable children were feasted on home-made wine and good plum cake. And the exhilaration to be had at one of these parochial gala occasions would be quite as great as that received when you heard him preach for grander causes, in grander places, such as the cathedral at Norwich. For the biblical text that he would choose, and then develop, would match exactly the activity that you had come to crown. Services of dedication for new church towers would occasion texts about building, services for new church organs texts about musical instruments. Thus your humble parochial endeavour seemed providential, part of the continuing cosmic drama purposed by God the Designer; thus you would contribute generously to the collection, so that usually it would total many times the weekly wage of an agricultural labourer.[50]

No wonder, then, he thought himself progressive in religion. He believed that to be 'Church of England' was to be protestant, and that to be protestant was to be free, politically and socially; that was why he was so anxious to convert the Irish from their wrong-headed Roman Catholicism. Thus he was a staunch upholder of the Church of England's *Book of Common Prayer*, which was resonant with intimations of his beloved natural world, and the truths of which he was prepared to teach. He would have had no truck with modern parsons inclined to say it inhibits the religion of

---

[50] For examples see Appendix I.

ordinary people.⁵¹ Indeed, in a sermon in Norwich cathedral in 1840 he commended specifically the Third Collect for Good Friday, which begs for the conversion of 'all Jews, Turks, Infidels, and Hereticks'. He was not, properly, anti-Semitic; it was simply that in the matter of Jesus Christ Jews were wrong and Christians right, so Jews must be converted. He would have thought peculiar the view of Canon Peter Schneider, a former curate of Sudbury, who in Holy Week, 1981, denounced the collect 'as giving a caricature of Judaism', saying that he had not used it in twenty-five years, and hoping that Anglicans would that week use a new one, which he had commissioned.⁵²

* * *

ALL THOUGHT led to Science, all Science led to God. Or so it seemed to Sidney. The newspapers dutifully intimated the particular teleological or philosophical mode of each of his addresses or scientific lectures, often at his behest. Considered sequentially they suggest that his old-fashioned views were held more defensively after the publication of *The Origin of Species* and, in 1860, of *Essays and Reviews*, that hugely controversial book produced by several famous Anglicans, which suggested (among other things) that a gap had appeared between Christian doctrine and what, thanks to science, educated people found it possible to believe.

The texture of Sidney's scientific lectures was analogous to the fragrance of Poll Sweedlepipe's easy shaving-shop, in that quite

---

[51] His great contemporary George Eliot would have agreed with him. The authentic voice of the Anglican uneducated is Dolly Winthrop's: 'Well, Master Marner, it's niver too late to turn over a new leaf, and if you've niver had no church, there's no telling the good it'll do you. For I feel so set up and comfortable as niver was, when I've been and heard the prayers, and the singing to the praise and glory o' God, as Mr. Macey gives out – and Mr. Crackenthorp saying good words ....' (George Eliot, *Silas Marner*, 1861, chapter x)

[52] *Church Times*, 16 April 1981, p. 1.

impartially and without distinction of persons, it exuded a composite whiff of many philosophies, the spotting of which in the following extracts may occasion much enjoyment. Whiffs of Butler, whiffs of Paley, a whiff of Ray (second extract), whiffs of Aristotle's Chain of Being (linear taxonomy) in 'Feeling and Hearing' and in the address on idiotcy (a whiff here, too, of Lamarck's environmentalism?) – all are there. In 'A Visit to the Tyrol' he discusses the important discoveries of flint instruments, made in 1847 by Boucher de Perches in the Somme valley. He endorses the published views of Henslow (*The Athenaeum*, 20 October and 3 November, 1860)[53] which, against the arguments of some geologists defiant of Scripture, had sought to salvage something of the view which Genesis presents concerning the age of man; having himself visited Amiens and Abbeville in order to investigate, Henslow had said that although we could no longer rely upon Scripture to reveal the age of the earth, received opinions concerning the time man had inhabited the earth must not be cast off without assurance 'that these hatchet-bearing gravels must be several thousand years older than the Pyramids of Egypt'. In 'The New Railway' (from Sudbury to Bury St Edmunds and Cambridge, opened in June 1865) there is something of the same excited awareness of the revelatory dimension of railway building as Dickens had discerned in the wonderful twentieth chapter of *Dombey and Son* (1848).

From a lecture on chalk and marl, Acle, 1846 (*Norwich Mercury*, 19 December 1846, p. 3):

> A farmer ... may also be assured that while he ransacks the globe for substances containing phosphates, they lie often at his feet, in

[53] The controversy is documented by George Kitson Clark, in G. M. Young, *Portrait of an Age: Victorian England*, annotated by George Kitson Clark, London 1977, pp. 337, 338 n. 13.

his soil, and only need proper plans for eliciting them. How wonderful all these things, and how should they lead us to adoration of the one Great Cause of all – "Nature is but a name for an effect / Whose cause is God".

From 'The wisdom and goodness of God apparent in the laws which regulate the revival of vegetation in the spring' – lecture for the Church of England Young Men's Society for Missions at Home and Abroad, London, 1853 (*Essex Standard*, 11 February 1853, p. 2):

> Mr. Sidney … began by observing that some of the most beautiful illustrations of the highest truths were taken in the Scriptures from vegetable life and productiveness. Hence the subject chosen was appropriate for an audience of well disposed young men, whose intelligence he hoped to see keeping pace with their zeal … Mr. Sidney introduced his explanations by adverting to the striking adaptations of the length of the year to the series of periodical changes which take place in plants, evidencing the widest adaptation of time to circumstance …. It was necessary therefore to explain the circumstances under which [vegetable] organism… will be called forth into that activity which may be regarded as the *proximate* cause of the revival of vegetation in the spring. He said *proximate* cause, because the secrets of vitality were in the hidden wisdom of God, and therefore the *most* physical and chemical forms failed to explain all.

From a lecture on the geology of Ballingdon Hill, Sudbury, to the Sudbury Literary and Mechanics Institution (S.L.M.I.), 1857 (*Suffolk and Essex Free Press*, 12 November 1857, p. 2):

> Mr. Sidney said he could not help remarking how strikingly the Word of God was testified to by Modern Geology, which plainly proved that the introduction of man was identical with the period assigned to his creation in the Mosaic history.

From 'The Life of a Plant' – lecture to S.L.M.I., 1857 (*Suffolk and Essex Free Press*, 3 December 1857, p. 2):

> All nature is one vast harmonious whole, the parts of which mutually depend on each other; and happy are they who regard it with the eye of Christian philosophy, and whose minds rise in the glorious view, to Him who made and upholds it.

From 'Oxygen, in the Air, Water, Earths [*sic*], and Plants' – lecture to S.L.M.I., 1858 (*Suffolk and Essex Free Press*, 18 March 1858, p. 2).

> Oxygen is not only vital, but continually assists in the continuous process of the elements of decomposing matter to their appointed end. As plants emit oxygen, so animals take it in, and expire carbonic acid gas...Nature has its circle; the animal sends forth, as was shown by experiment, carbonic acid for the plant, and the plant oxygen for the animal. Mutual dependence is a great law of nature, and it is a Christian law that we should mutually help each other, which is the foundation of all true benevolence, and of the good the well disposed desire to do. Every natural fact teaches some great moral lesson.

From 'The White Chalk of Sudbury' – lecture to S.L.M.I., 1858 (*Suffolk and Essex Free Press*, 18 November 1858, p. 2):

> Mr. Sidney hoped his audience would many of them find their town more and more interesting as they became acquainted with these subjects, and learn to admire that creative wisdom and goodness which had thus prepared the earth for man's service. God is wonderful in all his works, and happy are they who, in the spirit of true Christian philosophy, seek truth in its excellence, both in the things which he has made and in the Gospel which he has revealed in that Word which makes known to us Him by whom the world was made.

From 'Feeling and Hearing' – lecture to S.L.M.I., 1859 (*Suffolk and Essex Free Press*, 3 November 1859, p. 2):

> The first question was – What is feeling? It is the impression made on our organs by the instrumentality of nerves, which transmit it to the brain. In order to explain what nerves are, Mr. Sidney first exhibited a beautiful microscope view of a portion of a nervous fibre, showing its wonderful construction .... By the assistance of a succession of diagrams, the essential differences of the nervous system in different branches of the animal kingdom were clearly defined. In *radiate* animals it consists of connected nervous masses in a ring, in *molluscs* these maps are variously distributed over the body; in *articulate* animals they form a regular chain; and at length in vertebrate animals we find a brain and spinal column. But in these there is a regular gradation until we arrive at the highest perfection in man. Mr. Sidney traced and explained the regular advances from fishes to reptiles, from reptiles to birds, from birds to mammals, and then to our own brain and spinal column .... The bony framework of a man and a gorilla were contrasted, to show the superiority of the human skeleton, which is eminently a nerve skeleton .... Man stands alone, highest in intelligence and will, and his organisation shows it. He is a moral agent, destined for another state of being, and responsible. His brain indicates that no other creature is like him .... The organisation of man tells of higher things than belong to the other orders of creation, but sin degrades him, and to bring every faculty into antagonism to its evil influences should be the grand object with which we study the fearfully and wonderfully made body into which the great Creator breathed the breath of life.

From 'A Visit to the Hebrides in the autumn of 1861' – lecture to S.L.M.I., 1862 (*Suffolk and Essex Free Press*, 17 April 1852, p. 2):

> When Dr. Johnson visited these places with Boswell they could not enter into the geology of the tracts over which they passed, but modern science has clothed them with the greatest interest. Wherever the trap [lava] is found, has become decomposed, there

is always fertile soil. Thus the great outbursts of volcanic action have been made subservient to man's welfare, and even the terrific was preparatory of benefit. In this and kindred facts the Christian philosopher [i.e. the scientist who is a Christian] sees the analogy of his conviction that all the phenomena of the moral world are preparations for the destiny of the faithful, when this probationary condition should be exchanged for "the new heavens and new earth, wherein dwelleth righteousness".

From 'A Visit to the Tyrol, in the autumn of 1863' – lecture to S.L.M.I., 1864 (*Suffolk and Essex Free Press*, 7 April 1864, p. 2):

In adverting to the journey home through Bavaria and France, Mr. Sidney glanced at several matters of interest, but particularly to those discussions which have recently arisen relative to the antiquity of the human race from the discovery of the flint implements in the vicinity of Amiens. He said that he considered the hasty conclusions drawn from these and other localities much to be regretted, and could not concur in them. Time only permitted to glance at the arguments from the places near Amiens and Abbeville. Several eminent geologists had recently examined those *formations* and has [*sic*] pronounced them to be far more recent than others regarded them. It must be remarked that while these implements had certainly been found together with the bones of extinct animals, it could not thence be concluded that they were co-existent with man. It was admitted that there was nothing more to prove man more ancient than that the extinct animals were more recent than supposed. There had been no human bones, nor any ancient shells, found in these places. Indeed he believed causes had operated to cause the mixture not yet explained. He could show from the coast of East Anglia how such a stratum might be proved; for the crag is constantly wearing away and falling on the beach, carrying down the bones of the ancient mammals it contains, and mingling with the substance below and the remains of man and recent shells. In time a new stratum could be formed with only recent shells, and a few things from the hand of man. If future geologists should argue that these were co-existent, he knew they would be wrong, and Mr. Sidney believed the advocates of the great antiquity of man and his long continuance in a savage state were equally in error. If the men who built the lake habitations recently discovered did so with the rude implements found near them, they were possessed of more skill than has been assigned to them. Mr. Sidney expressed his assurance that no theories from discovery or science could ever ultimately interfere with the records of eternal truth, and it was his desire in all his lectures to make them auxiliary to the faith of the Christian, and by analogies of Nature to strengthen the hope in the glorious Maker and Redeemer of the world.

From an address to the friends and supporters of the Eastern Counties Asylum for Idiots and Imbeciles, Essex Hall, Colchester, 1865 (*Suffolk and Essex Free Press*, 30 November 1865, p. 2):

> There were many degrees of idiotcy.... They might ... be divided into three degrees. The lowest degree was a mere organism, having no power over the muscles, or the will. In the next class the idiot might have some partial control over these, but his reason is obscured and his speech imperfect; and then they came to that higher class who had the normal powers of animal action and perception to some degree, but were not capable of social relations or the duties of daily life .... He agreed that an idiot asylum should be a hospital, a school, a gymnasium, a farm, if possible, a garden, a large workshop, and a scene of harmless and exciting amusement .... First eradicate bad habits, give them some light employments, and award them praise instead of blame, and then classify the patients.

From 'A trip from Sudbury to Bury by the New Railway' – lecture to S.L.M.I., 1865 (*Suffolk and Essex Free Press*, 21 December 1865, p. 2):

> The lecture commenced by the exhibition of an illuminated geological map of England traversed by the railroads, and showing

the different formations respectively passed through. Without a knowledge of these, a traveller through a deep cutting could have no interest in his route where the distant prospect is shut out by the embankment. But to a person acquainted with various formations, it would be most instructive. The railway between Sudbury and Bury passes over an interesting series of recent and tertiary deposits contained in a basin of chalk which crops out at each end of the journey .... It is to the great phenomena of this tertiary period that we owe the fertile fields of East Anglia traversed by the new railroad, and we may see in all these result the beneficence of the glorious Creator in thus fitting our present abode for our use. Mr Sidney did not fail to point out this, nor the analogy of our being in a state of preparation for a nobler destiny through His atonement whose Advent we now thankfully commemorate.

From 'A visit to the Lizard and Land's End' – lecture to S.L.M.I., 1867 (*Suffolk and Essex Free Press*, 21 November 1867, p. 7):

He carried his hearers ... through the scenes of the new red sandstone, and other rocks on the road to Torquay. The first halt took place at Torquay, whence a short drive enables the explorer to reach the remarkable cavern called Kent's Hole .... Investigations have been made of it from 1824 .... The animals of which remains occur were bears, lions, hyenas, foxes, horses, deer, rhinoceros, badger and elephant. The last is of the species that was found at Cornard in making the rail-road [VI]. Mr. Sidney here described the three different species of fossil elephants found in England. Many *savan[t]s* argue from the things found the enormous antiquity of man, but Mr. Sidney could not allow their conclusions, but thought that the fact was the animals named became extinct more recently than many supposed. With regard to the cave, a half penny of 1806 and a sixpence of 1846 were found in it. Who would argue the antiquity of these!

* * *

RELATED CLOSELY to Sidney's wide concern with matters educative was his extraordinary concern with the problems and sufferings of the mentally handicapped, and for the Essex Hall Asylum in Colchester. It was extraordinary partly because, after all, the mentally handicapped could not have been so very numerous within the sphere of his immediate pastoral concerns in Little Cornard and the Sudbury area, but more especially because it derived from a remarkable combination of old-fashioned Aristotelianism and Christian evangelicalism – a combination, in the right hands, of great potential goodness.

The treatment of lunatics in the eighteenth century was cruel; in England its most famous victim was the king himself, George III. Those responsible for lunatics were mindful, consciously or otherwise, of the Great Chain of Being, the assumed existence of which permeated the culture of society at large. Upon the human section of the Chain the keepers of madhouses assigned to the lunatic a place higher than the places of, say, orangutans or lions or tigers, but lower than those of criminals or slaves or the natives of Africa, or the aborigines of Australia whom, in 1850, Thomas Huxley thought so great a blot upon 'the escutcheon of our common humanity' that he desired their 'elimination … from the earth's surface'.[54] Lunatics, in other words, were little better than what the marriage service referred to as the 'brute beasts that have no understanding'; so if necessary – and usually it seemed very necessary – they must be coerced and 'restrained' for their own good; cruel coercion and cruel 'restraint', it usually seemed, were efficacious forms of medical treatment.

But then things changed. Partly because of the evangelical revival of the eighteenth century (largely the work of the Wesleys and Whitefield and Sidney's relations, the Hills of Shropshire) the

---

[54] Desmond, *Huxley*, p. 144.

earlier nineteenth century was notably more humane than was the eighteenth; so, in the face of opposition from the medical profession and even many churchmen, the 'immoral therapy' for lunatics of the earlier period gradually gave way to a new kind of therapy – 'moral therapy'. 'Moral therapists' rejected the notion that lunacy was due to abnormalities in the brain, the blood or the nervous system. Instead they argued that it was due to psychological states, and that therefore it must be treated through appropriately contrived systems of communication, sympathy and understanding. Fortunately 'moral therapy' was endorsed by the Commissioners in Lunacy who, for the inspection of lunatic asylums, had been established under the Lunatic Asylums Act of 1845. Consequently, by 1856 there remained in the country only one county lunatic asylum still using mechanical restraint.

Edwin Sidney was passionate for 'moral therapy', not least for idiots who, for Victorians, were the lowest lunatics of all. His passion signified his naturalistic perception of Christ's love, rather like John Ray's; his evangelical conviction that every individual is unique and equal to all others at the footstool of the Lord; his boundless optimism; and a logic wobbling ever on the side of charity. Yet, as his 1865 address to the friends and supporters of Essex Hall showed, as though he were Aristotle he must always classify his lunatics, even, it seemed, before they were presented at Essex Hall; in the matter of lunacy the marriage of his kindly evangelicalism with his taste for classifying echoed St Paul's opinion (in Colossians) that the doctrine of salvation in Christ should be married with the Great Chain of Being. One day in Little Cornard he met an urchin. They had a conversation:

'You must not come to church next Sunday.'

'Why not?'

'Because you did not behave yourself last Sunday.'

'How do you know?'

'Because I saw you.'

'Then you should have looked at your book, and you would not have seen me.'

Quick as a flash Sidney contemplated the urchin as though he were Alice contemplating the Duchess's baby ('Now, what am I going to do with this creature ...?') and assigned him a place on the Great Chain of Being; very obviously the boy was not just a lunatic, he was worse – an *idiot* (who else would thus address a clergyman?). But he should be allocated to 'that higher class' of idiotcy, for which something might be done. Here was no cruelty, coercion, or restraint. After all, thought Sidney, like all of us such boys had minds, only they were in faulty bodies; the instruments were out of tune, like violins with flaccid strings, from which even a seraph could produce no harmony until they should be tuned. So, with kindness and appropriate medical treatment, tune the mind of the asylum lad who has executed a beautiful pencil sketch of Essex Hall for, had he his natural powers, he (whose father was born in – but *guess* where: Sudbury!) might probably have been a second Gainsborough; tune the mind of another lad he knows – a complete fool, unable to reason on the ordinary affairs of daily life – who glazes and frames the beautiful pictures that he draws, for he sent one to the queen who sent him two guineas, and now his drawings fetch five pounds each as fast as he can produce them.[55]

In 1848 a certain Dr Andrew Reed had created Park House, in Highgate, as England's first asylum specifically for idiots; it was maintained by private subscription. In the same year it acquired for use as a daughter establishment the hotel recently built outside Colchester railway station, which served the Colchester to London railway line completed in 1846. Essex Hall provided chiefly for children and young persons. It was administered by the Essex Hall

---

[55] *Suffolk and Essex Free Press*, 30 November 1865, p. 2.

INTRODUCTION

Charity, the leading light of which was Edwin Sidney, who with his magic lantern actually worked inside the place, teaching natural science to the children, and attracting national and international attention. By 1854, however, the Board of the Highgate Asylum wished to establish a new asylum near Redhill, in Surrey, big enough to provide for the whole country (XXXIII). It became clear that it would no longer support the institutions at Highgate and Colchester the inmates of which, it was proposed, should be transferred to Redhill. So, cajoled and advised by Sidney, leading public figures in East Anglia sought the financial means to establish Essex Hall as an asylum independent of London's control; it would provide, it was hoped, exclusively for the idiots of Norfolk, Suffolk, Essex and Cambridgeshire, and would not need to be associated with London's bold endeavour to serve the whole country. They were not immediately successful, though, and Essex Hall was closed from 1856 to 1859. Sidney was greatly vexed. But his formidable abilities as an organiser and fundraiser enabled Essex Hall to reopen on 1 July 1859, and to re-engage its former senior staff. It was officially renamed 'The Eastern Counties Asylum for Idiots and Imbeciles at Essex Hall, Colchester'. It flourished subsequently.

* * *

OXFORD IN THE 1840s was renowned for arguments about religion. In the University, Edmund Bouverie Pusey (1800–1882) was professor of Hebrew. In the 1830s he had helped to create the Oxford Movement, with John Henry Newman and others. In 1845 Newman left the Church of England to become a Roman Catholic. Anglo-Catholicism arose within the Church of England, largely out of the Oxford Movement. Pusey was one of its begetters, though he disliked its excesses, especially its excesses in ritual. Others too disliked its rituals, or thought it idolatrous or superstitious, or believed the pope to have a finger in it. So, wishing to be rude, they called it 'Puseyism', or 'Ritualism'.

Sudbury in the 1840s was less magnificent than Oxford. Its dreaming spires were few; Henry Bridgman's painting shows a compact little town, clean-cut and distinct, like Thomas Hardy's Casterbridge, with no suburbs in the modern sense, town meeting country if not precisely at a mathematical line then, largely, at lines devised by river and water meadows.[56] Yet in one thing Sudbury was like Oxford: in its Puseyism.

At six o'clock one Friday evening in July 1859, the coffin of a child with Latinate names was carried from a house in Stour Street. Preceded by three surpliced clergymen, a doctor, an undertaker and other gentlemen, it came to St Peter's church, upon the Market Hill. The church was crowded to excess. The bier with the coffin was placed in the chancel. One of the clergymen knelt at the head of the bier; stricken with grief, he was the father of the child. The burial service was conducted by the other two clergymen, one of them the curate of the parish. Psalms were chanted by the choir. When the coffin emerged from the church, upon the bier, it was surrounded by an arch-shaped frame, over which was draped a pall of rich white silk. In the centre of the pall was a large cross, some three feet long and of violet silk; at each corner was a smaller violet cross. A procession formed: first the surpliced choir; then the surpliced clergymen, wearing white scarves with violet bows; the doctor and the undertaker; the coffin; the two brothers of the child within the coffin; a carriage belonging to the famous Mr Andrewes, and containing the mother of the child, and a female attendant; three other carriages containing family and friends, the ladies attired in

---

[56] Thomas Hardy, *The Mayor of Casterbridge*, 1886, chapters 4 and 14.

INTRODUCTION

white trim with violet ribbons; and finally a large concourse of people, gathered sometime earlier upon the Market Hill. The procession wound through narrow lanes, to the church of St Gregory. In the churchyard, close to the church's north wall, a grave had been dug. The pall was removed from the coffin, which then was seen to be of plain oak, with a narrow head, and a silver coffin-plate and cross affixed to the lid. The clergyman who was the father was emotional, and scarcely able to pronounce the committal. Over 1,300 people were said to have been present. Some wept, others showed sympathy. All departed peacefully. But many of them murmured then, and afterwards around the town, that it was a very unusual funeral for the child of a clergyman of the Church of England.[57]

The police were there. For the child in the coffin was Isabella Louisa Molyneux. The grieving father was the Revd John Molyneux, perpetual curate of the united perpetual curacies of St Gregory and St Peter. He had come to Sudbury early in 1855. He had scandalised stout Protestants by declaiming Puseyism from his pulpits, and by inviting others to declaim it too. He had abused Evangelicals. He had declared for the abolition of pew rents, and for the redecorating of his churches in a Ritualistic manner. He had nagged the town concerning the spiritual destitution of its poor; indeed, as might a dissenting minister careless of Church of England conventions, he had preached to a crowd of eight or ten hundred, many of them poor, upon common land beside St Gregory's Church, so inspiring them to come to church, for the

---

[57] *Suffolk and Essex Free Press*, 21 July 1859, p. 2. George William Andrewes, JP, solicitor, was the grandson of the *Mr. & Mrs. Andrews* painted by Gainsborough. He is thought to have been the model for Mr Perker, the election agent in *The Pickwick Papers*. He was six times mayor of Sudbury, first during the year of Queen Victoria's accession (1837), and for the last time during the year of her Golden Jubilee. See C. G. Grimwood and S. A. Kay, *History of Sudbury, Suffolk*, Sudbury 1952, p. 117.

first time, for the Easter services of 1855. He had disposed many in the town to cry 'town pope', for he had engaged in rancorous litigation with two prominent parishioners – with Hodson, master of the National Society's boys' school, because he had dismissed him for incompetence and on account of a professed shortage of money with which to pay him, and with Cardinall, a churchwarden, because on 30 March before the funeral of the child, Cardinall had discovered Grimwood, a builder, under instructions from Molyneux alone, removing from St Gregory's church waggon-loads of old timber, partitions, pews and doors, to be sold for firewood and pig-styes, to make way for rush chairs (*popish* rush chairs, some thought) upon which to seat the converted poor. Blows had been exchanged, with bits of the old timber spiked with rusty nails, between seven or eight men following Cardinall, and the twenty or so working for Grimwood. The police had been called. Then, onwards from the end of May, news arrived of the anti-Ritualistic riots which were to recur in London, at St George's-in-the-East.[58] These were sad events; awareness of them complicated the sorrow of some among the hundreds who came to the funeral of Isabella Louisa Molyneux. A question arose: What crude unreason might this child in a coffin unleash? So the police were there.

Problems continued, into the 1860s and beyond. In the spring of 1866 Lord Arthur Hervey, archdeacon of Sudbury, and weary of Molyneux, declined to hold his visitation at St Peter's Church, because (he said) of lighted candles upon the altar during the service of Holy Communion. He went instead to Sudbury's third church,

---

[58] *Bury and Norwich Post*, 17 January 1855, p. 2, 18 April 1855, p. 3; *Free Press and General Advertiser for West Suffolk and North Essex*, 16 August 1855, p. 26; *Suffolk and Essex Free Press*, 7 April 1859, p. 2; *West Suffolk and North Essex Free Press*, 20 December 1855, p. 4, 3 January 1856, p. 4, 27 March 1856, p. 4; Michael Reynolds, *Martyr of Ritualism: Father Mackonochie of St Alban's, Holborn*, London 1965, pp. 50-70.

All Saints, which was Evangelical. In the autumn, excitable Charles Badham, vicar of All Saints, and Edwin Sidney's friend (XXXV), ascended into his pulpit, raised a rude eye in the direction of St Peter's, and delighted himself and half the town with a wondrous fiery sermon upon Ritualists, Puseyites, idolaters, popes of Rome, and yokes of bondage. Few, perhaps, in Sudbury shared the wry detachment of the wag who, observing the horological inconsistencies between the four clock-faces upon the tower of St Peter's, had remarked that the very clock itself had turned Puseyite, since, though some hands pointed to truth, more pointed to error.[59]

Broadly, then, there were two Church of England pastorates in early Victorian Sudbury. They were spectacularly different. One, Molyneux's, Ritualistic and inflammatory, yet efficacious in its way, was characterised most eloquently by that funeral of a child. The other embraced the ministry of Badham, together with the educational and agricultural missions in Sudbury of Edwin Sidney. Molyneux was a foil to Badham and Sidney, Badham and Sidney were foils to Molyneux. In so small a town the three of them together exemplified the potency, exuberance and robust diversity of early Victorian Anglicanism.

The Sudbury Literary and Mechanics Institution, called originally the Sudbury Mechanics Institute, was founded in 1834, 'to help those of limited means that Journeymen, Mechanics, weavers, apprentices, labourers and servants shall be admitted as readers on payment of 1s. a quarter'.[60] Its premises upon the Market Hill are now part of Barclays Bank. In his earlier years at Little Cornard Sidney was annually elected its president. As president, he lectured

---

[59] *Suffolk and Essex Free Press*, 19 April 1866, p. 2, 29 November 1866, p. 5; *West Suffolk and North Essex Free Press*, 8 November 1855, p. 1.

[60] Grimwood and Kay, *op.cit.*, p. 133. For the mechanics' institute movement see Colin Russell, *Science and Social Change 1700–1900*, Macmillan Press Ltd., 1983, pp. 154–73, 176–7.

there himself; procured others, such as Henslow and Owen, to lecture there too; and attended assiduously to its library, its museum, its membership and its business affairs generally. In October, 1857, its annual general meeting elected him life-president. The ponderous resolution passed was the affectionate tribute of workingmen gladdened in heart and, surely, enlightened in ways they had never expected: Sidney, they said,

> is now the Perpetual President of this Institute, and it is impossible not to look forward to the highest benefit which will result to the society from his acceptance of the office. Conversant as he is with those departments of literature which it is our chief object to encourage, this alone would have pointed him out as the right man to fill the Presidential chair. More than this by his extensive influence and large acquaintance with literary men, we believe him to be capable of benefiting us in a variety of ways. Since his election we have received proof that the public is inclined more than ever to sympathise with us ....[61]

The Sudbury Agricultural Association was apparently founded sometime in the first half of 1848, effectively by Sidney, aided by George Mumford, who became the more active of its two assistant secretaries. Earlier there had been a Sudbury Farmers Club and a South Suffolk Agricultural Association, based in Sudbury, but they had failed, evidently through want of leadership. Most country towns in the England of that day had their agricultural associations. Usually they met on market days, and disseminated information on farming topics generally. Often they would organise agricultural shows, with speechifyings and prize-givings, very like the one comically depicted in Flaubert's *Madame Bovary* (1857). But they were not always popular, for frequently they supported Tory Protectionism and were too indulgent in awarding fat-stock prizes to their members. In three editorials in December 1846 (the month

---

[61] *Suffolk and Essex Free Press*, 15 October 1857, p. 2.

that Pochin died), the anti-Protectionist *Times* newspaper had ferociously attacked the associations for these reasons, and had complained, too, of their patronising attitude to the honest endeavours of agricultural labourers: a trumpery medal, or a certificate for his cottage mantelpiece, was a mockery, the paper said 'to a poor fellow who you know has not five shillings to call his own in the world, and who also will have the grim alternative of death or a workhouse as soon as his strength begins to fail'.[62]

Through the 1840s Sidney was troubled by the plight of the English agricultural labourer, as were most other rural parsons. A very fateful year was 1848. Revolutions swept Europe. In February, in London, Marx and Engels had published the *Communist Manifesto*, wherein the ruling classes were admonished to tremble at the prospect of workingmen everywhere, with nothing to lose but their chains, uniting in the cause of communistic revolution. Till April it was uncertain what would be the effect of the Chartist movement upon law, order and stability in England. Sometimes Chartists came for parsons; lest they should come for him, every night in Yorkshire Charlotte Brontë's father placed a loaded pistol by his bed and in the morning discharged the bullet by firing it across the churchyard. Mrs Alexander kept no loaded pistol (we suppose) but, fittingly perhaps, she contemplated a phrase in the Creed ('Maker of heaven and earth') and published 'All things bright and beautiful', wherein little children were advised of the providential relativities, within Nature's world, of rich men, poor men, castles and gates.[63] In his

---

[62] For the wider significance of agricultural associations see Travis L Crosby, *English Farmers and the Politics of Protection, 1815–1852*, Hassocks, Sussex, 1977, pp. 11, 12.

[63] Modern clergymen are politically correct, so do not allow us to sing the third verse of Mrs Alexander's hymn, the whole point of which is therefore lost. The Roman Catholic bishop of Leeds, the Rt Revd David Konstant, was typical. In 1995 he told the Catholic Men's Society that the hymn was 'one of the most dreadful, even unintentionally wicked, commentaries on society', and that the third verse appeared 'to lay all the blame for social problems at God's door, and

Little Cornard rectory Edwin Sidney brooded: 'What should revolution come to Suffolk – to the Sudbury part of Suffolk?'. He recalled what he had once heard the great duke of Wellington say: 'No country in the world, where all classes meet together for the purposes of furthering benevolent objects, need fear for its national safety'.[64] So, perceiving that Suffolk's countryside, with its interdependency of social classes, corresponded to God's providential order of Nature, with its interdependency of plants and fishes and birds and animals and people, Sidney concluded that Suffolk's countryside must now be actively defended; to which end there had better be, say, an agricultural association in Sudbury, provided it should not attract the kind of hostility proclaimed by *The Times*. Therefore he created the Sudbury Agricultural Association, the prime and much vaunted concern of which was to be the encouragement and real rewarding of local agricultural workers for loyalty and effort in the various kinds of agricultural service, and for thrift, 'responsibility' and particularly 'self-help' in personal and domestic life. It was, advised the *Bury and Suffolk Herald*,[65] 'no portion of its aims to give prizes for stock, or highly-cultivated farms'.

> to take away the incentive to bring about change on the part of individuals and society – wholly contrary to Old Testament and Gospel teaching'. He was reproved, rather learnedly but ineffectually, by the Church of England provost of Newcastle-upon-Tyne, who said that if one observed the comma after 'them' and the comma after 'lowly', one would perceive that 'ordered their estate' meant 'brought them into being'. The bishop's underlying theme, the provost supposed, was that 'no Christian can escape the responsibility of carrying forward God's work of change in individuals and society. Had she been a drinking woman, Mrs Alexander would have drunk to that'. (*The Times*, 5 September 1995, p. 3, 7 September 1995, p. 17.) Mrs Alexander's essential point was of course valid, and was supported by Galatians iii 28. It was: The variety evident in nature is providential; so, by analogy, is the variety evident in our social structure; but God's grace is available equally to all. The mockery heaped upon poor Bishop Konstant on account of his remarks is merrily considered in Ian Bradley, *Abide with Me: the world of Victorian hymns*, London 1997, p. 266, n. 20.

[64] *Bury and Suffolk Herald*, 25 October 1848, p. 2.
[65] *Ibid.*

INTRODUCTION

On Wednesday, 18 October 1848, London newspapers on sale in Sudbury told of railway lines torn up around Vienna, the liberty-loving Viennese menaced by over 15,000 imperial soldiers, a mob in Leghorn determining to vanquish the government of Tuscany, and insurrection in Sicily, where three-fifths of Messina was in ruins, and the valuable libraries of university and Benedictine monastery had been consumed by fire.

In Sudbury it was different. In the morning, to the north of the town, a ploughing competition was held on the land of Thomas Meeking (X), of Woodhall Farm. There were three classes of competitors: ploughmen with wheel-ploughs, ploughmen with foot-ploughs, and ploughboys with wheel-ploughs. Each man and boy ploughed two stetches.[66] At three o'clock there was a prize-giving in the Corn Exchange, before the speechifying dinner and general meeting for subscribing members of the Association, at four o'clock. There were four classes of prizes: Class I – agricultural labourers; Class II – horsemen; Class III – 'Agricultural labourers having brought up large families without Parochial Relief, or only in case of Sickness'; Class IV – ploughmen and ploughboys. Twenty-nine prizemen received £41 between them, doubtless for each of them the equivalent of three or four weeks' wages. Six of the prizemen were from Little Cornard (five employed by Mumford, one by Sikes), including two Springetts (inevitably Springetts – a horseman and a ploughboy, employed by Mumford), a Scott, and William Moss, who received twenty-five shillings for having worked thirty-six years on the farm at Caustons Hall. At four o'clock the farmers and local clergy ate well, and drank toasts to the queen, Prince Albert, the prince of Wales and the rest of the royal family, and also, as if to prove the Church of England and

[66] A description of the stetch, and of the skills involved in ploughing it, is contained in George Ewart Evans, *The Horse in the Furrow*, London ed. 1970, pp. 30–36.

intellectual credentials of the occasion, to the bishops and clergy of the dioceses of Rochester and Ely – the dioceses respectively for the Essex and Suffolk environs of Sudbury. They contemplated their own benevolence. Sidney lectured them on drainage, on the question of rewarding *female* servants (he advised that they should think about it), and on ergot, helpful Nightingale having gathered some diseased grain on the ploughing field that day, for the purpose of illustration.[67]

So, labouring men had co-operated with the ruling classes, and the ruling classes had discerned no cause to tremble. In Sudbury, clearly, the precepts of Marx and Engels were no match for those of Aristotle and Mrs Alexander. But, for this labouring community alert to the subtleties of occupational and thus of social distinctions, surely something was accomplished beyond the handing-out of money; perhaps for a while some of the sixteen whose skills under Classes II and IV were on this occasion recorded in the newspapers perceived themselves as craftsmen, such as blacksmiths were, or thatchers, carpenters, or wheelwrights, and so a cut above their fellows in the field who had received no prizes, or who, alas, were never taken seriously by agricultural associations. If so, were they deluded? They alone could know; they alone were the true custodians of their own true worth and dignity.

Eventually the Sudbury Agricultural Association attached a horticultural show to the proceedings of its annual general meeting (XXXIV). For fifteen or twenty years the Association flourished – for as long, it seems, as Sidney and his co-founders were themselves young enough and energetic enough to attend to its affairs. Usually Sidney continued to insert one of his esteemed agrarian lectures into the proceedings of the annual general meeting. 'That the

---

[67] *Bury and Suffolk Herald*, 25 October 1848, p. 2.

Sudbury Agricultural Association has done much good in the neighbourhood is rendered absolutely evident to the traveller,' observed the Tory *Ipswich Journal*:

> As each village is passed, the cottage gardens, compared with the cottage gardens of ten years since, exhibit a neatness and improvement which indicate the provident habits of the humbler classes of the population. The encouragement of such habits may be said to form the principal basis of the Association, in conjunction with the fostering of those other moral and industrial habits, which, carried out in this and other parts of the kingdom, of late years have so abundantly brought into full relief....that spirit of courage and patriotism which has shown itself so conspicuously upon the heights of Sebastopol.

For what the Association had achieved, thought the *Journal*, credit must largely go to Sidney, who, at Acle and in Little Cornard, had

> commended himself as the good clergyman of the Church of England, who diligently pursues that great work which makes men not only good servants of the Queen, but at the same time qualifies them to become servants of God.[68]

* * *

---

[68] *Ipswich Journal*, 3 November 1855, p. 4.

EDWIN SIDNEY, servant of God, died on 22 October 1872. He was buried in his churchyard, under the west wall of his church's tower (XXXV), a situation corresponding to where Henslow had been buried in Hitcham. A comely memorial to him and to Eliza adorns the south wall of the church's nave. But more eloquent by far is a brass plaque, modest, misspelled and inconspicuous upon a wall within the tower:

C. NIGHTINGALE AND L. BUSSEY, LEFT the INTEREST OF 15L. IN THE P.O. SAVINGS BANK, SUDBURY, TO BE USED BY THE RECTORS of LITTLE CORNERD IN CLEANING & REPAIRING THE TOMB & MONUMENT of the REV. E.SIDNEY & ELIZA, HIS WIFE WHILE TIME ENDURES TO BE DONE BY A STONE MASON EVERY 2 OR 3 YEARS.

Fig. 9 '*Foursquare and prudent*': *Peacock Hall.*
Photo and © by Paul Matthews.

NEWSPAPER PORTRAITS

I   AUCTION 1843

Bury and Norwich Post, 8 February 1843, p. 3, and 15 February 1843, p. 3.

> PEACOCK HALL, CORNARD, NEAR SUDBURY, TO BE SOLD BY AUCTION By Messrs. Isaacson & Tattersall, Upon the Premises, on Friday, the 17th day of February, 1843, under a Power of Sale, The whole of the valuable FARMING LIVE and DEAD STOCK, AGRICULTURAL IMPLEMENTS, HOUSEHOLD FURNITURE, and miscellaneous effects, the property of MR. BIRD, who is leaving the above farm; further particulars of which will appear in a future advertisement.

II   FIRE AT PEACOCK HALL 1843

Bury and Norwich Post, 15 March 1843, p. 3.

> On Wednesday evening, about seven o'clock, the inhabitants of this town were alarmed by the appearance of a fire in the vicinity, which was shortly to be found at Peacock Hall, Little Cornard, belonging to Newman Sparrow, Esq. The engines from St Peter's and All Saint's [*sic*] parishes, set out immediately and soon reached the spot – about two miles distant. Great numbers from the town went and rendered assistance in extinguishing the flames, which in a few hours were wholly subdued, without any further damage, than the destruction of the horse shed, in which it commenced, and a cart-lodge adjoining, with a haulm wall. Happily but little wind was stirring at the time, or most probably the stacks, buildings, &c. would have been consumed. The horses in the shed

were saved by prompt assistance. It is supposed to have been wilfully set on fire. Many of the bystanders appeared to evince great satisfaction at the progress of the flames.

III   FIRE AT CAUSTONS HALL 1844

The trial and conviction of James Micklefield occurred at the Suffolk Summer Assizes, Ipswich, on Saturday, 27 July 1844, a day of grim proceedings. Micklefield's judge was Sir John Williams, who, after he had sentenced Micklefield, sentenced also those convicted on the same day of the firing of Norden's farm at Assington – namely, Isaac Everett, aged 21, and Layzell Hicks

Fig. 10   'Old' Caustons Hall, in its dilapidated state at the time of demolition in the 1960s. Royal Commission on the Historical Monuments of England. Crown copyright.

Randall, aged 16; Everett was given twenty years transportation, Randall fifteen. At the same time Williams sentenced two child incendiarists, John Woods and George Davey. Woods had fired some furze; he received six months' hard labour, and a whipping. Davey had fired a plantation; he received three months' imprisonment, and two whippings. In the same court on the same day Sir Edward Hall Alderson (Baron Alderson; a respected churchman) sentenced five other incendiarists to transportation for life; a sixth to transportation for twenty years; and a seventh, a woman, to imprisonment for two years.

Micklefield was transported on the Hyderabad to Norfolk Island, in the south Pacific. He arrived on 19 February 1845 and died on 6 April 1846, aged 18, having experienced the brutal administration of Major Joseph Childs, one of the most disreputable figures in British colonial and penal history.

Ipswich Journal, 3 August 1844, p. 4.

SUFFOLK SUMMER ASSIZES.
(Concluded from our last.)

SATURDAY, July 27.
• • •

(Before Sir JOHN WILLIAMS, Knt.)
• • •

INCENDIARISM AT LITTLE CORNARD.

James Micklefield, alias Lott, 17, was charged with having feloniously set fire to a farmstead, in the occupation of George Mumford, in Little Cornard, and destroyed certain barns, stacks of wheat, beans and straw, and a great number of sheep, calves, pigs and other property, belonging to the said George Mumford.

Mr. Gurdon appeared as counsel for the prosecution; the prisoner was undefended.

Mr. George Mumford, the prosecutor, deposed that, in April last, he occupied a farm at Little Cornard. He knew the prisoner at the bar. On Monday night, the 15th of April, there was a fire upon his premises. His premise and stock were all safe at 1/2 past 8 o'clock; the fire broke out at 9. A double barn, a granary, three large wheat stacks, all the agricultural implements, and 56 sheep were entirely consumed. About as many more sheep were obliged to be killed from the injuries they received. Besides these, 17 calves, nearly 60 head of swine, all the poultry, and a pointer dog were destroyed by the fire. The cows, bullocks and horses were saved. The prisoner lived in the parish; he had stolen some potatoes from the witness three-quarters of a year ago, for which he was imprisoned in Bury gaol for two months. No reward had been offered.

Golding Gallant, labourer, said he knew the prisoner: remembered his coming from Bury gaol. He said he had been to Bury for stealing Mr. Mumford's potatoes. Witness's wife asked him how he liked Bury gaol; he replied, "he did not care any thing about going to Bury gaol; Mr Mumford should not get any thing by sending him there, for he had plenty of lucifer matches at home, and he would be d——d if he would not have a flare-up." Three weeks before the fire he again came to witness's house. Witness said there had been a good many fires in the county, but they had been very good about Cornard, Assington, and Newton. The prisoner said, "there will be some by and bye: Mumford is a d——d bad'un; he will have one by and bye, and so he ought." Witness understood him to mean Mr. George Mumford: he knew of no other Mr. Mumford at Little Cornard. Two days before the prisoner was apprehended, he came again to witness's house, and said, "he did not know any thing about Mr. Mumford's fire;" adding that "on the night of the fire he came home from his master's at 7 o'clock, and was in bed three hours before the fire took place." The prisoner did not mention the Christian name of Mr. Mumford.

Prisoner (to witness): I did not mention Mr. George Mumford's name.

George Lorking, a labourer, who lived next door but one to the prisoner, deposed that the cottages in which he and the prisoner lived, were only three fields from the prosecutor's premises. When he saw the fire, it appeared to him to be just lit. The barn was on fire on the side next to his house. It was about a quarter past nine o'clock. He called the prisoner's brother Ted up on the night of the fire; at that time he did not see or hear anything of the prisoner. The Saturday before the fire, he had some talk with the prisoner down against Mr. Howlet's stile; he said, "Mr. Davy who lives at Bures, on the other side of my house, has had some threatening letters; Davy, Mumford, Siggers, and Sandalls, are to have fires." Witness worked at Mr Mumford's. Prisoner asked him "if there were not some potatoes in his master's barn." He said, "yes, there were." Prisoner said, "if there were he should have plenty of roasted potatoes, if there was a fire." Witness saw the prisoner at the fire; did not see him doing anything, but eating potatoes.

Prisoner (to witness): You told me that Mr. Davy and Mr. Sandalls had had threatening letters. Witness denied having done so.

William Lorking deposed that, at the time of the fire, he was in Mr. Mumford's employ. About a month before the fire, the prisoner went to his house; they were talking about fires, and he (witness) said "they had been very good; there had been no fire in that place." Prisoner replied "yes, they have been very good; but Mr. Mumford is a d——d bad'un; if I could see an opportunity, I would give him a flare-up." Witness observed, "sure enough you are not going to do such a thing as that?" Prisoner replied, "yes, that don't signify." About ten days before the prisoner was apprehended, he had a further conversation with him. Witness asked the prisoner "which way he went when he set his master's premises on fire?"

By the Judge: How came you to put such a plumb question as that to him? Witness: He said, "I went down Stench field, along the fen, and up the chase; when I got against the gate, I stood a minute or two." Witness then asked him whether he saw any body when he got there; prisoner replied "he did not," that he opened the gate, and went across to the barn, and took a couple of lucifer matches out of his pocket, and lit them and put them to the thatch of the barn – that he waited a minute or two, and returned home the same way that he went – that he went up the bean field, which is called Stench field, and added, "when my brother George called my brother Ted, I was standing on the other side of the fence, and I was waiting there to go to my own cottage."

Prisoner: I did not tell him so.

The Judge (to witness): Are you sure he made use of those words to you? Witness: I am quite sure he did. How came you to take it for granted that he had gone some particular way to fire the place? I had a mind to find it out if I could how he had done it. Then you put the question as soon as he had done it? Yes, my Lord.

Prisoner: I told him that I was in bed.

Witness: I don't remember that; he never told me he had been in bed at all.

John Jaggs deposed, that he recollected the night of the fire. He was in company with Lorking and the prisoner sometime after the fire. Witness said he had heard very little about Mr. Mumford's fire of late, and he thought the cause would not be found out now. The prisoner said, "Oh, no. I am not afraid they will come after me now, for if they do they will get nothing out of me, for I shall say I was in bed at the time." Witness said, they won't get much hold of you so, and he said, "Oh, no." Witness then said to him, he dare say that it did not cost a very long time to run up there to do that; prisoner replied, "Oh, no, it did not cost long to run up there and do that, whoever it might be. Witness said, he dare say he did not stay to tend the fire long after he had lit it. Prisoner replied, "Oh, no, I dare say they were pretty quick whoever they were." Witness then said to him, "I dare say you put the matches into the barn." He replied, "It was easy enough done with two lucifer matches; but you know Master Lorking I wont tell any one else, I'll have my d——d head knocked off before I will; if they come after me for that, they wont get anything out of me, only that I was in bed; I shall stick to that."

Joseph Hume, a labourer, deposed that he lived about 4 or 5 rods from the prisoner's house; saw him at Mr Mumford's fire; he was in the road a little way off his own house, at half-past 8 in the evening.

Prisoner: I did not see witness at all that night till I got to the fire.

The Judge (to the prisoner): Have you any witnesses to call, or anything to say in your defence?

Prisoner: No, my Lord, only my mother.

The Judge: Let your mother stand up.

The prisoner's mother was then examined by his lordship. The prisoner had been at work at Mr. John Bell's on the day of the fire; he returned home about 7 o'clock in the evening; he pulled off his shoes and stockings and sat down to rest himself. The prisoner remained at home till after the fire; he went to bed between eight and nine o'clock. He did not go out of the house till after the fire had broken out; that I will swear. My husband, myself, and my sons Edward and William, were all in bed by 9 o'clock. The prisoner slept in a room on the ground floor next to where my husband and self were sitting, and he could not have gone out without my seeing him. When we heard of the fire, the prisoner was asleep, and his brother Edward called the prisoner up; he got up and went with his brother and several others to the fire.

Mr. Gunning replied upon the case. He said it was impossible for them to believe the statement made by the prisoner's mother. They must either believe the testimony she had given, or disbelieve the evidence given by two most respectable witnesses, who had stated that they saw the prisoner from his home between 8 and 9 o'clock on the evening of the fire. It was very natural for a mother to endeavour to save her child from punishment, but it was for them to consider, from the evidence adduced, whether the prisoner was guilty or not.

His Lordship summed up, commenting upon the evidence as he proceeded; in the course of which he said, a most lamentable misfortune had occurred. The loss of property was very great – a large number of sheep and other harmless animals had been sacrificed. It appeared that there were three other persons in the prisoner's house on the evening of the fire, and it might appear extraordinary that they had not been brought before them to corroborate the evidence given by the prisoner's mother. However, that had not been done. Now if any one of the jury had been charged with having committed a murder, and he had been at home and asleep when the crime was committed, he would not only have brought one witness to prove his being at home and asleep, but he would, undoubtedly, have brought the others who were in the house, to corroborate the evidence given in support of such line of defence. It might be thought strange that the prisoner had not done so; but looking at his situation in life, he might not be able to bring them such a distance to give evidence; but it was for the jury to consider, from the evidence which had been adduced, whether the prisoner was guilty or not.

The jury found the prisoner guilty – Sentence deferred.

The Court adjourned about six o'clock.

―――――o―――――

MONDAY, July 29

• • •

SENTENCES OF THE INCENDIARIES.

About three o'clock, both Judges having taken their seats in the Crown Court, the following prisoners – *Saml. Jacob, Martin Turner, Edmund Botwright, Frederick Borley, Robert Hammond, James Lankester, James Micklefield, Isaac Everett,* and *Layzell Hicks Randall,* were placed at the bar, and amidst solemn silence were sentenced in the following impressive terms.

Mr. BARON ALDERSON: ….

Mr. JUSTICE WILLIAMS spoke as follows: — *James*

Micklefield, the circumstances attending your case, young as you are, possess almost every species of aggravation that can accompany the perpetration of this, one of the very worst of all possible offences. Of the motives which induced you to commit this act, the evidence leaves not the slightest shadow of a doubt – it was to gratify a long settled and deliberate purpose of revenge; and in the execution of that purpose ensued consequences of the most disastrous nature – consequences which involved in speedy ruin not merely an extensive property – the property consisting of farm buildings, the produce of a farm, and the implements of a farm, of great value; but a loss also of animal life, which is perfectly shocking and appalling. Without entering into the particulars of the details, no less than about 200 unoffending and harmless animals fell a sacrifice to your desperate act; and I must add that in the course of that scene of terror and devastation which it is hardly possible to conceive, there was a triumph exhibited by you, according to the witnesses, and a levity manifested by you, which strongly demonstrate the settled malignity of your heart. In a case of this sort it is in vain, after what had fallen from my learned brother, for me to add that it is impossible, with the slightest reference to public security, to entertain a doubt as to the sentence which I am to pronounce upon you – the sentence of the Court is, that you be transported beyond the seas for the term of your natural life...

IV   JOHN HUM 1845

Bury and Norwich Post, 14 May 1845, p. 2.

SUDBURY, May 12.

• • •

On Tuesday last, a man of the name of Elliston was found drowned near Lady's Bridge, on the Chilton side of Sudbury. He was a few years back a respectable baker of this place, but a man fond of drink. He lived in Plough Lane, was very low spirited, and had attempted to destroy himself two or three times lately.

Bury and Norwich Post, 28 May 1845, p. 2.

SUDBURY, May 26.

On Friday morning last, the body of a man named John Hum, of Little Cornard, 54 years of age, was found dead in a cut from, and close to the river Stour, near Ladies' Bridge, a very few yards from the spot where Elliston, the week before last, drowned himself. On the following day, an inquest was held on the body by Mr. William Dowman, coroner for the borough, when it appeared that the deceased had walked from Sudbury on the Cornard road with another man until they came to Ladies'-lane, and was last seen by the man at the bottom of it, when he proceeded on his way home, leaving Hum, who was rather intoxicated. As there was no evidence to prove that the deceased had either thrown himself into the water, or accidentally fell into it, the jury, through their foreman, Mr. John Hitchcock, returned a verdict of "Found Drowned." Hum was a man well known to the sporting gentry in the neighbourhood, as especially attached to the sports of the field. He had formerly been enabled to obtain a decent living by the occupation of a little land, keeping cows, and cattle dealing; but of late had been so much reduced in circumstances, as to apply for relief at the Union House, which is supposed to have preyed very much on his mind. He has left an afflicted widow and a large family of children.

V ENLARGING A SACRED EDIFICE 1847, 1848

Bury and Suffolk Herald, 8 December 1847, p. 2.

SUDBURY.

Since the appointment by the Bishop of Norwich of the Rev. Edwin Sidney to the Rectory of Little Cornard, the parish church has been insufficient to accommodate the number of persons that now frequent it, and a preliminary meeting was held on Friday last, to consider the propriety of enlarging the sacred edifice commensurate with the wants of the parishioners. All the influential inhabitants were unanimous in their opinion of the necessity for the enlargement, and offered to subscribe most

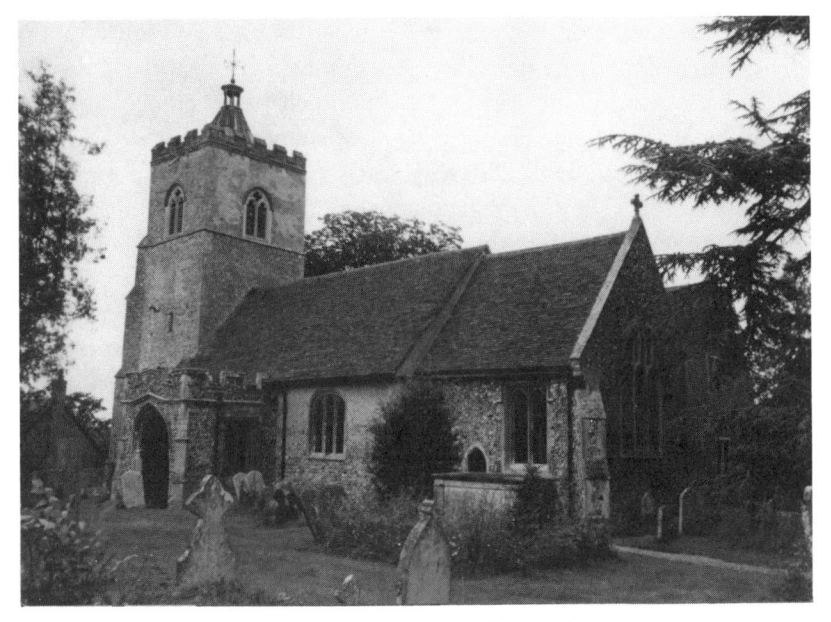

*Fig. 11 Little Cornard Chiurch.
Photo and © Paul Matthews.*

handsomely to carry out so desirable an object. Preliminary resolutions were then carried, and plans and estimates will shortly be submitted to the vestry.

William Ambrose, organist at St Peter's church, Sudbury, 1827–1874, advertised himself as 'pianoforte dealer & tuner & contractor for church organs, & organist to St. Peter's church, 5 North st'.

Bury and Suffolk Herald, 23 August 1848, p. 3.

RE-OPENING OF THE CHURCH OF CORNARD PARVA. — It having been found necessary to enlarge and improve the church of Cornard Parva, near Sudbury, a subscription was set on foot a few months since for that purpose, and the required amount most readily raised by subscription among the parishioners. The reparations were commenced with equal promptitude, and by dint of much perseverance are now completed. Divine Service was accordingly performed in the sacred edifice on Wednesday last, for the first time since its restoration. The congregation included most of the *élite* of the neighbourhood, and the church was so densely crowded that numbers were unable to obtain even standing room. Prayers were read by the Rev. E. Sidney, the respected rector, and a very able and most appropriate sermon preached by the Hon. and Rev. Lord Arthur Hervey, from 1 Peter, 1 chap. 24th and 25th verses – "All flesh is as grass, and all the glory of man, as the flower of grass. The grass withereth, and the flower thereof faileth away: but the Word of the Lord endureth for ever; and this is the Word by which the Gospel is preached unto you." The collection after the sermon amounted to £30. We should hardly have conceived it possible that improvements of such magnitude could have been effected in the church in so short a space of time, the repairs not having occupied more than about three months. That part of the building formerly used as the vestry, has now been made available for the accommodation of the congregation, and a new gallery erected. The whole of the original pews, which were alike wanting in uniformity and general neatness of appearance, have been removed, and modern ones substituted for them. A new altar piece has been erected, new pavement laid down, and, in short, the whole of the edifice completely restored; in addition to which a very fine-toned organ has been purchased, at which Mr. W. Ambrose presided. The performances of the Sudbury choir who likewise attended were most praiseworthy. Two sermons were also preached in aid of the funds on Sunday last by the Rev. E. Sidney, and a further collection obtained of £6 7s. 8d.

VI FOSSIL ELEPHANTS 1849

Early nineteenth-century comparative anatomists were much concerned to establish the precise origin and character of European fossil elephants (mammoths), partly because confused persons, who knew of Pyrrhus and Hannibal and the strange quadrupeds from countries tropical that sometimes appeared in Roman amphitheatres, were apt to say that fossil elephants were merely carcasses left around by conquering Romans.

The task of the Geological Survey for England and Wales was systematically to research the geological character of England and Wales, and to publish its findings. From its establishment in 1835 until 1845 it was controlled by the Office of Woods and Forests. By 1851 it had published accounts of the geological character of much of Wales and western England. 'Mr. Brown, who has a contact on the railway' is undoubtedly John Brown, FGS, of Stanway, near Colchester, who made an important contribution to the debate on the origin of the Felixstowe phosphates (IX).

George William Fulcher, Sudbury 'character', was a printer and publisher, and four times mayor of Sudbury.

Bury and Norwich Post, 14 February 1849, p. 2.

SUDBURY, Feb. 12.

• • •

As the railway labourers were this week excavating on the Colchester and Stour Valley line, in the parish of Great Cornard, nearly opposite the Five Bells Inn, they discovered, about 12 feet from the surface, embedded in gravel, a very large tooth and a tusk four feet long, of the Mammoth or Fossil Elephant. A similar discovery was made by the railway labourers in February last in an adjacent parish, and the head and tusks of a third Fossil Elephant were also taken out, all lying within a short distance of each other. Those first found were sent by the Rev. R. Dawson Duffield, Rector of Lamarsh, to the Geological Survey Office, London; and the Rev. Edwin Sidney, Rector of Cornard Parva, has the tooth discovered this week. We understand the tusk and a similar tooth previously found are deposited with Mr Brown, who has a contact on the railway.

VII   HANDSOME AND COMMODIOUS RECTORY HOUSE 1849

Bury and Norwich Post, 31 October 1849, p.2.

At a recent meeting at Little Cornard several of the most influential gentlemen agreed to raise the sum of £10 annually, to be expended in providing clothing for the best ploughmen and their families, an arrangement which will form another link in the kindly chain that unites the sympathies of the rich with the best interests of the poor. The pastoral care manifested by the Rev. E. Sidney is productive of the best results. Recently, increased and necessary accommodation has been provided in the church, at an expense of about £600; the education of the young is better attended to than formerly, and a large building has recently been fitted up by Mr. Sidney, in which the rev. gentleman intends delivering lectures, during the winter evenings, to the inhabitants of the parish: this is an exceedingly interesting feature, and cannot fail to be attended with the happiest results. A handsome and commodious rectory house is rapidly approaching completion, and everything indicates that the various means of usefulness now at work will render the population of this district as virtuous and intelligent as it was once degraded and ignorant.

VIII   LIGHTING A FIRE 1850

Bury and Norwich Post, 13 February 1850, p. 2.

SUDBURY, Feb. 11.

• • •

On Saturday last, in the afternoon, a barn belonging to the Peacock Hall Estate, Little Cornard, about 3 miles from Sudbury, was accidentally set on fire and speedily consumed, in consequence of the wind being strong at the time, and its standing on an isolated spot. Fortunately it contained only straw. The accident is said to have been caused by a boy having lighted a fire near by, a spark from which is supposed to have been carried by the wind to the barn and set it on fire.

IX   GEOLOGY AND FERTILISERS 1850, 1852

The second of these lectures is clearly the 'future lecture' referred to in the first.

In nineteenth-century Europe those who were not tillers of the soil often lectured those who were. In France such men were known to Flaubert the novelist; in *Madame Bovary* (1857) Madame Lefrançois asks Homais whether, as a small-town pharmacist, he is really qualified to go about lecturing the farmers on farming. Homais, gross and absurd, snorts that most certainly he is, for agriculture is within the domain of chemistry and all that chemists must know – the composition of manures, the fermentation of liquids, the analysis of gases, geological strata, the composition of soils and minerals and rain-water, the principles of hygiene and botanical classification, and so on, all of which may be learned from pamphlets and published papers. Homais was a charlatan. Sidney and Henslow were not; but in their roles as agronomists they were a recognisable type.

In England early Victorian farmers strove unceasingly to provide the contribution demanded from them towards feeding an ever-burgeoning British population. One aspect of their quest was their desire for improved fertilisers. Towards mid-century the supply of phosphate of lime used as agricultural fertiliser, and obtained from animal bones, became insufficient. Consequently the services were engaged of Dr Charles Daubeny, the holder simultaneously of the Oxford chairs of chemistry, botany and rural economy. Daubeny was dispatched to Spain, to discover whether the insufficiency could be remedied from the deposit of phosphorite in Estramadura. Apparently it could not. But the matter was considered so important that a second expedition was made, for further investigation. Then, in October 1843, Henslow drew attention to the occurrence of phosphate of lime in pebbly beds of the red crag of Felixstowe, in Suffolk. Thousands of tons of phosphate nodules (so-called) were lying between the rivers Orwell and Alde, particularly those parts around Woodbridge and Felixstowe. After raising, the nodules were ground, and reduced into superphosphate of lime by the application of sulphuric acid, in the same way as with bones, to produce a manure prodigiously good for many crops, but especially so for turnips. This processing of bones and of phosphatic nodules led eventually to the creation of the great firm of fertiliser-manufacturers, Fisons Ltd. But the superphosphate of lime thus produced encountered competition in the form of Peruvian guano – the rich, solidified, nitrogen-bearing excreta of Peruvian coastal birds which fed off the rich sea-life of the Humboldt Current. Guano became available to European farmers in the 1840s, and its fertilising efficacy was vouched for by the respected agrarian chemist, Justus von Liebig.

Concurrent with the widespread discussion as to the usefulness of the Felixstowe phosphatic nodules was a wider discussion, among professional agrarian chemists, as to the merits of farm-yard manure relative to those of mineral fertilisers in general. But also concurrent was a discussion, which rippled for some time through the published proceedings of the Geological Society and the British Association, as to whether the nodules were coprolitic and of the same age as the red crag, or whether they were non-coprolitic, detrital materials, found originally in the London clay. The matter was important, for it bore upon religion. 'We cannot believe in such things as coprolites,' cried one ruffled clergyman. 'The geological assertion that the Creator of this world formed it in some parts of coprolites savours very much of Satan or Beelzebub, the god of dung. Geologists could scarcely have made a more unfortunate self-refuting assertion than this.'

Henslow, as mineralogist, was one who originally thought that the Felixstowe phosphates were coprolitic. Wisely, however, he consulted Owen, as palaeontologist. Owen, as anatomist, examined the specimens Henslow sent him, and delightedly announced the discovery within them of portions (he called them 'cetotolites') of ear-bones roughly four inches square of three, probably four, species hitherto unknown of prehistoric whale. Since the markings on these 'cetotolites' were not compatible with their having passed through the digestive system of any other prehistoric creature, Owen was able hereby to dispose of Henslow's argument for coprolites. Important too for many religious people was the fact that the discovery in itself of three or four new species of *anything* obviously added *something* to the continuing agenda concerning the dimensions and purpose of God's created order.

When work-a-day farmers came to Edwin Sidney to learn about fertilisers and manure they were likely first to be instructed in formal geology, irrespective of whether or not the superior classes were present. For, believed Sidney, the prehistoric geological process (= Will of God) had produced mineral substances – phosphorites, for example – with fertilising properties. On their own or by the hand of man these substances had duly produced, or helped to produce, organic matter (= Will of God). Organic matter, besides being generative of further organic matter, was itself in one way or another eventually incorporated into further geological process (= Will of God). The total process was thus circular – reminiscent of the marriage ring, and somewhat reminiscent of the circularity of process implicit in the Prayer of Committal in the burial service, 'earth to earth, ashes to ashes, dust to dust; in sure and certain hope of the Resurrection'.

So, revealing of whales and suggestive of salvation through Christ's Resurrection: here was the wonder of the Felixstowe phosphates.

Other points:

* In 1841, prompted by the Royal Agricultural Society, Henslow had published a pamphlet entitled *Report on the Diseases of Wheat*. It was an up-to-date summary of existing published research (particularly continental research) on wheat diseases. It was addressed to the practising farmer, was matter-of-fact, and did not mention God or religion. In May, 1844, Sidney gave an illustrated lecture on 'the Diseases of Wheat' to a distinguished audience at the Royal Institution. He acknowledged his debt to Henslow. Then, in 1846, there appeared Sidney's *Blights of the Wheat and their Remedies*, wherein

he repeated his acknowledgment to Henslow, and made another, to the mycologist Miles Berkeley, formerly Henslow's pupil. Sidney's work covered ground similar to Henslow's, but it was longer. It was also teleological, and somewhat ecstatic, though a cautious title-page quoted Amos iv 9, on blasting, mildew, and palmer-worm as instruments of a chastening God; appropriately, perhaps, Sidney was gratified that his 'plain treatise' was published by the Religious Tract Society (*Blights*, p. iii).

* In the 1852 lecture one sentence is especially notable: 'They are the Cambrian, Silurian, Devonian, Carboniferous, and Permian systems...'. Here Sidney, ever up to date, describes the nomenclature that during the 1830s and 1840s came to be agreed among British geologists as being applicable to geological systems more or less the world over. The thrilling story of how this agreement emerged is the subject of Martin J. S. Rudwick's *The Great Devonian Controversy: the shaping of scientific knowledge among gentlemanly specialists*, Chicago and London 1985, an important monograph in the history of science. The Devonian system, says Rudwick (p. 459), 'is regarded as the first period in which terrestrial vegetation and vertebrae animal life became relatively abundant and diverse'. Furthermore, investigation of its invertebrate fossils revealed that they were transitional between those of the Silurian system and those of the later Carboniferous system. This evidence of the gradualism of faunal change confirmed Sir Charles Lyell's uniformitarianism, which (as we have seen) helped to pave the way for Darwinism. Edwin Sidney could hardly have affirmed the existence of the Devonian system to his Little Cornard audience without at the same time commending to them an acceptance of the related

circumstance of gradualistic change in the geological process. If, therefore, we place this fact alongside Sidney's approval of Richard Owen and his archetypal vertebra we surely have proof aplenty that Sidney's audiences, in Little Cornard and in Sudbury, were being treated to doctrines of evolution which would have dismayed the scriptural literalists among his brother clergy, even though Sidney fell far short of endorsing the teaching of Charles Darwin.

* Both Henslow and Sidney were much exercised by the tiny wheat midge, which, said Henslow, 'may be seen in myriads, in the early part of June, between seven and nine o'clock in the evening, flying about the wheat, for the purpose of depositing its eggs within the blossoms' (*Report*, p. 24). William Kirby, vicar of Barham near Ipswich, had first discerned its habits, in 1798.

* The poem appearing in Sidney's 1850 lecture is a misquotation of lines from *The Temple of Nature*, a poem by Charles Darwin's grandfather, Erasmus Darwin (1731–1802) – 'Last, at thy potent nod, Effect and Cause / Walk hand in hand accordant to thy laws; / Rise at Volition's call, in groups combined, / Amuse, delight, instruct and serve Mankind'. Erasmus Darwin was a physician, a philosopher, a poet famous for his rhyming couplets, and a scientist accomplished in many fields. But because he was also a deist who rejected the God of Christianity in favour, simply, of a First Cause he was regarded in the early nineteenth century as a dangerous subversive; not until around the middle of the century was he considered 'safe'. He contemplated caterpillars turning into butterflies, tadpoles turning into frogs, cows with one head producing calves with two, and so on, and concluded (though he could not prove it) that species could be mutable over very

long periods of time. *The Temple of Nature*, published posthumously in 1803, was a long, detailed and poetic tribute to nature seen as evolution from crude matter to the intellectual and social sophistication of late eighteenth-century Europe. Surely it was naughty of Edwin Sidney to quote one little bit of it which, out of context, seemed to suggest the existence of the God of Christianity in which Erasmus Darwin did not believe!

Many notable English poets admired Erasmus Darwin, among them Blake, Wordsworth, Coleridge, Shelley and Keats. Wordsworth in his early twenties was infatuated with both Darwin the scientist and Darwin the radical political thinker. In 1798 Wordsworth wrote a lengthy poem called *Peter Bell: a Tale*, in the Prologue of which he celebrated an imaginary journey about the Earth and around the stars in 'a little Boat': 'There's something in a flying horse, / There's something in a huge balloon; / But through the clouds I'll never float / Until I have a little Boat, / Shaped like the crescent-moon'. This part of his Prologue was apparently based on the description of a balloon-journey in a poem by Erasmus Darwin, *The Loves of the Plants*, published in 1789. The three lines of verse in Sidney's 1852 lecture are a misquotation of lines 248–250 of *Peter Bell*. A few weeks later, in Sidney's presence, at the annual general meeting of the Sudbury Agricultural Association, these lines were misquoted again in a speech by Sidney's crony, George William Fulcher (IV).

So, from Erasmus Darwin in 1789 to Wordsworth in 1798, from Sidney in 1850 to Sidney (and his crony) in 1852 – it really does seem that Sidney was as keen as most of his leading scientific contemporaries systematically to validate science not only with Scripture but also with the most popular English poetry of his day.

* The dean of Norwich in 1850 was the Hon. George Pellew. Owen Chadwick records his role in the affair of the coffins at Ketteringham, in 1853 (*Victorian Miniature*, London 1960, p. 143).

Bury and Norwich Post, 2 October 1850, p. 4.

THE REV E. SIDNEY'S AGRICULTURAL LECTURES.

The last lecture of the season by the Rev. E. Sidney in his parish of Cornard Parva, was attended on Friday week by a large audience of principal inhabitants of the district, which completely filled the spacious room fitted up for the occasion.

The subjects of this lecture were Lime and Chalk, with a continuation of Vegetable Structure, illustrated, as before, by the illuminated diagrams, most beautifully executed by Messrs.

Fig. 12   The rectory barn.
Photo and © Paul Matthews.

Carpenter and Westley. In the course of the description of the elements and combinations of lime, the sulphates and phosphates were brought before those present in a very interesting manner, and amusement was afforded by tying the rib bone of an ox, out of which the bone earth had been dissolved, in a knot. The nodules of phosphates found at Felixstowe were also described, but Mr. Sidney reserved the chemistry of the phosphates for a future lecture. The following practical hints as to the application of lime and chalk will be found valuable: With regard to lime, as it expels ammonia from fermenting manures, it should never be applied with them. A neat experiment made in the room clearly proved this danger; but it hastens decomposition, and revives it when it flags, in all organic matter. It gives fertility to soils, improves the quality of crops, helps dormant manures, kills certain weeds, makes the grain thin-skinned, gives mealiness to potatoes, to peas the disposition to soft boiling, while it hastens the maturity of all vegetable produce. A compost of quick lime, earth, and recent animal or vegetable matter, is very desirable. The saline compounds of lime, which are soluble, supply the plant with food, first, the carbonates, particularly chalk and marl, the latter of which was defined as an earthy mixture, containing carbonate of lime, often of different colours. Marls vary so exceedingly in composition that their effects are far from uniform, depending on the carbonate of lime, the sand, the clay, and the phosphates they contain. But let the farmer remember one thing – all marls exhaust the land unless organic matter is well supplied to it. To know the quantity of chalk that may be prudently applied, much depends on the quality of the soil, and the previous crumbling of the winter's heap. The objects of applying it are, mechanically, to render gravelly soils tenacious and close, the stiff clays more open and free, and sandy more firm. For these purposes, at first, a large supply of 400 bushels and more per acre is often required, while about half this quantity is enough for marshy grass lands. *But afterwards let all additions be small, and at short intervals.* If quick lime is applied, let it be borne in mind that clays, marshes and vegetable soils, need much; those of opposite character little. The quantity also should in some degree be regulated by the depth of the ploughing. Lime should be modified in its forms of application to meet different objects; for clayey and boggy soils slake quickly, and put it on at once, as also on the heaths, but for grass let it be slaked by exposure to air, and in a fine powder; for fallows all that is required is minute division. The value of a compost with earth is that small quantities of lime are more easily spread, and, by the smallness of the quantity, injurious running into hard lumps of hydrate is obviated, while the action on tender herbage is gentler. The older the compost, and the more vegetable matter is in it, the better. The standing rule for lime should be thorough mixture, and always to be within reach of the atmosphere. The quantity already in the soil should be ascertained, as too much is a great mistake; for it will sink and harden around the roots of plants. The ultimate effects of caustic and mild lime being equal, the advantages of the quick are – it more readily crumbles; it sooner neutralises injurious acids; is soluble in water, losing half its weight in burning; is more cheaply carried where chalk or lime stone or lime kilns abound; it kills insects, and also tends to keep off disease from the feet of sheep. Salt is often excellent with it, lime in the state of carbonate slowly decomposing the salt, and producing carbonate of soda of chloride of calcium. In all these things (Mr Sidney observed) we have wonderful evidence of the beneficence, power and wisdom of God; and the more we study these things under the pious influence of His Word, the more we shall admire and adore Him

> "At whose potent nod effect and cause
> Walk hand in hand according to His laws;
> Rise at volition's call, in groups combined,
> Amuse, delight, instruct and serve mankind."

As soon as the applause subsided, Professor HENSLOW rose, and prefaced his motion of thanks by some interesting observations on the wheat midge, which he said was most accurately figured in the diagram shewn in the lecture. The *larvae*, he said, appropriated the juices of the young grain and caused its shrivelled condition, and this year produced most extensive mischief. It was agreed by eminent entomologists that there were three or four species of this midge, and after long and patient investigation, it was found that they prospered in the ground, whence the flies emerged to do their injurious work in June, when they might often be seen of an evening flying about the ears in myriads. For a time the *larvae* remain in their cases attached to the husk. When thrashed out therefore and thrown away, they entered the ground and lived to produce the injuries described by Mr. Sidney. They should be sifted out with small sieves into heaps with the dust, and destroyed. The Professor expressed his high admiration of the lecture, and moved the thanks of the audience to Mr. Sidney, which was responded to with enthusiasm.

The Dean of NORWICH seconded the motion, as an old friend of the reverend gentleman, whom he had often listened to with delight in Norfolk, where his loss was sincerely deplored by all classes. He begged to say how deeply he felt the importance of the religious tone of these addresses, leading them to the great analogy of the Divine and natural truths, which were calculated to awaken the most beneficial reflections.

Mr. SIDNEY said the only reward he desired was the edification and enjoyment of his neighbours, and the only proof of the appreciation of his efforts their reassembling when he should, please God, call them together another year.

The large company separated with the most gratifying expression of the enjoyment of the day.

Essex Standard, 17 September 1852, 2nd ed., p. 2.

THE REV. E. SIDNEY'S LECTURE AT CORNARD PARVA, FRIDAY, SEPT. 10.

Notwithstanding the heavy rain of the morning, this lecture attracted a brilliant assemblage from all quarters within reach. We observed among these Lord and Lady Arthur Hervey and son; Lady Rowley and party; N. C. Barnardiston, Esq., and Mrs. Barnardiston and party; J. Berners, Esq., of Wolverstone; J. Poley,

Esq., Mrs. Poley, and party; Rev. J. C. Blair Warren and large party; F. T. Yelloly, Esq.; Rev. Messrs. O. Raymond, Roberts, Forster, Henley, Weightman, Fearon, Robinson, Kirby, Green, Byng, &c.; the Mayor of Sudbury, R. W. Bevan, Esq.; J. Sikes, Esq.; W. Mason, Esq.; and many respectable inhabitants of Sudbury, besides several most intelligent agriculturalists, with members of the families of Halifax, Johnson of Lavenham, J. Garrad, Esq., of Bures, and party; and a party from Liston Hall, and numerous others, filling the large room specially fitted up with apparatus and everything complete for these meetings. Mr. Sidney's principal parishioners were also present, and afforded every facility they could to the company.

The lecture was divided into two parts; first, a geological outline of the several strata of the earth, with a view to explain the characteristics and position of upper tertiaries near Sudbury; and secondly, phosphorus, to describe those important manures – the phosphates. Mr. Sidney began by alluding to the great modifications and changes to which the crust of the earth has been subjected. The principal causes had been the rising of mineral matter in a molten state from beneath, the wear and removal of this to other localities by various means, and the accumulations of deposits in originally horizontal layers under waters, where the remains of animal and plant have been preserved; as also convulsions of the earth's crust itself, areas of large extent having been raised above and depressed below the level of the ocean. These had occasioned likewise the squeezing, bending, plicating of masses of mineral matter ridged up into mountain ranges. The several formations of the earth's crust, of whatever kind, are called *rocks*; and they are either aqueous, igneous, or metamorphic: the aqueous are stratified, and the igneous often unstratified; the latter are either volcanic or plutonic, but contain no fossils. The aqueous rocks are fossiliferous, and some of them have been derived from the igneous rocks, and spread over areas of different extent and form by water, succeeding each other as detrital deposits in lakes as seas do now. The divisions, for the western area of Europe at least, are the primary or paleozoic, secondary or mexocoic, tertiary or cainozoic. The periods of the primary comprised the reign of fishes; they contain shells mostly extinct, with molluscs, corals, trilobites. They are the Cambrian, Silurian, Devonian, Carboniferous and Permian systems, and are all marine except the Carboniferous, which are marine, estuary and terrestrial. The secondary formations were the ranges of great reptiles, with some fishes and other curious creatures, too many to enumerate, and comprise the Trias, Iurassic or Oolite, the Wealden and the Cretaceous group. With the tertiary commences the reign of great mammals. The divisions of the tertiary are well known to the most superficial student of geology – namely, the eocene, signifying dawn; miocene, signifying the less new, and pliocene, or more new; in fact these three terms, which, ingenious as they are, will fall into disuse, represent the lower, middle, and upper tertiaries. To the first, which are marine, fluviate and estuary, belong the Plastic clay and London clay; to the second the Coralline crag, which is marine. The third is divided into pliocene, pleistocene, or more new, and modern: to the pliocene the red crag and Norwich crag pertain; to the pleistocene belong the various cavern deposits, the brick earth in the Thames valley, and the drift, till, or Boulder clay of Norfolk and Suffolk, to which last the observations now to be made were chiefly to be directed. Mr. Sidney, who had before illustrated his subject by a pair of most splendid new scientific lanterns and illuminated diagrams, by the eminent opticians Messrs. Carpenter and Westley, to whom he paid a great compliment, proceeded to show a series of five diagrams, for the idea of which he said he had to thank Professor Henslow, which rendered intelligible the changes from the pleistocene period to the modern. The present era immediately followed the glacial epoch; and the drift in this district Mr. Sidney said belonged to the last complete chapter of the earth's history. The Alpine chain itself had originated since the beginning of the tertiary period, and shows that the intensity of the causes disturbing the crust of the globe has not diminished since the older fossiliferous ages. The changes under review were stated to equal in amount the conversion of sea into land of a continent of [*sic*] at least as broad and lofty as Europe, Asia, and North America. During the same periods there has [*sic*] been vertical substances as well as elevations of the same area. Though some of the tertiary strata are heaved up to great elevations on the flanks of mountain chains, they preserve their original horizontal position in the London clay, the Paris basin and the plastic clay. In the tertiaries monstrous reptiles disappear and mammals are found. Those of the Paris basin belong to the eocene; the largest animal of the miocene is the tremendous dinotherium; and in the older pliocene we have elephants and other great mammals of the living genera, but lost species. In the pleistocene period which succeeded this a great part of the European continent was covered by an ocean full of floating ice, and at the end of this period the bed of the glacial sea rose. This ice transported portions of rocks as glaciers, floating ice down rivers, and coast ice, while sometimes enormous masses would get aground full of detritus and capsize. The Boulder clay, drift, till, are deposits of an arctic clime, advancing south during the subsidence of the land, and north during its elevation. Ballingdon Hill is a fine specimen, and contains fragments of numerous rocks thus transported. In the days of the great mammals, whose bones have been found in this neighbourhood so recently in excavating for the railroad, the intersecting branch of the sea now dividing our island from the continent did not exist; then came the subsidence and the icy sea, the refrigeration which occurred being to be expected when large portions of Europe and North America were submerged, and the gulf stream not running as now. At the bottom of this sea, and in small islands, by the descent of glaciers, the erratic tertiaries were no doubt formed. Mr. Sidney, in conclusion, said a few words on the agricultural character of these soils, and on the importance of draining the clays. The whole subject led to many serious reflections. It seems as if the ground on which we stand is placed but a few miles above seas of liquid fire, subject to secular tides – now ebbing, now flowing; and as all things have their time, so have we; but our's [*sic*] is one of probation for eternity, and the only way of escape, when the last hour arrives, is through the method opened to us in the

Gospel revelation.

The second part of the lecture was on phosphorus and phosphates. Phosphorus was discovered by Brandt in 1669, at Hamburgh, and is best procured from bones. It oxidises, as was shown by some very striking and successful experiments, including some beautiful and surprising combustions under water. Phosphoric acid was also formed in several ways, and the phosphates of lime, magnesia, soda, potash and other bodies were noticed. Mr. Sidney pointed out in this part of his lecture the quantities of phosphates in the several kinds of bone, and the importance of obtaining from them soluble superphosphates, by the action of sulphuric acid, for manures. The most remarkable portion of this division of the lecture was the use of clear phosphorus in obtaining ozone for experiments. Mr. Sidney obtained it before his audience, and showed its decomposing powers and the curious way in which they are destroyed by heat. He had discovered the existence of ozone in plants, and showed the similarity of the tests employed in the plant to those used this day in the laboratory. He believed ozone, which is an *allotropic* state of oxygen, performed most important functions in the economy of nature. In conclusion Mr. Sidney pointed out the wrong arguments which had been in vogue as to the applications of phosphates, showing that the knowledge of the composition of a crop is not a certain guide to the constituents of manures, as has been so often asserted. Turnips contained five times as much alkalies as phosphoric acid, but phosphates are better for them than alkalies. The same unsuspected results appeared in other cases, and were now on the eve of being satisfactorily accounted for. Thus we were daily seeing new truths opening up before us, and happy was the man who read the works of nature in the spirit of a Christian. Of men who have no love for nature it may be said, as it was of a dull rustic,

> "The primrose on the river's brink
> A yellow primrose was to him,
> But it was nothing more."

On the other hand the Christian philosopher —
"Exults in joys to grosser minds unknown,"
and anticipates brighter scenes than these that have passed away.

N. C. BARNARDISTON, Esq., returned Mr. Sidney his own thanks, and proposed those of the present audience in a neat and appropriate speech, in which he enlarged on the benefits conferred by the exertions of the reverend gentleman on his neighbours of all classes. At the conclusion of these observations, which were warmly cheered,

Lord ARTHUR HERVEY rose to second the vote of thanks proposed by Mr. BARNARDISTON, and made some excellent observations on the religious tone which pervaded Mr. Sidney's instructions of this kind, which met his sincere approbation. He most heartily concurred in what Mr. Barnardiston had said, as he was sure they all did. When the applause had ceased,

Mr. SIDNEY said his great encouragement was the presence of his friends and neighbours, and he hoped to summon them next year again. He then dismissed them with the blessing, and the large audience separated with many expressions of gratification. Mr Sidney, we understand, has since given a lecture to the working classes and one to children.

X   SILVER SALVER 1851

The mayor elect was George William Fulcher (IV). Gainsborough Dupont was descended from Sarah Dupont, sister of the painter Thomas Gainsborough, native of Sudbury.

Bury and Norwich Post, 19 November 1851, p. 2.

SUDBURY.

PRESENTATION OF PLATE TO THE REV. EDWIN SIDNEY.

At a meeting at the Town Hall, on the 29th of Sept., Thomas Meeking, Esq., Mayor, in the chair, it was unanimously resolved

"That the congregations of the churches of St Gregory and St Peter, having learnt with much regret that the Rev. Edwin Sidney will not preach as usual in that town on the evenings of first Sunday in each month, are anxious to mark the grateful sense they entertain of his kind services for the last four years by presenting him with some testimonial of their esteem and regard, and that a subscription be commenced for that purpose."

In pursuance of the above resolution, on Friday week a deputation, consisting of the Mayor, the Mayor Elect, G. Dupont, Esq., sen. Churchwarden of St Peter's, and John Sikes, Esq., one of the Magistrates of the Borough, waited upon Mr. Sidney at his residence, with a silver salver, very elegantly chased, weighing 98 ozs., and bearing the following inscription:–

"Presented, November 7th, 1851, to the Rev. Edwin Sidney, M.A., Rector of Cornard Parva, by the congregation of the Churches of St. Gregory and St. Peter, Sudbury, Suffolk, to mark the high sense they entertain of his kind and faithful ministerial services, gratuitously rendered, in the Church of St Peter in that town, on the first Sunday evening in every month, for a period of four years."

It was accompanied by a copy of the resolution and the names of the subscribers, beautifully written on vellum by Mr. Gibbs. In presenting it the Mayor thus addressed the rev. Gentleman:–

"REV. AND DEAR SIR, – I have the pleasing duty, from the office I have the honour to hold, and which I assure you I value the more because it has given me the privilege of being deputed with the gentlemen around me to present to you, in the names of the subscribers, this piece of plate, as a testimonial of their appreciation of the valuable and gratuitous services you have rendered us by your occasional ministry among us, and which we hope have been the means of promoting not only the moral, but we trust, under Divine blessing, the spiritual improvement of many among us. Nor can I avoid alluding to your unwavering adherence to the great and essential doctrines of the Gospel: your affectionate manner of proclaiming them, and your great kindness manifested to us upon so many occasions will, I am sure, ever secure a place in our most grateful remembrance. Permit me, then, Sir, with this Testimonial, to present you with a copy of the resolutions, together with a list of the subscribers, and to accompany them with our sincere, earnest, and united wish that you and your amiable lady may enjoy every temporal and spiritual blessing, that your life may continue to be a life of usefulness, and that your last days may be your best."

Mr. Sidney, who was evidently much affected during the delivery of this address, replied to it as follows:–

"MR. MAYOR AND GENTLEMEN, – The kindness so generously manifested in this munificent token of regard will cause you to give me credit for receiving it with every feeling yourselves and its other donors could desire. I shall ever treasure it with extreme gratitude and a vivid recollection of my friends in Sudbury, whose names are enrolled in the list of contributors. The humble services, of which this is indeed a far more than adequate memorial, were given with a most sincere pleasure, enhanced by the attention I was rejoiced to notice in the congregation, of whose best interests I can only say I have not been unmindful in my prayers. I beg you will not only accept yourselves my warmest thanks, as those who have undertaken to convey to me this gratifying token of esteem, but that you will add to the favour the further one of expressing the same to those who deputed you, and to whom I am so deeply obliged."

After the presentation of the salver the deputation were most hospitably entertained by Mr. Sidney, who reiterated the deep sense he entertained of the kindness of his many friends, and particularly desired that his warmest acknowledgements might be communicated to all the subscribers.

XI   LATE LAMENTED DUKE 1852

The first duke of Wellington, victor of Waterloo, died aged 83 at Walmer Castle, Kent, on 14 September 1852. He was buried in St

Paul's cathedral on 18 November. He received a state funeral unprecedented in splendour; a million and a half people lined the route of the procession, from the Royal Hospital, Chelsea, to the cathedral. Local communities performed their own obsequies, to coincide with those in London.

Essex Standard, 26 November 1852, 2nd ed., p. 2.

SUDBURY.

Thursday, the 18th, being the day of the public funeral of the late lamented Duke of Wellington, there was a total cessation of all business in this town. The bells of the churches were tolled from an early hour in the morning; all the shops, except those of the Society of Friends, were closed; and sermons were preached at the churches of All Saints' and St. Peter. In the surrounding villages the day was also observed by the tolling of the funeral bell, and suitable sermons were preached in several of the churches on the following Sunday. At Cornard Parva the Rev. E. Sidney took for his text the 8th ver. of the 8th c. of Ecclesiastes – *"There is no man that hath power over the spirit to retain the spirit, neither hath he power in the day of death; and there is no discharge in that war."* In the course of his address the Reverend Gentleman, was enabled, from his connexion with the family of Lord Hill, to introduce several striking characteristics of the lamented Duke not generally known to the public, which excited the deepest interest in the congregation.

XII   SEASONABLE BENEVOLENCE 1854

Essex Standard, 13 January 1854, p. 2.

SEASONABLE BENEVOLENCE. – During the late inclement weather the principal parishioners of Cornard Parva set on foot a subscription for their poor neighbours, and collected the handsome sum of £22, which has been distributed in coals, and most gratefully received by the recipients of their bounty. This sum was in addition to their usual gifts to the Clothing Society.

XIII JOHN BELL 1854

John Bell was the tenant of John Gurdon (of Assington), at Yorley Farm. He had been the employer of James Micklefield (III).

Bury and Norwich Post, 21 June 1854, p. 3.

> SUICIDE. – On Tuesday morning Mr. John Bell, farmer, of Little Cornard, aged 64, left home, about 6 in the morning, avowedly to water some cattle; but his daughter seeing him go in a different direction, proceeded in search of him, and in about half-an-hour after found him in a pond of water, her attention having been attracted by his hat lying upon the bank. Her screams brought assistance, and the deceased was got out, but he was quite dead. An inquest was held on Thursday last, by G.A. Partridge, Esq., when it appeared that he had been in a low state of health and spirits for some time, arising from disease of the brain, and in the opinion of Mr. Bestoe Smith, surgeon of Sudbury, who attended him, was at times insane. The jury returned a verdict of "Temporary insanity."

XIV DUCAL VISITS 1856

The second duke of Wellington (1807–1884), eldest son of the victor of Waterloo, had been MP for Norwich, 1837–1852.

In 1844 parliament passed the Regulation of Railways Act, which said (for the benefit not of dukes, but of the poorer classes) that on all future railways there was to be covered-in third-class accommodation on at least one train a day (the 'parliamentary train'), travelling the length of the line, each way, stopping at every station, and charging a maximum of one penny a mile for the third-class passenger. It is possible that on this occasion the duke had his own private carriage hitched to the parliamentary train.

West Suffolk and North Essex Free Press, 16 October 1856, p. 4.

> THE DUKE OF WELLINGTON AT SUDBURY. – The Duke of Wellington arrived at the Sudbury Station on Tuesday morning, by the parliamentary town train, and proceeded to pay a brief visit to the Rev. E. Sidney, at Little Cornard Rectory. We understand that his Grace left the same day by the 12.20 train (which halted at Cornard to take him up), and pursued his journey to Norwich.

West Suffolk and North Essex Free Press, 30 October 1856, p. 4.

> On Monday, his grace the Duke of Wellington made another visit to the Rev. E. Sidney, and was accompanied by that gentleman to the Idiot Asylum, Essex Hall, Colchester.

XV JOHN NEWMAN SPARROW 1857

Suffolk and Essex Free Press, 12 March 1857, p. 4.

> LITTLE CORNARD. — AWFULLY SUDDEN DEATH. — On Saturday last, an inquest was held in this parish, before G. A. Partridge, Esq., Coroner, on the body of Mr. John Newman Sparrow, a highly respectable landed proprietor and farmer, residing at Peacock Hall. It appeared that on the Thursday previous, Mr Sparrow left his house during the afternoon, in his usual state of health, and, about five o'clock, was discovered by his youngest son, sitting in a field, apparently very ill. He requested that a cart might be fetched to convey him home, and assistance

being procured, he was placed in a small tumbrel, but, before the house could be reached, it was discovered that the spark of life had fled. – W. B. Smith, Esq., surgeon of Sudbury, stated that he had attended deceased for a pulmonary infection, which was, undoubtedly, the cause of death, and the jury returned a verdict accordingly.

XVI   IN MEMORIAM 1857

Charles Clutterbuck (1806–1861) was a prominent stained-glass artist, criticised in his own day for favouring the *cinquecento* style, which he employed at Little Cornard. The Spanish painter Bartolomé Esteban Murillo lived from 1617 until 1682.

Suffolk and Essex Free Press, 15 October 1857, p. 2.

LITTLE CORNARD.

MEMORIAL WINDOW. — In this neat little church, a splendid painted window, by Clutterbuck, has lately been erected, by order of J. Sykes [*sic*], Esq., in memory of the late Mrs. Sykes. The centre contains a very fine figure of Our Lord and Saviour, after Murillo; on the left, the Saviour is represented pointing to the vine, "I am the vine," &c.; and on the right, as the good Shepherd. In the upper compartments are representations of the four Evangelists. The beautiful colours in this window render it worthy of special notice.

XVII DISSOLVING VIEWS 1857

The magic lantern was invented in the seventeenth century. It became an important entertainment in public and in private. The glass slides were hand-drawn or painted until 1880, but subsequently engravings and drawings were transferred to slides by photographic methods, and then coloured. The quality of the projected picture consequently deteriorated.

Throughout the period covered by this book, Messrs Carpenter and Westley, opticians, of 24 Regent Street, Waterloo Place, London, were renowned suppliers of magic lanterns and their accessories, and of a wide variety of slides. Edwin Sidney was their frequent client. Sometimes, it appears, he devised the content of his lectures to suit whatever slides he could hire from the currently available stock of Carpenter and Westley. But sometimes (particularly in the 1860s, it would seem) Carpenter and Westley prepared specially for him slides copied from his own photographs.

Sidney's lectures of the popular kind were usually illustrated with 'dissolving views', though he did not enlist the chorusing support of choirboys as did the high church Parson in the extract which follows.

The extract conveys the principle of 'dissolving views', and confirms the impression given by newspaper reports of Sidney's lectures that 'dissolving views' could arouse great excitement among country people. The extract is from an imaginary dialogue entitled 'The Parish and the Priest: Colloquy the Second: Christmas Customs', which in 1857 appeared in *The Churchman's Companion*, a fervently Anglo-Catholic, 'family' periodical which ran from 1847 to 1883, and upon which the Evangelical Sidney would surely have frowned. In the extract young Ernest, of priestly vocation, has just graduated from the University of Oxford. To discover the soundest principles of priestliness and seasonal endeavour he visits the 'little retired country village' of Fisherford, to converse with the good and Ritualist Parson. As the Parson agrees, the apparatus required for showing 'dissolving views' was expensive: on the front page of the *Suffolk and Essex Free Press* of 14 November 1861, Messrs Carpenter and Westly advertised 'a pair of Dissolving View Lanterns, No. 2, with Apparatus, Reflectors, &c.', for the princely sum of £12 6s., and 'a good assortment of paintings for Dissolving Views ... from £15 and upwards, in addition to the Lanterns'.

Childermas Day (Holy Innocents' Day) is 28 December. 'Friday and Childermas are two cross days in the week,' said Jonathan Swift, 'and it is impossible to have good luck on either of them' (Swift, *Directions to Servants in General*, 1745, 'The Cook').

The Churchman's Companion, vol. xxii, December 1857, pp. 441–3.

• • •

ERNEST. – I know you have a dinner of roast beef, and plum pudding, and apple-pie in the Christmas week for your schools.

PARSON. – Yes, thanks to our kind-hearted neighbour at Fisherford Hall. And it is one of the most pleasant sights of the year. And not the least pleasurable part about it is to see the care with which every child almost always stows away a great lump of pudding, so that "mother," and all at home, should have a taste of it for supper. We hold our feast usually upon Childermas-day, – thus setting at defiance the old superstition which held it to be the unluckiest day in all the year. And instead of adopting the ancient discipline which whipped the school all round upon that morning, in order that the memory of Herod's murder of the Innocents might have a more vivid place in the scholars' remembrance, we devote the evening to the Christmas-tree, (on which we suspend the school prizes), or to an exhibition of such Dissolving Views as may be suited to children's tastes and capacities. That evening is a very happy one: and education owes a great deal to Messrs. Carpenter and Westley, for the improvement which they made in the magic-lantern; and the high art which they have called into requisition for the production of their pictures, has enabled us to bring subjects of interest before the people, from which, till of late, they were hopelessly excluded. We can now elucidate by pictures on a very large scale, scenes and processes, which formerly could only be shown through the medium of very expensive books, that could only be inspected by a few persons at time. Formerly, the slides of a magic-lantern were, nine times in ten, coarse and vulgar, if not offensive and profane. *Now*, the phantasmagoric paintings are made subservient to the best and noblest purposes. And of such representations our people never seem to tire; and the beautiful manner in which, by the simplest contrivances one view "dissolves" into another, is as much a marvel to them here at Fisherford, as on the first evening on which it was exhibited, when they came to the sage conclusion that the parson painted each picture, as he went on talking to them.

ERNEST. – This sort of apparatus is very expensive, is it not?

PARSON. – Yes: and I fear necessarily so, for each picture being a perfect miniature, the artist who executes it must be paid accordingly. Poor folks, therefore, like the country parsons, must be content to make their collection of sliders slowly. It has taken me a good many years to get a series illustrative of the chief localities of Scripture: but I have had my reward in the assurance of many of my people that they had been unable to form any notion of Bible-lands, or to understand many passages in the Bible till they had seen these views.

ERNEST. – Of course you accompany each scene with a *vivâ voce* description, or embody them in a lecture?

PARSON. – Yes, and I relieve my audience of the sound of a voice of which they must be very tired, by interspersing the narrative with such choruses and other sacred music by our choir-boys, as can appropriately be introduced. Our school will hold an assembly of a hundred and fifty people, or thereabouts, and there is always a great press for tickets for the two or three nights on which the dissolving views are displayed.

• • •

XVIII SAPIENT DECISION 1858

George Lorking was the son of 'Master' William Lorking (in parish records described variously as husbandman, or labourer), and of his wife Catherine. Father and son had been witnesses at the trial of James Micklefield (III). George Lorking was baptised by William Pochin on 17 September, 1826. On 25 October 1851, he was married by Edwin Sidney, in the church, to Mary Baldwin, a parish girl aged 21, the daughter of a thatcher. The church's register of baptisms records the baptisms by Sidney of four children of George and Mary: Arthur (15 May 1853), Caroline Lucy (7 January 1855), David (22 February 1857), and Margaret Lucy (10 April 1859). Caroline Lucy died aged fifteen months, and was buried by Sidney on 28 December 1855. Sidney buried her father on 4 December 1858.

On 2 August 1858, the royal assent was given to the Act of Parliament establishing the General Medical Council, for the control of the nation's medical profession. 'It is expedient,' observed the Act's preamble, 'that persons requiring medical aid should be enabled to distinguish qualified from unqualified practitioners'. In general, as from 1 January 1859, only medical practitioners registered with the Council, on the basis of qualifications specified in the Act, would be able to claim legally qualified status, and sue at law for the recovery of professional fees, charges, etc. For purposes of registration the Act became operative on 1 October 1858. All in all, therefore, 'a man who pretended to be a doctor' in November 1858 was perhaps well advised to settle for a couple of pullets, and disappear.

Suffolk and Essex Free Press, 9 December 1858, p. 2.

LITTLE CORNARD. – Mr Greene, deputy coroner, held an inquest last Thursday, upon the body of George Lorking, 31, farm labourer. It appeared from the evidence that the deceased had been for some years subject to pains in the head, and epileptic fits. About a fortnight previous to his death, a man who pretended to be a doctor, called at the deceased's house, and, having sapiently decided that the malady arose from his having a large *tape-worm* in *his inside*, succeeded in palming off upon the poor people a bottle of his mixture, in payment for which, as money was not obtainable, he consented to take a couple of pullets. After taking the medicine for three or four days, and suffering with the pain even more than usual, he discontinued taking it. He had four fits, the last on the morning of the day on which he died. Mr. Symmons, surgeon, of Bures, stated that he had attended the deceased for epileptic fits about six or eight months since; he considered that the brain was affected, and was softening, or that he had a scrofulous tubercle upon it; he had examined the bottle of medicine, and found that it contained a great deal of cayenne pepper, green mint and lamb mint, but no laudanum or any other narcotic. It might have irritated his stomach, but, in his opinion deceased's death was not caused by the stuff he had taken – The Jury returned a verdict of "Natural Death."

XIX SPARROW'S LOSS 1859

Suffolk and Essex Free Press, 20 October 1859, p. 2.

LITTLE CORNARD

FIRE, – on Tuesday, the 11th inst., a straw stack, value about £148 [*sic*], the property of Mr. Sparrow, of Peacock Hall, was destroyed by fire. It appears that a boy 10 years old, who was taking care of sheep for Mr. Seggers [*sic*] in an adjoining field, made a fire to warm himself, and the flames spreading along some loose straw reached the stack. Mr. Sparrow's loss is covered by insurance in the Globe Fire Office.

XX BRAMBLES AND CRINOLINES 1859

At the annual general meeting of the Sudbury Agricultural Association held in Sudbury's town hall on 14 October 1859, Edwin Sidney, secretary, responded to the toasting of his health, and considered local issues.

His criticisms of recommendations 'from high quarters' concerning the improvement of the morals of the lower orders pandered to coarse prejudice. It was surely directed at Prince Albert (Queen Victoria's consort), who throughout the decade before his death (1861) was greatly involved with the application of the considerable surplus revenue which had accrued from the Great Exhibition (1851) to the building of the museums area of South Kensington; the object, largely, was popular improvement. 'All the Prince's schemes for Museums of Science and Art were devised,' says his biographer, 'with the view of putting the working-classes in as favourable a position as the rich for seeing for themselves what science and art had achieved, and the steps by which they had advanced to their present state.... That the arrangement of Museums of Art as well as of Science should be such as to afford the means of methodical study was a point on which the Prince justly laid the greatest stress.' Sniping thus at Albert was of course wholly at odds with the fact that many a rustic bumpkin must have been elevated beyond his station by Sidney's characteristic endeavours in the field of popular instruction. But then Sidney raised low minds to visions of the Great Designer; Albert (whose children Henslow taught) raised them merely to a sense of their own capabilities. The difference was important.

Girls of the parish school in Spout Lane, Little Cornard, were importuned by fashion. 'Crinoline' was, properly, the stiff fabric of horse-hair from which were made the so-called crinoline petticoats used in the early 1850s to distend ladies' skirts. Through most of the 1850s fashionable ladies were desiring their skirts to be more and more filled out; 'if ladies' dresses continue to increase in breadth,' observed a wag, 'it will be absolutely necessary to widen all the public thoroughfares'. Inevitably, the crinoline petticoat, even with three or four rolls at the bottom, became inadequate to its task. So, in October 1856, there appeared the first advertisement in England for the cage-like, so-called artificial crinoline – 'Whalebone skeleton skirts, 7/6'. The artificial crinoline became a vogue, promoted in France by the Empress Eugénie. Thus encouraged, by 1857 the artificial crinoline (of whalebone, wire, or even 'new Paris watch-spring' wire) might be supporting anything up to eighteen yards of silk skirt material. The year 1859 saw the high-point of this vogue: whilst girls in Little Cornard hunted brambles, Sheffield was producing sufficient crinoline wire a week for half a million crinolines, and even your lady's maid and factory girl, it was lamented, had now to have their crinolines.

Other points:
* Among the celebrated works of Sir Francis Legatt Chantry (1781–1841) is the group of sleeping children in Lichfield cathedral, and statues of George IV (at Windsor and in Trafalgar Square) and the first duke of Wellington (the Royal Exchange).
* John Singleton Copley, first Baron Lyndhurst, 1772–1863; Lord Chancellor 1827–1830, 1834–1835, 1841–1846.
* It was customary in Suffolk to plough a field in stetches, the width of which varied according to the heaviness of the soil.

Suffolk and Essex Free Press, 20 October 1859, p. 3.

SUDBURY AGRICULTURAL ASSOCIATION.

• • •

THE DINNER.

...The Rev. Edwin Sidney had been their willing, and he might say their devoted, friend for nearly twelve years, and had ever received from the President and members of the Association the most kind and cordial assistance...It had been thought by some persons that their institution was opposed to education, but such was not the case, and he had on all public occasions advocated the education of the poor. He had himself during the year preached twenty-eight sermons for National Schools, without omitting his other duties. (Cheers.) Under some systems of education there was danger of its unfitting its recipient for the state in domestic life which Providence had called on him to fill. (Hear, hear.) It had been recommended from high quarters to improve the morals of the lower orders by arts, literature, and science, giving them a mouthful of everything and a bellyful of nothing. (Laughter.) Such an education inflicted injury to the individual, and no benefit to society. The vanity which pervaded a great number of the female portion of the village population was most striking. They saw the mother washing the skin off her knuckles, ironing till she could not stand, and proud to see her daughter sitting in the room there – proud because she did nothing. (Hear, hear.) He knew a parish, not ten miles from that town, where the girls from the school even went to the woods to get brambles to make themselves crinolines. (Laughter.) He wished the boys to read their Bibles, to cast accounts, to write letters, and not chemistry and the arts and sciences, which only put them out of their places; and as for the girls, instead of crochet and other nonsense, teach them to make butter cloths, which was a much better thing. (Loud cheers.) Let them be educated suitable [*sic*] to their station, with a practical knowledge of the pursuit they were to be engaged in. To plough well, for instance, might appear to some people a very easy matter, but let them try their hands, and they would see how much practical knowledge was necessary. Sir Frances [*sic*] Chantrey, the great sculptor, was a ploughboy, and one day at Holkham Lord Leicester said, he would give a hat to any one who should draw the best and straightest furrow. Chantrey said, "Let me try my hand," and drew the furrow, and won the hat. As Lord Lyndhurst had said, if a gentleman thought it very easy to write a leading article, let him only try his hand at it; and if he thought he could plough a stetch, let him first try his hand. He would mention Saffron Walden, where twelve ladies had undertaken to take in twelve girls for two or three hours a day, to learn domestic labour. He mentioned these things to show he had no wish to impede the progress of education in a right direction ….

XXI   UNUSUAL PROPORTION OF PERSONS 1860

Frederick Charles Bell, of Yorley Farm, was the son of Charles and Maria Bell, and the grandson of John Bell (XIII). Sidney baptised him on 22 April 1859, and buried him, aged nine months, on 19 November. Charles and Maria Bell, who died in 1899 and 1864 respectively, are commemorated by a fine tombstone, near the path from the Sunday school room to the lychgate.

Suffolk and Essex Free Press, 12 January 1860, p. 2.

> A HEALTHY LOCALITY. – In the parish of Little Cornard, containing a population of between four and five hundred, only one death, that of a child, occurred during the year 1859. This parish, we believe, has amongst its inhabitants an unusual proportion of persons who have reached the age of 80 and upwards.

XXII   FOR THE CHURCH MISSIONARY SOCIETY – FOUR LECTURES

The Church Missionary Society was created at the end of the eighteenth century by William Wilberforce and his friends of the (Evangelical) Clapham Sect. In Little Cornard and elsewhere Sidney lectured in its support. His audiences were often packed. Sidney's C.M.S. lectures sometimes titillated, but over the years they must have constituted an impressive panorama of overseas missionary endeavour and prodigious Christian heroism, against their background of European colonialism.

Japan 1861

From about 1640 the rulers of Japan commenced a policy of peaceful isolation with regard to the rest of the world, chiefly because they believed that the stability of Japanese feudal society was threatened by European Christian influences. Thus for two hundred years or so Japan was largely outside the mainstream of world history. In 1853, however, four American warships commanded by Commodore Perry steamed into Yedo (Tokyo) Bay; in 1858 a treaty of 'amity and commerce' was signed between Japan and various European powers (including Britain); later, there were manifestations of anti-foreign feeling in Japan (indeed, the British legation was murderously attacked on 4 July 1861, the very day of the *Free Press* report of Sidney's lecture); in May 1862, the first Japanese official mission to Britain arrived in London; and after the revolution of 1868 the westernisation of Japan began in earnest. So, in Little Cornard Sidney's 'very attentive audience' of 30 June 1861 may be viewed as part of a wider early Victorian audience, excited by what *The Athenaeum* fervidly called 'a wonder and a jealousy of the travelled Thanes who explore the pillared, painted, broad-eaved, cottage-decorated, garden archipelago, with its fanciful ways and inexplicable means of human life'.

The published account of Sidney's lecture is regrettably short. But most of the lecture was evidently a synthesis of accounts already published by the bishop of Victoria, and 'the eldest son of Mr Veitch'.

The colonial see of Victoria, Hong Kong, was created in 1849. George Smith ('a travelled Thane'), from Goole, in Yorkshire, was its first bishop; his jurisdiction covered the island of Hong Kong, and the Anglican congregations in China. In 1860 Smith had under his charge seventeen missionary clergymen, most of whom were nominees of the C.M.S. Smith's lengthy account of his visit to Japan was published in London in 1861, under the title *Ten Weeks in Japan*; it was reviewed in *The Athenaeum* of 25 May that year. It dealt with Japanese geography, government, culture and religions. Its eight illustrations were attractive woodcuts, five of them copied from photographs provided by Messrs Negretti and Zambra, manufacturers of cameras and scientific instruments. (Did Messrs Carpenter and Westley perhaps reproduce these woodcuts for Sidney, as supporting magic lantern slides?)

John Gould Veitch (1838–1870) was the eldest son of James Veitch (1815–1869), himself the 'Son' of the firm of Messrs James Veitch and Son, distinguished nurserymen of Exeter and (from 1853) of Chelsea. In April 1860, young John Veitch began his voyage to Japan and China, whence he sailed to the Philippines. He returned to England two years later, bringing with him many choice plants for the enrichment of British horticulture, among them the japonica. Extracts from Veitch's letters and diaries relating to his journeyings in Japan were published as eleven items in *The Gardener's Chronicle* between December 1860 and August 1861. Between 1864 and 1866 Veitch made another voyage, similarly fruitful, to Australia and the South Sea Islands.

Suffolk and Essex Free Press, 4 July 1861, p. 2.

MISSIONARY LECTURE. – On Sunday evening last a very interesting lecture on "Japan" was delivered by the Rev. E. Sidney, Rector of Little Cornard, in a large barn attached to the rectory, in aid of the funds of the Church Missionary Society. The rev. lecturer, in his introductory remarks, stated that he had derived much original information from the Bishop of Victoria, at Hong Kong, and also from the eldest son of Mr. Veitch, the eminent florist, both of whom visited Japan in 1860. He described the geographical and physical features of the country, its natural products, and the peculiar manners and customs of the people; the extraordinary circumstances attending its isolation from the rest of the world, and hostility of the government and people to Christianity. We regret that our space will not permit us to give a more extended notice of this lecture, but may add that Mr. Sidney concluded a very remarkable sketch of the Island[s] and people of Japan, given in a lucid and felicitous style, by stating that efforts were about being made to send missionaries out there, by whose aid it was hoped to evangelise numbers of the people in the same manner as had been so successfully carried out in China. The large barn was thronged with a very attentive audience, including several ladies and gentlemen from Great Cornard, Sudbury, &c. The collection amounted to £4.13s., additions to which have been made by some friends who were unavoidably absent.

Islands of the Pacific 1862

The modern history of the Pacific Ocean falls into three periods. The first, from 1796 to 1850, was the time of trading and Protestant missionary settlements; the power of the native chiefs was undisturbed, since the European powers had not yet realised the political importance of that ocean. The French annexation of Tahiti and the British annexation of New Zealand closed the period. The second period, from 1850 to 1875, was characterised by white commercialist activity, and consequent political interest on the part of European powers and Australia. This period ended with the British annexation of Fiji. The third period, after 1875, has its place within the saga of European and American colonial imperialism which unfolded during the forty or fifty years preceding the First World War. During this period the independence of native political chiefs broke down. The period closed with the German annexation of Samoa, and the establishment of a British protectorate over the Tonga Islands.

Sidney's audience would have understood perfectly that geological formations, tropical vegetation and protestant (but not Roman Catholic) missionaries were the equal fruits of God's Providence. 'The King of Tahiti, named Pomari [*sic*]', so circumspect in the matter of conversion, was King Pomare II, who reigned from 1803 to 1824. Pomare became a Christian in 1812, and three years later, with European support, triumphed over other Tahitian chiefs. A 'missionary' kingdom was established, with a scriptural code of law, and by 1818 infanticide had been suppressed. For a time protestant missions held sway. Captain Cook was held to be the discoverer, further north, of the Hawaiian Islands, in 1778; he named them the Sandwich Islands, and was killed there in 1779. The bishop mentioned by Sidney was Thomas Nettleship Staley, formerly a clergyman from Wandsworth; he was consecrated first bishop of Honolulu in London in December, 1861, and sailed from Southampton in the following August.

Suffolk and Essex Free Press, 3 July 1862, p. 2.

MISSIONARY LECTURE BY THE REV. E. SIDNEY, M.A. – The quarterly parochial lecture in connection with the Cornard Parva Church Missionary Society was delivered by the Rev. E. Sidney, rector of the parish, in his large lecture barn, on Sunday evening last. The building was quite filled by the villagers and others as well as by some ladies and gentlemen from Sudbury and adjoining parishes. After singing an appropriate hymn, and a prayer by the Rector, he delivered a very interesting lecture on the "Islands of the Pacific, and their history, past and present, as connected with missionary operations." He described the organic formation on these islands, some being composed of coral, some of limestone rock, and others of high volcanic origin, several volcanoes being 13,000 feet high. The vegetation was on a gigantic scale, varied and most splendid; there were cocoa-nut trees, palms, bananas, and bread fruit trees, &c. The natives were very savage; but the King of Tahiti, named Pomari, embraced Christianity, conquered his enemies, and encouraged the missionaries. Infanticide was common, one woman stated she had killed eleven of her children. France gained possession of some of these islands, and introduced the Roman Catholic religion. Several missionaries had been murdered at the different islands. An English bishop had just been appointed to the Sandwich Islands. Mr Sidney, who was listened to with much attention and evident marks of interest, concluded a very interesting address with an earnest appeal to his auditors for support for the Society whose cause he loved to advocate. The collection amounted to £4.10s.9d.

Madagascar 1863

King Radàma I of Madagascar reigned from 1810 to 1828. He favoured the education and civilisation of his people; with British support he imposed his authority over a large part of the island. Christian teaching was begun in the capital in 1820. But in 1828 the young Radàma died, and one of his wives, Rànavàlona, seized power. Rànavàlona was opposed to the policies of Radàma. In 1835 she declared the profession of the Christian religion illegal, and persecuted those who resisted. About 200 (not 2,000) Christians died, and numerous others suffered severely. Rànavàlona's successor in 1861 was her son, Radàma II, a Christian, who opened the island to missionaries.

The bishop of Mauritius in 1863 was Vincent William Ryan, consecrated in 1854; after his resignation in 1868 he was for twelve months archdeacon of Suffolk. Sidney's friend Ellis was the Revd William Ellis, distinguished and much travelled missionary, and writer on missions. The Revd Rowland Hill (not to be confused with Sir Rowland Hill, the inventor of the penny post introduced in 1840) had been one of the pioneers of the eighteenth-century Sunday school movement, and in due course his schools had become associated with the training of missionaries. 'Have you read Ellis's book on the South Sea Islands?' the aged Hill would enquire of visitors; 'oh! worthy, sensible, good creature – he was a teacher in our Sunday schools; he is an honour to us'. Two things especially prompted Ryan to avail himself of the situation in Madagascar, changed in 1861, and to visit there in July 1862. First, there were many Malagasies among the Christian community in Mauritius. Then, Ryan had been impressed by Ellis's two published works on Madagascar; indeed, in 1856 Ellis and Ryan had met. Sidney's lecture of 28 June 1863 was of topical interest in that, quite recently, Ryan had been enthusiastically received at the annual general meeting of the British and Foreign Bible Society, at Exeter Hall, in London, during a discussion on Madagascar.

Suffolk and Essex Free Press, 2 July 1863, p. 2.

LITTLE CORNARD.

MISSIONARY LECTURE. – On Sunday evening the Rev. E. Sidney, rector delivered a lecture in aid of the Church Missionary Society, in the large lecture barn attached to the rectory. The building was crowded, including a number of ladies and gentlemen from the adjoining parishes, Sudbury, &c. Amongst these were S. Higgs, Esq., Mayor of Sudbury and family; the Rev. J. B. Sparrow and party; Mr. Mumford and the Misses Mumford; Mr. Garrad and party, Bures; Mr. Fitch sen. and jun. and family; Mr. Newman Sparrow, &c. A missionary hymn was first sung, with accompaniment, a collect and the Lord's prayer. Mr. Sidney took for his subject the Island of Madagascar, of which he gave a most interesting and lucid account. He described the great natural beauties of the island, its geographical position and productions; the character of the natives and the many difficulties encountered in the establishment of Christianity. The principal missionary, Mr. Ellis, was formerly a teacher in the Rev. Rowland Hill's school, who was his (Mr. Sidney's) relative and guardian and with whom he spent his early years, having lost his parents when very young. The rev. lecturer described the success of the missionaries under King Radama, but who unfortunately dying in 1828, his Queen, a most cruel and wicked woman, succeeded him, and persecuted the Christians, putting nearly 2,000 persons to death who had refused to abjure the Christian faith. Nothing could be more herioc [*sic*] than the death of these martyrs, hundreds of whom were speared, whilst others were thrown from a high rock. At length the Queen died in 1861, and her successor was anxious to do all the possible good in his power. Mr. Ellis and the Bishop of Mauritius went to the Island, and were received with great honour. The Queen of England also sent a magnificent bible as a present to the King. At the present time there were nearly ten thousand Christians in the Island, and the good work was progressing with entire success. Mr. Sidney's very excellent address was listened to most attentively throughout, and appeared to afford much gratification. The collection amounted to £5 16s.8d.

Arabia and the Arabs 1865

Suffolk and Essex Free Press, 27 July 1865, p. 2.

CORNARD PARVA CHURCH MISSIONARY SOCIETY. – On Sunday evening the rector, the Rev. E. Sidney, delivered a lecture in the large lecture barn attached to the rectory. The subject chosen was "Arabia and the Arabs," which Mr. Sidney treated in his usual lucid and effective style. There was a large attendance, over 100 people being unable to gain admittance. The collection amounted to £5.

XXIII BURGLARS? 1862

The first of the courtroom occasions was Friday, 17 January, when the magistrates were Sir William Parker, of Melford Hall, and John Sikes, who farmed in Little Cornard. The second was Wednesday, 22 January, when they were Parker and the Revd N. W. Hallward, rector of Milden since 1827.

Norman and Keeble were tried at the Suffolk Quarter Sessions at Bury St Edmunds, on Monday, 17 March 1862. 'The Jury,' said the *Suffolk and Essex Free Press* (20 March, p. 3), 'found a verdict of Guilty against both prisoners, but recommended Norman to mercy on account of the weakness of the evidence. (Laughter.)'. Said the chairman of the court: 'Just lay your heads together again – if you think him guilty find him so; if you have any doubt give him the benefit of the doubt'. So, they found Norman not guilty. Keeble was then sentenced to three years' penal servitude.

Little Cornard Victorians would have found this rigmarole report splendidly titillating – theatrical 'script', stealth across country by night, 'escape' by railway, London's East End, shady Jew, 'two men ... haggard from their confinement' (a sure sign of criminality!), and so forth.

Other points:
* The firm of Lefley & Sons, Ltd., conducted their business from 17 North Street, Sudbury, until the 1980s; they were respected vendors of fish, fruit and vegetables.

* The first edition of *A Summary of the Law Relative to Pleading and Evidence in Criminal Cases*, by John Frederick Archbold, renowned legal writer, 1785–1870, was published in 1822; the fortieth edition was published in London in 1979.

* The London terminus of the Great Eastern railway from Colchester to London was Shoreditch, until the construction of Liverpool Street station in 1875. (The Great Eastern railway absorbed the Eastern Counties railway in 1862.)

* 'Mr W. D. King's house, near Norman's house' was the house now designated 33 Friars Street, where Matthew Arnold stayed, as a school inspector, in 1853. William Doubleday King was a prominent Sudbury Quaker and Suffolk ornithologist. There was something of Poll Sweedlepipe about him, for, wrote Arnold to his wife, 'his collection of stuffed birds is really splendid. I could have passed days looking at it; every British bird you could name he has, and the eggs of all, which is almost as curious. He has stuffed all the birds himself, being an enthusiastic amateur; the collection of sea-fowl, and of all varieties of the hawk and falcon, was beautiful.' And later: 'I have fallen on my legs here, being most hospitably entertained by a Quaker who has a large house here. It is a curious place, and I am writing in the hall of it, at which all the pupil teachers are gathered together at their work. The hall is completely covered over as to its walls with a vast collection of stuffed birds, which gives it a ghastly effect enough'.

Suffolk and Essex Free Press, 23 January 1862, p. 3.

THE HOUSEBREAKING CASE AT LITTLE CORNARD.

Charles Norman, labourer; *Samuel Upson*, higgler; *Alfred Piper*, rag and bone collector; *George Piper*, newsvendor; and *Daniel Keeble*, silk weaver, all of Sudbury, were placed at the bar charged with the burglary committed at Prospect House, Little Cornard, the residence of A. R. Stark, Esq., which was plundered on the 7th inst. of a quantity of household furniture. The house was uninhabited at the time, and it is supposed that the prisoners procured a key to fit the street door, and removed the articles at different times. Three of them were taken into custody by Supt. Sach, of the Sudbury borough police, and two by Inspector Scholefield, of the county force. They had been twice previously remanded.

P. J. Wates deposed he was agent i.e., clerk to the prosecutor; Mr. Stark had a residence called Prospect House, Little Cornard; on 7th Jan. Mr. Sparrow, the owner of the house, came to witness's offices and informed him that a robbery had been committed; he knew the property; there were four feather beds stolen, five counterpanes, blankets, pillows, bolsters, carpets, table covers, books, and various other things; witness would be able to identify some of the articles, but not those produced (beds and bedding); witness had very good reason to be certain that if the prisoners were remanded he should be able to have important further and sufficient evidence to connect the prisoners with the robbery; he asked for a remand, and should be prepared with the further evidence by Wednesday next.

James Rogers said he was a furniture broker at Sudbury; he bought the bed produced the night before the robbery was known of George Piper; it was between six and seven o'clock; witness said he would rather he waited till the morning, but prisoner, who had told him he had a feather bed to sell, said he had some money to make up; witness went and looked at it; prisoner asked 30s. for the bed; witness, after looking at it, saw the feathers were very coarse, it was not worth near that, and prisoner then offered to let him have it for 24s.; he gave him 21s. for it; it was a common cotton tick, stained, with about 30lbs. of common feathers in it.

Ellen Carter said she had lived in service with Mr. Stark two years since; the bed belonged to Mr. Stark; she knew it from the stains in the middle of the bed, and recollected it when living with Mr. Stark; was quite confident, could swear to the bed.

Supt. Sach stated he had been engaged in investigating the case of the robbery at Prospect House; from information obtained he had reason to suspect all the prisoners to be connected with the robbery; a bed (produced) had been identified by a young woman, which had been obtained from a furniture dealer, named Rogers, at Sudbury, to whom it had been sold by one of the prisoners, George Piper; he had reason to believe Piper bought it of Norman, one of the other prisoners, for 15s; Ellen Carter, a servant, who formerly lived with Mr. Stark, had identified the bed; witness had reason to believe that they could collect further evidence; he also believed he could connect all the prisoners, and be able to produce evidence to satisfy the magistrates; Mr Gooday was engaged as solicitor for the prosecution; he asked for a remand till Wednesday next.

Robert John Leffley, who said he went about selling nuts and oranges, and sprats and herrings in the season: On Thursday, the 9th of January, the prisoner Keeble came about seven in the evening, and asked him if he would like to earn 6d., witness replied "Yes;" he told him to go and fetch Piper's truck, and trundle it down to his house; witness did so; Keeble and Alfred Piper put three parcels on the truck; two of the parcels were big ones, and one a small one; one was done up in oil cloth, and the other in a piece of bagging; they did not appear very heavy; they told him to go down the street, and they would overtake him; they overtook him near Mr. Tovell's, Ballingdon; Keeble's yard, where they took up the things, is in Cross Street, Sudbury; it is called Goody's yard; Piper and Keeble helped him to shove up Ballingdon Hill; Piper went on with his newspapers to sell, and Keeble and witness went on to the Fox public-house, by the turnpike, where they had two pints of beer and some bread and cheese; they afterwards took the truck to the Hedingham railway station. Piper met them two miles before they got there; they unloaded the goods, and put them in the station, Piper told one of the porters they were for a gentleman to whom they belonged, there was a name on the parcel, but witness is no scholar, and does not know what it was; Piper said the gentleman would come for them; he thinks, Keeble said to Piper he would be back from London, on Friday night; witness and Piper left Keeble at the station, Keeble borrowed witness's coat to go to London, promising to give him 6d. for the use of it: prisoner has the same coat on now, witness exchanged coats till the following Saturday, when Keeble gave him back the coat and 2s. for his day's work; witness asked him if he had been doing nothing wrong, as he had heard some beds and several other articles of furniture had been stolen and he might get into as bad trouble as he; Keeble said he had not been doing anything wrong and he (witness) need not be afraid of that; this was at Lawrence's house, on the Saturday, when he paid him the 2s.; Piper came back to Sudbury and he took the truck back.

The magistrate said this witness had given his evidence very well, and in a straightforward manner.

This was all the evidence offered, and the five prisoners were further remanded till Wednesday next.

After the prisoners were taken out of the justice room, Inspector Scholefield returned and said that Geo. Piper wished to speak to Mr. Sikes, and he had a statement to make. The magistrates consulted the clerk, and decided that they could only hear Piper in the presence of the other prisoners. They were then all brought in again, and Sir Wm. Parker having cautioned them that anything they said would be at their own peril, and would probably be used as evidence against them, –

Geo. Piper made the following statement, after first saying that he had told Mr. Gooday all he had to say: – I did not do the robbery; on the 7th of January, Norman asked me if I could sell a bed for him; I did so, and sold it to Mr. Rogers, all I made over 15s.

I was to have for myself; I sold it to Mr. Rogers and gave Norman the 15s. on Tuesday night; on the same evening Keeble and Norman asked me to go up to Cornard with them to bring a parcel home. I did so. Keeble told me he would pay me for my trouble. That's all just now. I wish to say nothing else. I understand the caution given by the magistrates, and will sign to what I have stated.

Upson said all I have to say is will you let me have bail, as my father is very bad. There is nothing against me, and I will defy the whole world to say anything against me. I shan't be far off. I should wish to see my father who lives at Acton, and is very bad. I have goods and can give bail.

Mr. Almack (Magistrates' Clerk) inquired if prisoner's father was in a dangerous state, and was informed by the police that he was not.

The magistrates declined to take bail, but said as Upson was going to Boxford, he could be taken by an officer to see his father, but it must be in the presence of a police constable.

The prisoners were then removed.

Three are kept in the cells at Melford police station, one at Boxford, and one at Sudbury, in order to their separate confinement, and to prevent any communication passing between them.

TWO OF THE PRISONERS TURNING QUEEN'S EVIDENCE.

The prisoners were again brought up at Melford on Wednesday before Sir Wm. Parker and the Rev. N. W. Halward [*sic*]. It was stated there were no less than fourteen witnesses to examine. Mr. Gooday appeared for the prosecution.

Mr. Gooday addressed the Bench, and stated that he did not know how far he could carry the case, whether the robbery went to the extent of a burglary or not. The house was empty at the time Mr. Starke principally residing at Woolwich. It was completely furnished in an expensive style, and the carpets and furniture were all new. Property to a considerable amount in value had been stolen, but he found that he should have to rest the grounds of the case chiefly on the evidence of the two of the men in custody, who indeed were *participes criminis* in the affair, although not actually perpetrators of the robbery, which there was no doubt was committed in the middle of the night. He proposed to admit George Piper and Alfred Piper as evidence against the others. (The learned gentleman gave outline of the facts as will be found detailed in the evidence.) He thought it right to mention that the Sudbury police, which was a very effective force, closely watched the streets throughout the night, and it was almost impossible for any person to convey stolen property into the town without detection. The prisoners knowing this had taken the precaution to enter the town early in the morning by Friars meadow, on the right hand side of the railway. As regards Upson there was scarcely any evidence, and he should leave that part of the matter to the discretion of the bench. If the magistrates thought it well he should admit the two Pipers to give evidence.

Mr. Halward considered Mr. Gooday must drop the charge of burglary, and called his attention to Archbold, where it stated that to constitute a dwelling house, for the purpose of convicting for burglary, it must be occupied by the family. If the persons had their meals in the house, but slept elsewhere, it cannot be a burglary. Some one must be sleeping in the house.

Mr. Almack said in this instance the house could not be considered a dwelling on which to found a charge of burglary. It must be for housebreaking. (It may be stated a charge of burglary can only be tried at the assizes, housebreaking at the quarter sessions.)

The two Pipers were then discharged, and went into another room, previous to being admitted as Queen's evidence.

Percy John Wates was first called, and recapitulated his former evidence, adding that he had visited the house within two months of the robbery, when he saw the furniture all safe. Everything was then undisturbed, and the beds were made up ready for use. On

Tuesday, 7th Jan., he visited the house again, and then found that a quantity of things had been stolen, carpets, bedding and ornaments. He gave notice to the police, but on going to the house on the Wednesday morning, about nine o'clock, he found that a further robbery had been committed since the previous evening; the drawing and dining room carpets were gone; he noticed especially the drawing room carpet, a large Brussels one about 20 by 15 feet; the piece produced is the same pattern; it had lain rolled up opposite the door; the dining room carpet was also rolled up and lay under the dining table; the breakfast room carpet was also gone, and all the bed room carpets; is not certain that these latter carpets were there on the Tuesday night; the doors of the wardrobe were open; he missed about a dozen large books, bound in red calf and gilt; they were stolen; the title of one was "The Faiths of the World," published in 7s.6d. parts; the drawer was full of books on Tuesday night, and he noticed on Wednesday morning that it was empty; a quantity of chimney ornaments were gone; he observed a timepiece was also stolen and some strips of carpet stained with oil.

The prisoners were separately asked if they had any questions to ask the witness, but they declined, and said they knew nothing about it.

Alfred Piper, sworn, said he lived in Plough Lane, Sudbury; Keeble lived in Cross Street; recollected Saturday night, 21st December; about ten o'clock he was at the beershop kept by Joseph Green in Church Street; he had a basket at the time selling nuts, oranges and women's shoes; Daniel Keeble, one of the prisoners, opened the door and called him out; he asked him when he got on the pavement if he had a mind to earn a shilling or two; Witness replied it all depended upon what it was; he said we don't want you to do anything, only to go along with us. He went home, leaving his basket at the beerhouse; they met the prisoner Charles Norman near the Angel, Friars Street, at 11. They all three went across Friars' meadow; they went down Lady's Lane, past Mr. Seagrave's, the Pot Kilns and across some fields till they got to the hill – this was not the direct way. Keeble and Norman went up to the house; he waited for an hour against the gate, does not know how they got in, nor did he see a light; they came back with two bags and a small bundle; Keeble gave him the small parcel. They returned nearly the same way across the fields out of the footpath to Norman's house in Bullocks Lane, back of Friars Street; Witness saw the things unpacked; there were three white bed rugs, two large tea pots, some candlesticks, glass lustres for chimney ornaments, there were some hair rugs like what they put in gigs. They mentioned about going to London, and Keeble said, you are a stranger, they wont take any notice of you, you had better take them to London, I will pay you for your trouble – this was on the Sunday morning, they got home to Norman's about six o'clock. Witness was to go to London by the first train that morning at five minutes to nine; he went home, washed and had breakfast, returned at a quarter past eight and saw Norman; the things were all packed; Witness's brother, George Piper, came to the house with his truck, one parcel was put into the truck, Witness took one on his back, and Norman carried one containing the time-piece to the back of the Rose and Crown; Witness then took it and went to the Station. As they went to the station, Witness saw Peter Davies in his garden. He went to London by train, and proceeded from Shoreditch to Petticoat Lane; down the lane he asked a Jew if he would buy them; he replied, Let me look at them, and then they both went up an ally [*sic*] way. The Jew looked at the things and asked him what he wanted for them; he said £8; the Jew said I'll give you £5; Witness replied give me your money, and sold them to him. Witness returned on Tuesday to Sudbury, he went to his own house, and Keeble and Norman came, and he divided the money between them; there was £3 odd in silver and a sovereign. Keeble said he knew witness had made more of them, and some words ensued. Witness said I wish I'd stuck to the lot. Keeble said If you had I'd be d———d if you should have walked about Sudbury alive; on Wednesday night, 8th January, about nine o'clock, Keeble came to witness and he went to his house in Cross-street, Keeble took him into a front room, showed him a lot of carpeting and said "This ain't a bad lot is it? Will you help me to pack them up? I'm going to London in the morning;" there was one very large carpet, as much as witness could lift; the piece produced is similar to the pattern; there was [*sic*] four or five spotted rugs; pieces of carpet; several large red covered books about the Crimean war; Keeble said he had looked at them; there was [*sic*] beaded mats, the size of a plate, such as ladies make; witness helped him to pack two parcels; Keeble said he had nothing to pack the large carpet in and it was worth 15 or 16 guineas; he again went to Keeble's house, his wife having come for him, and saw him; he went and called Bob Leffly [*sic*] to help witness with the truck.

Mr. Halward here remarked that the prisoners were undefended, and Mr. Gooday was perhaps going a little to[o] far.

Mr. Gooday said he had no wish to go beyond the strict limits of evidence.

Witness resumed; Keeble told Leffly, to get Piper's truck from the Ship and Star; he did so; the parcels were directed. "Mr Burnley, passenger, London;" they loaded the truck; the large carpet was then packed up; Leffly took the truck to Ballingdon Hills [*sic*]. Witness with Keeble overtook them and helped them up the hill; witness had his newspapers on his back, the *Free Press* newspapers, which he carried for sale; they saw a policeman at Hedingham; Keeble said, "If he says anything to us I shall own the goods;" they went to the station, and afterwards they had some beer; Keeble said he was going up to London by the next train at 4.15; he showed witness a direction on a piece of paper, and said, "This is where I am going to;" it was No. 8, Burn Street, Hackney Road, so he understood; he said, "Take the things to the station, and say they're for a gentleman going by the next train," and he would remunerate him for his trouble; he never had one penny, or saw him again until he was in custody.

Keeble said he never went to Green's beer-house; it was all false.

Norman said he never went to Cornard with him in his life; there were no witnesses to prove it.

By Mr. Gooday: Witness and his brother went to the Angel on

Wednesday night, and ordered some pork chops; Keeble and Norman were there; they had some rum and beer; Mr. Hale, the landlord, said it was too late to give them the pork chops; it was nearly twelve o'clock when they left; he saw his brother George sell a bed to Mr. Rogers.

George Piper said he was a silk weaver; on Sunday morning, the 22nd December, he went round the Back Fields, and saw Charles Norman, who told him that his brother Alfred was going to London; witness said, "Yes, I know it, he told me he was;" witness went with his truck to the back of Mr W. D. King's house, near Norman's house; witness's brother brought out the parcel from the direction of Norman's house; next day he saw Norman and Keeble, who asked him if his brother was come home; he met his brother at the station, and Keeble and Norman came to the house; they asked him if he had parted with the things; he said, "Yes, he had sold them for £5 to a Jew;" Keeble said he would not believe it, they were worth more, and some words arose; he must have made more Keeble said; his brother Alfred gave them the money into their hands; his brother said if he had known what he did he would have stuck to the lot; Keeble said, "If you had you shouldn't go about alive;" they had some beer at the Ship and Star, and there were some words there also about the money; on Tuesday, 7th January, he went to Norman's house, as he had asked him to sell a bed; Norman told him all he made over 15s. he was to have; he and his brother took the bed to his house, and in the evening he went to Rogers, who bought the bed for 21s; that same evening they all met at the Ship and Star, and went afterwards to the Angel; they stayed till twelve: Keeble had some bread and cheese; they could not get some pork chops which were asked for; Keeble asked him if he would go to Cornard; he had heard where the other things came from; Keeble said he was to stop outside; witness and Keeble went up alone; it is called Prospect House; Keeble said if anybody comes you are to call; Keeble went in by the front door, for he heard him unlock it; there was a light in the house; witness waited an hour, and Keeble brought out two large parcels and a small one; witness took one and Keeble the other two; they were two or three hours, and got home a little before six to Norman's house; the parcel was so heavy he could not carry it, and threatened to throw it down; the parcels were left at Norman's house; witness then went home; Keeble said he would pay him for his trouble when he had parted with the things.

Keeble said this witness had varied from his statement on Friday, but Sir Wm. Parker referred to it, and there was no material difference.

To Norman: I never accompanied you to Cornard in my life.

Robert Leffley repeated his former testimony.

Peter Davies, confectioner, Friars Street, Sudbury, deposed that on Sunday morning, 22nd December, he was in his garden, which is not far from Norman's house, at the back of Mr. Dowman's, and about half-past eight saw George Piper coming round with an empty truck; Alfred Piper brought a sack or bag, which appeared very heavy, and placed it on the truck; George Piper took the truck towards the railway station; the elder Piper went back; witness went towards home, and again met him, this time with a sack on his back; witness thought Mr. Dowman's premises were being robbed, and inquired of neighbours.

Lydia Playle stated that she lived in the same yard as the prisoner Keeble, in Gooday's Yard, Cross Street; she recollected last Thursday morning week, at half-past seven, she saw the witness Leffley in the yard take out a truck; Keeeble [sic] was in the street; does not know what was in the truck; it was covered up, and the things appeared heavy; soon after she saw Keeble and another man come out of the yard one after the other; they all went towards Ballingdon; that's all she saw and all she heard.

Geo. Mitchell, ostler at the Angel Inn, recollected the fore part of the week, a short time ago, the prisoners Keeble and Norman, and the Pipers being in the taproom, and asking for pork chops late at night; a day or two after this he heard of the robbery; his master refused to draw any more beer for them, as he said it was late; they appeared a little freshy; they left about midnight when the house was shut up.

To Norman: You refused to have some beer, and had

two-pennyworth of rum.

Chas. Sylvester, landlord of the "Ship and Star," said prisoners were frequently in his house; he recollects Upson being there the night before the robbery was known; would not swear as to any particular night the others were there.

Supt. Sach, of the Sudbury police, stated he went to Prospect House on the 8th of Jan. in company with Inspector Schofield [*sic*] and tried the windows outside first; they were all fastened; he then went in by the door, and saw that a great many lucifers had been struck, and thrown on a marble sideboard; there were spots of candle grease dropped about, and matches strewed about; the rooms were all in confusion; he went up stairs and examined all the doors; there was a chest of drawers which had been attempted to be forced, the others were all open; there was a large japan deed box which had been apparently attempted to be forced; there was some wet also on the floor of recent date; there were cobwebs upon all the windows inside; all the doors and windows were secure, and in witness's opinion no one had entered the house except by the front door; knows Norman for three years; he is a labourer, and work[s] sometimes on the barges at the Quay; Keeble is a weaver by trade; witness went to his house and saw he had some work, but it appeared to have been left some time, the shuttle was covered with thick dust; witness and Inspector Scholefield apprehended Norman; he afterwards apprehended Keeble; all the prisoners said they knew nothing about it; he produced the bed had from James Rogers.

Chas. Holland, bricklayer, recollected Keeble coming to him three weeks ago, to ask him for the direction of his brother James who live[s] in London; witness got his direction from his daughter, and gave it to the prisoner; Keeble is his son-in-law; he is 74, and cannot remember the address.

Jas. Holland stated he was a baker, and lives at No. 8, Bath Grove, Bath Street, Hackney Road, London; on Thursday night, the 9th of January, about eight o'clock, Keeble came in a cab to the house; he said he had come from the Eastern Counties, and that he had brought some things up from the country to sell for two men; witness asked him how he knew his direction; he said he got it from witness's brother; witness saw three large bundles in his room, and a parcel of books tied up in a handkerchief; they were red morocco covered; the handkerchief did not quite cover them, and he noticed on one of the backs of the books the figures 7s.6d. in gilt; witness did not touch them, they were tied up with ropes; Keeble went to Bethnal Green Road to get a bed; witness wrote down to his niece, stating that Daniel Keeble had come to his house with some bundles of carpeting and rugs; he wished to ask a question about it; as soon as he began to ask a question about them, he (witness) found Keeble had not come honestly by them.

Mr. Halward said not a word of this letter could be evinced against the prisoner.

Witness: Mr. Keeble told him there were rugs and carpets in the bundle; did not see him afterwards; the parcels were taken away by him the next morning; he read on the back of another book the words "Crystal Palace."

Ellen Carter, in the service of Mr. R. Strutt, Great Waldingfield, said she formerly lived with Mr. Starke, three years since; she knows the bed she slept upon, and made it every morning; remembers a mark or stain upon the ticking when she went; she knows this mark well; the bed produced is the same, and she has no doubt whatever about it; the piece of glass produced by Inspector Scholefield is similar to the ornaments in the best parlour of Prospect House; they were marked in the same way with two gilt lines.

James Rogers deposed to purchasing the feather bed produced of George Piper for 21s.

Celia Starke, daughter of the prosecutor, recollected the carpets in Prospect House; the Brussels carpet in the drawing-room was a green pattern like the piece produced; the Kidderminster carpet in the bed-rooms is nearly the same as the pattern, only the stairs were diamond-shape instead of round; the piece of glass produced is like the bottom of the lustres which stood on the chimney-piece in the drawing room; it is marked in the same way; her father has not given up the house.

Inspector Scholefield, Melford Station, stated that he apprehended Alfred Piper, and searched him at the Police Station, Sudbury; in his frock pocket he found the piece of glass now produced.

Alfred Piper, recalled, said he got the piece of glass off one of the images (the lustres), and brought it back from London; it was broke going to London; he did not know he had it in his pocket; it came out of the bag when he emptied it in Petticoat Lane.

The prisoners were duly cautioned.

Keeble said: I have nothing to say to the charge.

Norman said: I have nothing to say, only what Alfred and George Piper have said about me is quite false. I never had a thing in my house, I'll take my oath, – not concerning that robbery. I know nothing about that; I'm as honest as anyone in this room. I can swear they never took anything from my house. That's all I have to say.

Samuel Upson was discharged.

Daniel Keeble and Charles Norman were both committed to take their trial at the next Quarter Sessions at Bury, on Tuesday, April 15th.

The witnesses, fourteen in number, were all bound over, and the hearing, which lasted nearly four and a half hours, terminated.

The case has excited great interest in the district, and the small court room at the Melford station was crowded on each occasion. The two men, Norman and Keeble, looked haggard from their confinement, and showed much anxiety, especially whilst the Pipers were giving their evidence.

XXIV   DOCTOR OF MEDICINE 1863

Suffolk and Essex Free Press, 1 January 1863, p. 2.

On Monday, the 22nd. ult., Mr. W. L. Mumford, M.R.C.S. and L.S.A., of Cornard Parva, having passed the usual examinations, was admitted to the degree of Doctor of Medicine at the University of St. Andrews.

XXV WEDDING 1863

Edward Albert, prince of Wales (later King Edward VII) married the Danish princess, Alexandra, in St George's Chapel, Windsor, on 10 March 1863. The nation rejoiced. Yet up and down the kingdom churchmen high and low were troubled by the thought of public merriment in Lent. In Sudbury, quarrelsome Molyneux, incumbent of the benefice of St Gregory and St Peter, and highest of High Churchmen, provoked the displeasure of the townspeople by forbidding the ringing of his churches' bells, and compounded it by causing to be published in the *Suffolk and Essex Free Press* (5 March, p. 2) a letter which he had elicited from Archbishop Longley of Canterbury, saying that the prince's mother, Queen Victoria, 'quite feels the difficulty there may be respecting festivities and rejoicings during Lent', and that he (Longley) 'should like this to be as widely known as possible'. But Longley was disingenuous. For such distaste as the Queen at that time felt for 'festivities and rejoicings' derived not from considerations of Lent, but rather from the death of Prince Albert (December 1861). Indeed, when Longley had ventured to argue that there should be no marriage at all during Lent, the Queen had reproved him: his objection rested on 'fancy and prejudice', she thought, and (here a reproof for Molyneux, had he known) reflected an attitude which was 'very Catholic'.

In Great Cornard, nevertheless, jollities at Gray's Hall were just about as far from the centre of the parish as it was possible for them to be. In Little Cornard the respected rector was surely discreet: he did what rectors were supposed to do regarding the aged and poor widows, etc., and remembered to take up the church's desk-sized *Book of Common Prayer* (parson's copy; donated in 1748) and write in the margin of the Prayer for the Royal Family the words 'Albert Edw Prince of Wales the Princess of Wales'. Mr. C. J. Simpson, 'furnishing ironmonger, lamp and chandelier manufacturer, bell hanger, iron, tin & zinc plate worker & gas fitter, & agent for Ransomes' & Bentall's agricultural implements, 2 Old Market place', pillar of Sudbury Conservatism and renowned songster at Sudbury social functions, did not come to sing.

Suffolk and Essex Free Press, 12 March 1863, p. 2.

> LITTLE CORNARD. – We are informed that on the memorable 10th of March Mr. N. Sparrow supplied the persons in his employ, and several old people, with a good substantial dinner. Mr. Mumford also kindly supplied wine and cake to the school children.
>
> GREAT CORNARD. – *The Eventful Tenth*. – The marriage of the Prince of Wales and the Princess Alexandra was celebrated in this parish in an interesting manner. A bountiful tea was, through the kindness of the inhabitants, provided for all the poor parishioners. It took place in a barn, kindly lent by T. Fitch, Esq., of Gray's Hall, tastefully decorated for the occasion with flags and evergreens. The barn was also heated by means of a stove, kindly lent by Mr. C. J. Simpson, ironmonger, Sudbury. At the conclusion of the tea the National Anthem was sung by the whole assembly, and three hearty cheers were given for the Prince and Princess of Wales.

Suffolk and Essex Free Press, 19 March 1863, p. 2.

> THE 10th MARCH AT LITTLE CORNARD. — Some particulars were omitted in our last. Mr. Mumford, in addition to giving all his men a dinner, presented their wives with tea and sugar. Mr. Sikes gave a good substantial dinner to 36 of the men in his employ. Mr. N. Sparrow also gave a dinner to his employees.

Mr. Seagrave gave meat and 1s. in money to each family. The Rev. E. Sidney, the respected rector, in the kindest manner provided for the aged and poor widows, &c., giving them wine and cake, tea and sugar, &c., so that there was not a single family in the parish but what participated in the festivities of the day.

XXVI   LECTURE TO JUVENILES 1863

Sidney's 'Lectures to Juveniles', given regularly to Sudbury children in the 1860s, were clearly inspired by (though more diffuse than) the Christmas Juvenile Lectures which Michael Faraday gave regularly at the Royal Institution, commencing, apparently, in 1826. Faraday's lectures in this *genre* were the precursors of the Royal Institution's New Year Lectures for children given in our own day, and televised. They were renowned not just among children, but also among the higher classes of London society; two of the courses which he gave – *The Chemical History of a Candle*, and *Lectures on the Various Forces of Matter* – were published, became particularly famous, and ran into very many editions.

In *The Sunday Times* of 29 August, 1982 (p. 7), Norman Harris likened a representation of a swimming Rhine maiden in a forthcoming Bayreuth production of Wagner's *Rheingold* to 'a once-renowned nineteenth-century theatrical trick, Pepper's Ghost'. He wrote:

> John H. Pepper was director of the Royal Polytechnic Institution – "a place of popular scientific entertainment" – and he patented his Illusion after using it in theatrical performances in 1862 and 1863. Plays were written for the device, and Dickens used it during readings of The Haunted Man.
>
> The trick ... employs a sheet of transparent material placed at an angle on the stage like an inclined shop window. The audience sees through this sheet of glass or plastic to the actors on the stage. The screen thus has a two-way effect: it is transparent and reflective.

When Sidney spoke, Pepper had recently entertained the people of Bury St Edmunds for three nights.

Suffolk and Essex Free Press, 31 December 1863, p. 2.

JUVENILE LECTURE BY MR. SIDNEY. – On Monday evening the Rev. E. Sidney, M.A., the highly esteemed President of the Literary Institute, gave his annual Christmas lecture to juveniles at the Town Hall. The lecture was illustrated by dissolving views and other illuminated diagrams, kindly lent by the eminent opticians, Messrs. Carpenter and Westley. They consisted of views of the principal buildings in Europe, fables (affording scope for some trite remarks from the lecturer) and comic slides, which highly amused the children present. Also portraits of eminent men, the late Lord Elgin, Earl Russell, the Prince Consort, and others, concluding with Mr. Sidney, himself which elicited great applause. The printing of these slides reflects very great credit on the firm of Messrs. Carpenter and Westley, one in particular was a *chef d'oeuvre* in itself. It was a view of the Needles, Isle of Wight, with the sun in the foreground, the waves rippling perfectly true to nature, and the sea gulls flying overhead. How the water was made to move and the birds to fly we are quite unaware, but the illusion was most extraordinary, and what is more it was highly pleasing, certainly far preferable to Pepper's famous ghost. It would be difficult to find as good an illustrator as Mr. Sidney, and so the audience seemed to think, to judge from their frequent applause. We are glad to hear that the same firm is having views of the Tyrol painted to illustrate Mr. Sidney's lecture in the spring.

XXVII   HENRY GAME 1864

Allan Mumford, aged twenty in 1864, was the third son of George Mumford. The tombstone of Ambrose Game is near the churchyard lychgate.

Suffolk and Essex Free Press, 14 April 1864, p. 2.

A BOY DROWNED NEAR SUDBURY.

Early on Tuesday morning week a boy named Henry Game, about fifteen years of age, the son of Ambrose Game, shoemaker, Little Cornard, was accidentally drowned in a ditch by the side of a road called Morse's [i.e. Mosses] road. There was only four or five inches of water in the ditch and it is supposed that the unfortunate lad, who has been subject for some time to fits, was taken with one, fell in, and being quite helpless was smothered in the mud, the body being found with the face downwards and the water reaching only to his ears. Deceased had been in the employ of Mr. Geo. Mumford, farmer, Little Cornard.

The inquest was held on Thursday (before J. W. I. Ion, Esq., one of the Coroners for the Liberty of Bury St. Edmunds), at Mr. Bell's public house, Little Cornard. The following jury was sworn:- J. Wakelin, foreman; W. Abrey, Jacob Jones, H. Carrington, Jas. Buggs, Chas. Bell, Newman Taylor, Alfred Segers, Henry Segers, Samuel Segers, C. Bell, jun., A. Bell, and Wm. Turner.

The jury having viewed the body –

Arthur Game, a boy about ten years old, was examined. He said he was brother of the deceased and lived with his father at Little Cornard; last Tuesday morning, a little before six, deceased left home by the gate whilst witness was going to work; he spoke to him, but did not recollect what he said to him; he appeared in his usual health, and walked down the lane by himself; witness never saw him alive again.

Allan Mumford said: I live with my father, Mr. George Mumford, at Little Cornard; I knew the deceased Henry Game; I was walking along the road last Tuesday morning at half-past six, when I saw a bag and cloak by the side of the road and knew it to belong to the deceased; the road is called Morse's Road; I went up to the ditch on the left side of the road and saw the deceased in the water; the ditch is ten yards from Morse's House [?*Moss Cottage*]; he was lying on his face; he didn't move; I pulled him out of the ditch, but the body was quite cold and he appeared to me quite dead; I called to Alfred Mose, who was working close by, and sent him for deceased's father; they moved the body to the house; witness didn't observe any marks by the side of the ditch or indications of a struggle, or where he might have stumbled; deceased's lips were blue and the nose bleeding a little.

By Mr. Wakelin: The face was under water up to the ears and covered with mud; he had worked for my father about a month.

Ambrose Game deposed: I am a shoemaker and live at Little Cornard; the deceased, Henry Game, is my son; being informed that my son was dead I went and took him home and immediately sent for the surgeon, Mr. Lynch; the deceased has been subject to fits for two years; he would drop down suddenly helpless and I used to put him to bed; the fits generally came on in the morning; the fit would last about ten minutes or a quarter of an hour before he came to himself again.

John Cox Lynch, surgeon, Sudbury, deposed: I saw the deceased between eight and nine on Tuesday morning; the body presented all the external appearance of death by suffocation and life had evidently been extinct upwards of two hours: I am aware that deceased has been subject to epileptic fits, and I have no doubt that he fell into the ditch during one of these attacks; the state of unconsciousness which the fits induced would not have allowed him to make any effort to extricate himself.

The coroner said there could be very little doubt but that the deceased was accidentally drowned. Nothing was more feasible than that he was taken with one of these fits, to which it appeared he was subject to [*sic*] in the morning, and that he fell into the ditch and was accidentally drowned.

The jury immediately returned a verdict of "Accidental Death by drowning."

XXVIII   HARVEST HOME 1860, 1864, 1865

The Victorians invented the Church of England harvest festival, chiefly in the 1850s. It was one aspect of their continuing reaction against the dreary slothfulness which had characterised much of the Church in the eighteenth century, and in the earlier nineteenth. But particularly it was a means by which some of the more conscientious rural clergy sought to turn from days of drunkenness and vice the poor committed to their charge.

In the middle ages, and in Tudor times, jollifications were prompted by many occasions in the agricultural and liturgical calendars. By the mid nineteenth century all these celebrations other than those associated with the harvest had apparently fallen into desuetude. But, as if to compensate, the customs of the harvest were by then characterised, over much of the country, and often with the collusion of farmers themselves, by an unrivalled elaborateness and colourfulness, and usually by a crude drunkenness thoroughly at odds with the soundest principles of Christianity. The climax of these harvest festivities was the horkey, or harvest supper. Often in the 1840s, in Norfolk and Suffolk, horkeys were kept in public houses or cottages; but when practised to their full extent, at the farmstead, they were very elaborate indeed.

Several Victorian clergymen around the country claimed to have invented the harvest festival. In the Sudbury area of Suffolk and Essex the new-style festivals began to appear in the late 1850s. Little Cornard was conspicuous and, under Sidney's inspiration, celebrated the first of its new-style festivals in September 1857. The local newspapers usually reported them in full.

The Little Cornard harvest processions were manifestly the product of an old-fashioned rural paternalism, exercised jointly by the parish's church and farmers. They were affirmations of the existing social order; this kind of thing was what Marx and Engels in the *Communist Manifesto* ridiculed as 'feudal socialism', or 'waving the proletarian alms-bag in front for a banner'. The venerability of the custom is suggested by portraits etched in literature, of obedient lower orders in one style or another marching to and fro, as they did in Little Cornard. For example, in Ben Jonson's 'To Penshurst', of 1616:

> But all come in, the farmer and the clown,
> And no one empty-handed, to salute
> Thy lord and lady, though they have no suit.
> Some bring a capon, some rural cake,
> Some nuts, some apples; some, that think they make
> The better cheeses, bring 'em; or else send
> By their ripe daughters, whom they would commend
> This way to husbands, and whose baskets bear
> An emblem of themselves in plum or pear.

And in book iii, chapter iv, of Benjamin Disraeli's novel *Coningsby* (1844), where almsgiving day at St Geneviève is described (was this passage parodied knowingly in the report of the Little Cornard celebrations of 1864?):

> They came along the valley, a procession of nature, whose groups an artist might have studied. The old man, who loved the pilgrimage too much to avail himself of the privilege of a substitute accorded to his grey hairs. He came in person with his grandchild and his staff. There also came the widow with the child at the breast, and others clinging to her form; some sorrowful faces, and some pale; many a serious one; and now and then a frolic glance; many a dame in her red cloak, and many a maiden with her light basket, curly-headed urchins with demure looks, and sometimes a stalwart form baffled for a time of the labour which he desired. But not a heart there did not bless the bell that sounded from the tower of St. Geneviève!

The splendid '"Harvest Cart" in Suffolk' appeared in *Punch*, of 17 September 1864 (p. 115), two days after its appearance in the

Suffolk and Essex Free Press. Its author was John Impit Lushington (alias 'Quill'), who served at different times in the East Suffolk police and in the commissariat department of the army in the Crimea. From 1860 to 1868 he lived at Theberton, near Yoxford and Saxmundham, whilst employed as clerk to the chief constable. Later he was appointed to be master of the workhouse at Braintree, in Essex. He died aged 51, a Norwich auctioneer, in 1881. In 1865 he published a volume of poems entitled *A Suffolk Largess by Quill*, which contained '"Harvest Cart" in Suffolk'.

Other points :
1864:

* 'The earth is the Lord's, and the fulness thereof': Psalm 24, v.1, biblical version.

* Deuteronomy xxviii 2–7: 'And all these blessings shall come on thee, and overtake thee, if thou shalt hearken unto the voice of the Lord thy God. Blessed shalt thou be in the city, and blessed shalt thou be in the field. Blessed shall be the fruit of thy body, and the fruit of thy ground, and the fruit of thy cattle, the increase of thy kine, and the flocks of thy sheep. Blessed shall be thy basket and thy store. Blessed shalt thou be when thou comest in, and blessed shalt thou be when thou goest out. The Lord shall cause thine enemies that rise up against thee to be smitten before thy face: they shall come out against thee one way, and flee before thee seven ways'.

* '[W]ho praised him for thy creation, preservation, and all the blessings of this life, but principally for their redemption': the reporter has picked up an echo of part of the General Thanksgiving, appointed to be read after the Litany and the Orders for Morning and Evening Prayer, in *The Book of Common Prayer*.

- * 'The Rifles' were the Sudbury Volunteer Rifle Corps, in the formation of which, in January 1860, Sidney had been involved (*Essex Standard*, 27 January 1860, p. 2).

- * 'Mawther', 'mauther' or 'mor' is Saxon in origin and means 'young woman'.

- * William Brock was a butcher, of 16 North Street, Sudbury.

1865:

- * 1 Timothy iv 4, 5: 'For every creature of God is good, and nothing to be refused, if it be received with thanksgiving: For it is sanctified by the word of God and prayer'.

Suffolk and Essex Free Press, 18 October 1860, p. 3.

CORNARD PARVA.

The annual Harvest Home for this parish was held on Friday last, and as the day was very propitious, the usual out-door rural sports, which generally are so much enjoyed on similar festive occasions, were engaged in with much zest by the villagers, and indulged to their hearts' content. The proceedings very appropriately commenced with divine service at half-past eleven o'clock, at the neat and clean church, which has recently been thoroughly cleaned and painted, and all the wood work varnished, but which is far too small for the Sunday congregations. The service consisted of mornings prayers, litany and sermon. The indefatigable rector, the Rev. E. Sidney, officiated, and preached a very appropriate sermon from the words of St. Paul to the people of Lystra, found in the 14th chapter of the Acts and 17th verse, "Nevertheless, he left not himself without witness, in that he did good and gave us rain from heaven and fruitful seasons, filling out hearts with joy [*sic*] and gladness." Service being concluded, the congregations wended their way, if not in martial array, yet in very picturesque confusion through the church[yard], lane, farmyard, and road to the rectory barn, used occasionally for church missionary lectures on Sunday evenings by Mr. Sidney, and formerly, before he was president of the Sudbury Literary Institute, for lectures in connection with the Agricultural Association.

The customary good fare of roast and boiled joints of mutton and beef, and hot plum puddings, was prepared, furnished excellently and liberally by Mr. Brock, our Sudbury caterer on such occasions, and after grace by the rector, who officiated as chairman at a cross table at the end of the commodious *impromptu* dining hall, the rustic guests fell to, and soon the clatter of knives and forks, and the occasional soft hum of conversation (which, however, soon increased and waxed loud and joyous) were the only sounds heard except when at intervals the Bures band performed suitable music. The employers, Messrs. Mumford, Sikes, Segers (father and two sons), Sparrow, Fitch, &c., &c., carved for the men, and their servants waited upon them.

After dinner various loyal toasts were proposed by the chairman, and heartily responded to by the men, who drank the healths of the Queen, officials, churchwardens, rector and others with as much enthusiasm out of their earthenware mugs, as if it had been sparkling champagne from crystal goblets. The men then vacated their places, which were soon filled by the women and children, the barn not being large enough for all to dine together. The females had dinner and tea in one, and the school children were served with buns and cake, the ladies enjoying the scene and doing the honours of the feast. The afternoon quickly sped away, and its last hours and some of the evening were spent by the cottagers on a meadow adjacent to the rectory, where the sports already alluded to were indulged in, hearty and vociferous laughter testifying the enjoyment of all at the ludicrous nature of some of the pastimes. Dancing also took place, to the notes of the band, and two fine balloons, let off by Messrs. Adams, of Sudbury, created much surprise among many of the guests, and well finished the day's programme

Suffolk and Essex Free Press, 15 September 1864, p. 2.

"HARVEST CART" IN SUFFOLK.

Yow, Jack, bring them 'ers hosses
   Get this 'ere waggin out;
I think the weather mean to cleare,
   So jest yow look about!
Come put old Jolly to right quick —
   Now then, hook Di'mond on,
(There, chuck yow down that plaguy stick),
   An' goo an' call old John.

John bo', the "Cart-shod close" we'll try
   (Get yow upon the stack);
I'm sure the whate's by this time dry —
   Bring them 'ere folks here, Jack.
Blarm that 'ere chap! Where is he now?
   Jest look you here, my man,
If yow don't want to have a row,
   Be steady, if you can.

Ope that 'ere gate. Wish! Jolly – Wo!
   Cop that 'ere rope up, Sam;
Now I'll get down an' pitch, bo', so
   Jump yow up where I am.
Load wide enough, mate, – that's the style -
   Now hold ye! – Di'mond! – Wo'o!
Jack! – that 'ere boy do me that rile -
   Jest mind yow where yow goo!

There goo a rabbit! Boxer, hi! –
   She's sure to get to grownd.
Hold ye! Now then, bo', jest yow try
   To turn them nicely round.
Don't knock them shoves down! – Blarm the boy!
   Yow'll be in that 'ere haw!
That feller do me so annoy;
   But *he* don't care a straw.

* * * * *

How goo the time? I kind o'think
Our fourses* should be here.
Chaps, don't yow fare want some drink? -
There's Sue with the old beer!
The rain have cleared right slap away;
An' if it hold out bright,
Let's work right hard, lads (what d'ye say?)
An' clear this field to night! – *Punch.*

*The harvest men leave off at four o'clock for refreshment, which they call their "fourses."

HARVEST HOME AT CORNARD.

The annual celebration of the ingathering of the harvest was held at Little Cornard, in the barn usually occupied by the Rev. E. Sidney for the delivery of his instructive lectures, which on this occasion was tastefully decorated with various flags, banners, mottoes, flowers, &c., under the kind superintendence of the Misses Mumford. From the centre beam was displayed a white banner, bearing the inscription, "The earth is the Lord's, and the fulness thereof." The day's proceedings were commenced with [a] service in the church, which was well filled, and even the spacious porch and large west and children's galleries were occupied, there being no room to spare. The prayers were read by the Rev. J. Bailey, Rector of Great Waldingfield, the sermon being preached by the Rector, the Rev. E. Sidney. The rev. gentleman took for his text 28th Deut., v. 2 to 7, and delivered a short but very appropriate discourse. He first alluded to the occasion of his parishioners assembling in the house of God that day, and then proceeded to notice – 1st, the persons to whom the blessings named in the text are promised, and 2ndly, the promises themselves. The promises were for those who harkened to God's word, who praised him for their creation, preservation, and all the blessings of this life, but principally for their redemption, and who saw both in the voice of nature, and in the revelation of His word, the glory and love of their Creator. The discourse was listened to with much attention by all present.

After the service a procession was extemporised, led by the band, composed of several musicians, from Bures and Sudbury, with the big drum of the Rifles, followed by the school children and their teachers, headed by two banners; the girls carrying one, with the inscription "Cornard Parva Harvest Home," and the boys, with "God Save the Queen," the poles being ornamented with branches of wheat. Then came the men and women, the grandsires and grandames of the parish, the father and the matron, and the rustic beau and his sweetheart, or, in Suffolk vernacular, his "mawther." The farmers, with labourers and their families, and the visitors, with the Rector, Mr. Sidney, and the Rev. Bailey. Arrived at the Rectory gates the children soon dispersed, and were quickly merrily at play. The men and women were speedily, on presenting their tickets, admitted to the "Banqueting Hall," and took their places side by side at the well spread boards, the Rector taking the chair, and Mr. Mumford the vice-chair; Messrs. Sikes, W. Sparrow. H. and A. Segar [*sic*], – Fitch, &c., also sitting down and carving for their guests. The caterer was, as usual, Mr. Wm. Brock, of North Street, who provided the best of fare, and plenty of it. There were roast beef and mutton, bread and beer, and hot plum puddings.

After dinner various toasts were drunk and short speeches made.

The Chairman gave the customary loyal toasts, and the health of Mr. Mumford.

Mr. Mumford responded, and gave some excellent advice to the men, and gave the health of the Rector, which was received with three times three.

Mr. Sidney responded in a humorous speech, observing that an old friend opposite him said he had hollaed himself hoarse and had asked an old woman to help him, and another had significantly observed that they could not drink toasts out of empty glasses, which was a hint they must be replenished. Mr. Sidney then proposed the health of Mr. Sikes, which that gentleman acknowledged, and proposed the healths of Mrs. Sidney and the ladies, which was [*sic*] also drunk with three times three; and for which Mr. Sidney gave thanks, gracefully alluding to their work in the parish in the way of education, teaching in the Sunday School, visiting the poor, &c.

The barn was then cleared, when the children entered, and had a plentiful dinner and tea combined, of meat and pudding, tea, bread and butter, and cake, many also receiving presents from the Misses Mumford, &c.

The evening was spent in rural sports, racing, dancing, &c., while those that liked smoked in the booth and while they sipped their ale and enjoyed the "baccy," could watch their boys and girls at play; or the younger bachelors could, as the ale excited pleasurably their feelings, discuss the excellence of their "mawthers." All was merriment and harmless fun; the gentry united in trying to make all happy, and the day passed off pleasantly throughout. As dusk came on the merry party separated and soon all was still in the Rectory glebe. A large party was entertained by Mr. and Mrs. Sidney at the Rectory. About 330 men, women, and children were present and dined. Among the visitors, &c., were J. Sikes, Esq., and Mrs. Sikes, G. Mumford, Esq., and family, the Rev. J. Bailey and Miss Bailey, W. Garrad, jun., Esq., Miss Adams, Mr. Fitch, jun., Messrs. W. and A. Segers and Miss Segers, Mr. Bowers, Mr. and Mrs. Sparrow, &c., &c. The weather proved most propitious throughout the day, a cool refreshing breeze tempering the heat of the sun.

Suffolk and Essex Free Press, 14 September 1865, p. 3.

HARVEST HOMES

• • •

GREAT [*sic*] CORNARD.

The celebration of the ingathering of the fruits of the field was held at this village, on Friday, the 8th instant, and commenced with Divine service in the church at a quarter before one o'clock. The prayers were read by the Rev. H. Mumford, and a sermon preached by the rector, the Rev. E. Sidney, from 1 Timothy iv., verses 4–5. Afterwards a procession was formed, preceded by flags and banners, and a band of music which proceeded to the rectory.

The Dinner to the harvest men and their wives, was liberally supplied by Mr. Brock of Sudbury. The dinner took place in the large barn which has been fitted up for public meetings. It was admirably decorated with bouquets of flowers, banners, flags and evergreens. The flags were partly supplied by Mr. Mumford's family, and partly lent with great kindness by friends in Sudbury. After the removal of the cloth the Rev. E. Sidney gave the usual loyal toasts and that of the Queen was responded to with enthusiastic cheers on the part of the workmen. Mr. Mumford replied to the health of the Churchwardens, himself and Mr. J. R. Sparrow, and made some appropriate remarks on the duty of Christian thankfulness, and said, that notwithstanding the difficulties of the harvest, he hoped the poor man would have a sound and good loaf this winter. He then gave the health of the Rev. E. Sidney, in very kind terms, and the toast was received with enthusiasm. Mr. Sidney congratulated his parishioners on the success of the day, and said that from what he had heard from the gleaners he had hopes that Mr. Mumford's expectations would be realised. He said that having just returned from a continental tour, he could not but contrast the condition of the labourers' wives here, with that of the poor women in other countries. Every female present ought to be thankful that she was born an

Englishwoman. After some other remarks, Mr. Sidney gave the health of Mr. Sikes, a constant promotor of the festivities of the day, and returned thanks to the Rev. H. Mumford for his assistance. Mr. Mumford proposed the health of Mr. [?Mrs] Sidney and the ladies, which was received with loud cheers, and the labourers and their wives made way for the children of the school for whom an ample repast had been provided. They were most heartily waited on by the ladies of the parish, and were as happy as juveniles can possibly be. The day terminated with the usual out-door games, and the party separated with many expressions of satisfaction at the kindness shown them. The extreme heat of the weather seemed almost forgotten, and the whole passed off without a single occurrence to mar its success and pleasure.

XXIX   VALUABLE PIONEERS AND COADJUTORS – A LETTER FROM DR LIVINGSTONE 1866

It is possible that Sidney had met Livingstone through the social network of Henslow. For Henslow was rector of Hitcham, which is close to Stowmarket. At Stowmarket lived Anne, Catherine, and Susanna Ridley, and also two brothers, Thomas and Manning Prentice. Thomas Prentice had been a friend of Livingstone when both were students at the training institution of the London Missionary Society at Ongar, in Essex. It is highly likely that Henslow knew his near-neighbour Thomas Prentice, for Prentice was not only an evangelical Christian but, as a prospective missionary turned Stowmarket corn merchant, was also connected with agriculture. In due course Livingstone had become a regular visitor to the home of the Ridley sisters in Stowmarket. Probably he had hoped to marry Catherine, but instead she married Thomas Prentice. There was a voluminous correspondence between Zanzibar and Stowmarket; perhaps that between Zanzibar and Little Cornard was a by-product of the friendships that produced it.

Suffolk and Essex Free Press, 19 April 1866, p. 2.

DR. LIVINGSTONE. — The Rev. Edwin Sidney has recently received a letter from Dr. Livingstone, the celebrated African traveller, now on his third great exploration. It was announced at a recent meeting of the [Royal] Geographical Society that the Doctor had reached Zanzibar; from his communication to Mr. Sidney it appears that he has taken with him a number of tame Indian buffaloes, to introduce into Africa; and as, like the African ones, they do not suffer much from that terrible pest the Tzetze, it is hoped they may be acclimatized. Hitherto there have been no beasts of burden as such in Central Africa. The intrepid explorer and missionary has also taken with him nine converted Africans, educated in the Government Schools at Bombay, who are Christians and willing to work, and the Doctor has great hopes that they will prove valuable pioneers and coadjutors. A hope has been expressed that on Dr. Livingstone's return, Mr. Sidney, as president of the Literary Institute may induce him to favour Sudbury with a visit and give a lecture on Africa.

XXX   ISAAC MOWER 1866

Suffolk and Essex Free Press, 8 November 1866, p. 5.

Fatal Accident at Little Cornard.

We are sorry to have to record a sad accident which occurred in this parish on Tuesday last, by which a poor man named Isaac Mower has lost his life. The unfortunate deceased was in the employ of Mr. Henry Smith, builder, as a bricklayer's labourer, and was engaged in sinking a well on the farm belonging to George Mumford, Esq. He had got down to a depth of about 26 feet, when the earth suddenly caved in and buried him. Unfortunately the soil was of such a fine and loose nature that there is little doubt but that he was quickly smothered, the sides giving way for some

12 or 14 feet and forming a dense mass of earth, affording but little chance of digging the poor fellow out, and indeed the men who arrived on the spot seemed afraid to venture down the well. It would unquestionably have been highly dangerous for them, and only probably have led to further loss of life, and it seems there were no proper appliances at hand to shore up the sides and excavate sufficient to recover the body. Wooden cylinders were, however, obtained, it being considered too great a risk to trust to the ordinary shoring up, owing to the sandy nature of the soil, and the body was recovered last (Wednesday) evening. The deceased was found in an upright position, with his arm extended as though to ward off the earth. We regret to have to add that the deceased, who was a sturdy, hard-working man, leaves a widow and five children to mourn his untimely fate.

XXXI BRICK YARD

200,000 Superior White Drain Tiles 1851

Bury and Norwich Post, 1 October 1851, p. 3.

AT LITTLE CORNARD BRICK YARD.
TO AGRICULTURALISTS.
MR. W. R. ROLFE

Has received instructions from the Proprietor

TO SELL BY AUCTION,

On the Premises, the Brick Yard, Little Cornard, on Friday, October the 3rd, 1851, at Eleven for Twelve o'clock, in Lots to suit the convenience of purchasers, 200,000 Superior White Drain Tiles, in five different sizes.

The Auctioneer particularly invites the attention of Agriculturalists to the above sale, the Ware at this Establishment being generally acknowledged as the best in the neighbourhood. The Yard abuts immediately on the high road between Bures and

Sudbury, affording great facilities for carting. Buyers will be allowed any reasonable period for removal

Further particulars may be had on application to the Auctioneer, North-street, Sudbury.

Henry Segers 1868

The tombstone of Henry and Sarah Segers stands a yard or two behind that of Charles and Maria Bell (XXI).

Suffolk and Essex Free Press, 12 March 1868, p. 8.

DEATHS.

• • •

March 7, Mr. H. J. Segers, Cornard brickworks, aged 49.

Carrying on the business 1868

Suffolk and Essex Free Press, 9 April 1868, p. 4.

LITTLE CORNARD BRICK WORKS.

MRS. H. SEGERS

Returns her sincere thanks to the Public for the favours received by her late Husband, and begs to inform them that she intends carrying on the business, and hopes by strict attention to all orders she may be favoured with to receive their continued patronage and support. March 18, 1868.

*Fig. 13   Michael Faraday in 1857.
By courtesy of the National Portrait Gallery.*

XXXII MICHAEL FARADAY 1868

In the 1790s England was at war with revolutionary France and many of the English upper classes were worried lest the lower classes should become insubordinate. Might not the promotion of applied science be one of many things that, at a domestic level, would be advantageous to the lower classes, and so make them more amenable?

So wondered many of the leading aristocracy. They therefore supported the founding of the Royal Institution, in London, in 1799. Quite soon, however, 'applied science' at the Royal Institution became mostly 'agrarian science', and remained so for the first decade of the nineteenth century. From 1803 to 1812 Sir Humphry Davy was the leading figure at the Institution, and during that period it was his brilliant lecturing (felicitous of phrase, lively of motion and language, dramatic and well structured) that largely sustained it, rather than the Royal Society of London, as the centre of English science. From 1825 (when he was appointed director of the laboratory of the Royal Institution) until 1862 (when he delivered his final Friday Evening Discourse) Faraday was the presiding genius.

Faraday was the greatest, most sober 'popular' lecturer and the greatest experimental scientist of the nineteenth century; he refused the presidency of the Royal Society in 1857 through increasing mental debility, not through false modesty. But he was also a Sandemanian, a member, that is, of an evangelical sect named after Robert Sandeman (died 1771) and founded in 1728, the theology of which was teleological, and which originally had been expelled from the Church of Scotland for holding that national churches, being 'kingdoms or this world', were unlawful. Sandemanianism was at the root of Faraday's analogical procedures in matters of scientific experimentation: apprehension of the Divine origin of nature, and of the rationality and goodness of God, Faraday argued, could lead to apprehension of the intelligibility, beauty, economy, and unison of the physical world. (Paley, of course, had argued the other way round.)

Faraday had had little formal education, but he devoted much thought to the quality of education available generally in early Victorian society. Despite the impression that he sometimes gave, he regarded as facile any rigid demarcation between imagination and fact; in 1818 he had written an essay entitled 'On Imagination and Judgement', in which he had argued that it was the function of *imagination* to produce possibilities and *analogies*, upon which it was the function of *judgement* to be exercised, so to produce *facts* which, at least provisionally, could be regarded as proven: *assertion* was not

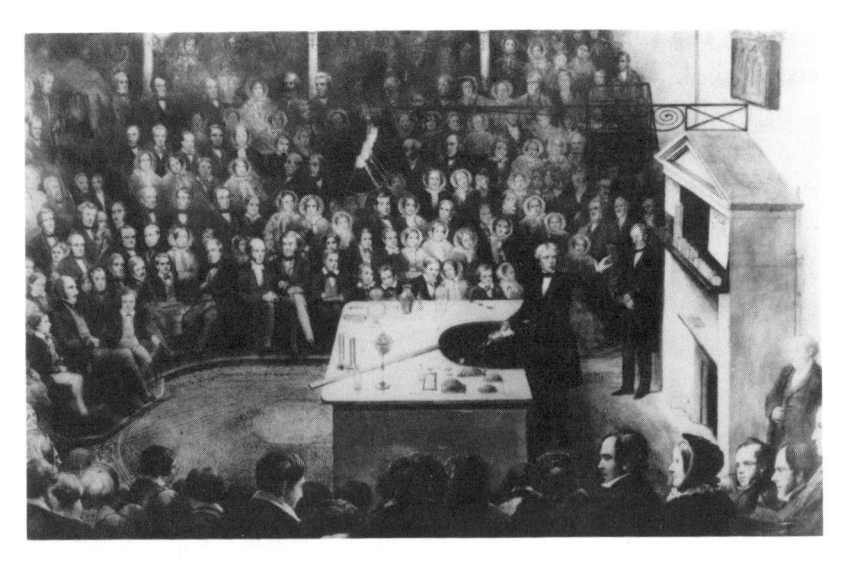

Fig. 14   Michael Faraday lecturing at the Royal Institution, with Prince Albert and sons in the audience. This is the lecture theatre in which Edwin Sidney also lectured. Courtesy of the Royal Institution.

fact, it was theory. But proven *facts* (and, of course, unproven *assertions*) were the concern of scientists ('philosophers'); therefore the role of science was crucial in education which, after all, was concerned, thought Faraday, with the development of *judgement.* Faraday returned to these ideas in a series of discourses on the general subject of education, delivered at the Royal Institution in 1854; one of these discourses was entitled 'Observations on Mental Education' ('Education of Mind', as Sidney called it).

Lack of *judgement,* according to Faraday, caused many 'educated' people (among them Queen Victoria and Prince Albert) to be credulous in the matter of the automatic movement of tables and other items of furniture, which was one aspect of the spiritualism a craze for which ('the present morbid condition of public thought', as *The Athenaeum* described it) descended upon London in the early 1850s. The phenomenon came to be called 'table-turning' in deference to Faraday, who had investigated a group of people determined to prevent a table moving, by pressing down upon it with their fingers; Faraday's observations led him to proclaim (not very convincingly) that the group was in fact assisting the table to turn, by *'quasi* involuntary muscular action'.

MRS JANE MARCET (1769–1858) first published her *Conversations on Chemistry* in two volumes in 1806. Widely read and acclaimed, and many times republished, these 'conversations' were between an instructress, 'Mrs. B.'. and young girls, Caroline and Emily. They popularised the lectures on chemistry delivered by Davy at the Royal Institution. Faraday read them at the age of 18, and so was introduced to the subject of much of his life's work – electro-chemistry. The 'little volume' which Sidney submitted to Faraday was published in 1867.

N. C. Barnardiston was prominent in Sudbury affairs. He lived at The Ryes, Little Henny (Essex), and was founder-chairman of Sidney's Sudbury Agricultural Association.

Suffolk and Essex Free Press, 29 October 1868, p.7.

SUDBURY MECHANICS AND LITERARY INSTITUTION.

The opening lecture of the above-named society for the present season was delivered on Thursday evening in the Town Hall, by its highly-respected President, the Rev. E. Sidney, Rector of Cornard Parva, and chaplain to Viscount Hill. There was a large and most respectable audience, among whom we noticed N. C. Barnardiston, Esq. (in the chair), and party; J. St. Geo. Burke, Esq., and party; the Mayor, S. Higgs, Esq.; Jno. Sikes, Esq., and party; Rev. G. Coldham, Glemsford; C. Badham, All Saints, Sudbury; J.E. Fell, Acton; J. Fenn, Henny; W. K. Borton, Wickham; — Wilson, Sudbury; J. A. Bridgman, Dr. Williams, J. Alexander, H. C. Canham, H. S. Pratt, W. D. King, M. Mason, G. Mumford, F. Fitch, Garrad [*sic*], R. G. Dupont, J. Parmenter, and — Sparrow, Esqrs.; Messrs. Harding, Fox, N. Sparrow, S. Brown, Bridgman, Wright, J. Hunt, &c., with a large number of ladies.

The subject of the lecture was "Professor Faraday and some of his discoveries."

The CHAIRMAN, in introducing the lecture, spoke of the services which had been rendered to Society by the discoveries of such men as Brunel, Stephenson, Cook, and Faraday, and of the great loss which, especially in scientific circles, their deaths had occasioned. To such investigators the whole world was indebted, and their names and works ought ever to be had in remembrance (cheers).

The Rev. E. SIDNEY, before commencing his lecture, expressed the satisfaction he felt at again meeting the members of the Society to which he wished all possible prosperity. He mentioned the indebtedness of the institution to their worthy president of that evening, who by liberality had assisted to defray the cost of the experiments; to Mr. Burke, who had also generously assisted; to Mr. Sikes, and also to Mr. J. Hills. He then proceeded with his lecture, of which the following is a *resume* [*sic*].

Michael Faraday, said Mr. Sidney, was born at Newington Butts, on September 22nd, 1791, and died at Hampton Court, on August 25th, 1867. He was apprenticed to a bookseller and a binder for some years, but he longed for science, and was fond of experiments. His thoughts were turned to chemistry by reading the well-known "Conversations" on that subject by Mrs. Marcet, with whom he Mr. Sidney also was well acquainted. A member of the Royal Institution kindly introduced young Faraday to the lectures of Sir Humphrey [*sic*] Davy, of which he made notes, and sent them to Sir Humphrey for perusal, by whom he was engaged as an assistant, accompanying him to the Continent, from 1813 to 1815, when he returned to the Royal Institution, and remained in office there until his death. The great secret of his fame seems expressed in one of his sayings, "I could trust a fact, but always cross-examine an assertion." Mr. Sidney gave a brief outline of Faraday's early career, and of his marriage, glancing at his first contributions to science till 1821. He also noticed Faraday's admirable assistant, Mr. Charles Anderson, who helped him for forty years. It was in 1820 that Oersted made his discovery of a voltaic current on a magnetic needle, without which we should never have had the electric telegraph, nor many of the discoveries of Faraday. This was the first experiment shown by Mr. Ladd, and explained by the Lecturer. This was followed by an exhibition of the rotation of a magnet around the current, Faraday's first great discovery in this line. On Christmas Day 1821 he led his young wife in triumph to his laboratory to show her his achievement. Next came his grand discovery of the induction of electric currents, the foundation of many wonderful inventions, one of them the marvellous machine of Mr. Ladd, a working model of which he exhibited and explained. To understand this it was necessary to be well understood, namely the action of induction on two separate wires of the coil, magneto-electric induction; and the induction of an electric current on itself. By the smallest application of such a current to Mr. Ladd's machine, and rapid rotation the power might be exalted from the smallest beginning in an infinite degree, giving intense electric illumination and other effects, some of which were beautifully shown, the rotations of the two armatures being 2000 a minute, including 4000 charges in the machine. It gained the silver medal at Paris. Generally, for the full effects it must be worked by steam when used by light-houses or other great lights. It is constructed on the double armature principle, both armatures being placed end to end, so that their magnetic axes cross each other at right angles. Its power of decomposing water was well shown. Mr. Ladd next showed his large electro-magnet, due to the discovery of induction by Faraday. The spark given out between the poles was very striking. He also showed the curious experiment called "Faraday's Saw;" and his own medical machine with a circular magnet. By way of a little variety Mr. Sidney called the attention of the audience to Faraday's discovery of the hydro-carbon called Benzol which was the foundation of the splendid aniline dyes – thence came fine colours, mauve, magenta, &c., so much admired by the ladies. These colours were brilliantly exhibited by the aid of the electric light. Mr. Ladd had brought with him 60 cells of Grove's powerful battery, the effects of which may be imagined. This was followed by Faraday's observations of the lines of magnetic force which are shown with extreme skill, and greatly surprised those who saw these remarkable effects. After this came the grand subject of the magnetism of all matters, except perhaps nitrogen, which seems to be different. Faraday called all matters *magnetic*; those substances which arrange themselves from pole to pole are called *paramagnetic*, and those at right angles to the line between the poles he called *decimagnetic*. All those were illustrated by attractive experiments. One of Faraday's last and most wonderful discoveries was the magnetization of light. By the aid of a polariscope and a powerful electro magnet, Mr. Ladd succeeded in showing this extraordinary phenomenon, one of the most difficult and surprising that can be conceived. We have no space for more than this brief allusion to these admirable experiments which were fully explained by Mr. Sidney. He also called attention to other matters relating to this great and good philosopher. He described his excellence as a lecturer, and mentioned his exposition of the follies of the table turners at the time their practices were in vogue. Mr. Sidney also quoted Faraday's pointed remark – "I think the system of education which could leave the marked condition of the public body in the state in which his [*sic*] subject has found it, must have been greatly deficient in some very important principle.['] Mr. Sidney spoke of Faraday's remarkable lecture on the "Education of Mind" and especially noticed the distinction he drew between the truths relating to science, and those of religion. Faraday was fully persuaded that the Christian believer is taught by a higher than human power, and that the truths of the eternal world are received by faith. He was a most humble believer, in the revelation of the word of God, and the effects of his conviction of the truths of Christianity, were manifest in his humble, self-denying and holy life. The greatest experimental philosophers [*sic*] the world ever saw, was a sincere and lowly believer in the truths of Christianity, and an example of the humblest piety. His views were peculiar, and he was remarkably silent on the subject of religion. In a letter to Mr. Sidney advising him to publish his little volume called "Conversations on the Bible and Science" he said, "though as you know it is not my place to speak on such matters, I think of them." Though mild in the extreme and kind, he was a man of energy and spirit. He refused the Presidency of the Royal Society and said, "No; I must always remain plain Michael Faraday." Though Faraday had many honours, he bore them meekly, and his character as an eminent man of science was felt by every one, from the deepest philosopher to the simplest child who never had the pleasure of seeing him in his home, the Royal Institution of Great Britain.

At the conclusion of the lecture, which was very frequently applauded, a unanimous vote of thanks was given to the Rev. E. Sidney for the interesting information he had afforded; to Mr.

Ladd for his numerous, costly, and most successful experiments; and to the Chairman for his kindness in presiding, and his liberality to the institution. Mr. Sidney announced that the next lecture would be delivered by Dr. Williams, Vice-President of the Society.

XXXIII   MOVEMENTS IN ORGANIC LIFE 1869

John Langdon Haydon Down, 1828–1896, was an eminent Victorian physician and morbid anatomist, with a special and very compassionate interest in the mental illnesses of children. The illness 'Down's syndrome' is named after him.

The son of a village apothecary in Devon, Down arrived in London at the age of 18, becoming an assistant to a surgeon in the Whitechapel Road and a student in the laboratory of the Pharmaceutical Society. He came to know Faraday, whom he helped with his work on gases. In 1853 he became a student at the London Hospital, where his career was distinguished. He qualified as an apothecary and as a surgeon in 1856, and obtained higher qualifications in 1859. Meanwhile, though, in 1858, he had taken the startling decision to exchange the glittering promise of a career in medicine for the dismal promise of a career in mental illnesses, and accepted the post of medical superintendent of the Earlswood Asylum for Idiots, in Surrey, which at that time was still absorbing inmates from the closed asylums at Highgate and Colchester (see above, Introduction). Down's self-sacrifice was recognised, for in 1859 he was elected assistant physician to the London Hospital. For the next ten years, however, he continued to live near Redhill, and to practise both there and in London.

It was probably through his indirect link with Essex Hall that Down came to know Sidney. In 1866 he produced a classical description of what he called 'the mongolian type of idiot', in a

XXXIII MOVEMENTS IN ORGANIC LIFE 1869

Fig. 15   John Langdon Haydon Down.

paper called 'Observations on an Ethnic Classification of Idiots'. In this paper he argued that the totality of the physical characteristics of a 'mongol' boy whom he had examined were such that 'it is difficult to realise that he is the child of Europeans, but so frequently are these characters presented that there can be no doubt that these ethnic features are the result of 'degeneration'. To argue thus – to assume implicitly, that is, that the people of Mongolia are self-evidently 'inferior' to the people of Europe, and then to erect upon this assumption the argument that through some kind of heredity a particular human being is 'degenerate', or has reverted in a *Darwinian* or evolutionary way to some kind of human stock 'lower' than the stock of a 'normal' human being – is to dress up in clinical language the *pre-Darwinian*, Aristotelian attitude of mind (with its notions of 'higher' and 'lower') that Sidney revealed when he told of his conversation with the urchin in Little Cornard (see above, Introduction).

A wider notion that human stock could 'degenerate' became prominent in the later nineteenth century when it was believed by many that the inhabitants of the poor inner-city areas would, through the generations, 'degenerate', mostly through their slothfulness and inbreeding; they would develop, that is, waxy complexions, narrow chests, bad teeth, weak eyes, weak physiques in general, and even weak moralities, unless from time to time they were 'regenerated' with the blood of wholesome country people. This notion led straight to the sinister doctrine of eugenics, and to the doctrines of Adolf Hitler. On the other hand, Down's notion of 'degeneration' could produce humane results. Undoubtedly it fortified Edwin Sidney in his work for the mentally handicapped. And undoubtedly if you believed that a European could 'degenerate' into a 'Mongolian', then by analogy you could in principle believe that a white European could 'degenerate' into a black African; indeed, in 1887 Down claimed publicly that he *had* treated 'white negroes, but of European descent': 'I have had under my care typical examples of the negroid family, with the characteristic malar bones, the prominent eyes, the puffy lips and retreating chin. They have had the woolly hair, although not black, nor has the skin acquired pigmentary deposit. They have been examples of white negroes, but of European descent'. If you could believe that, then you believed that racial differences were not in fact racially specific – that is, you believed that the world's various ethnic families were *not* distinct species. And if you believed that, then you had better oppose negro slavery in the Southern states of the U.S.A., and support the notion of the Unity of Man. Which is precisely what Down did. So the line between good and evil in the doctrine of 'degeneration' was wobbly, finely drawn, and full of paradox.

But Charles Kingsley the children's novelist made merry with paradox. In *The Water Babies,* of 1861, he cleverly summarised Victorian notions of 'degeneracy' (or 'degradation') , when Tom the water-baby asks the gentleman salmon and the lady salmon why they so dislike the trout. Their reply embraces Aristotle's notion of the Great Chain of Being (for Kingsley claims that trout are 'lower' than salmon); Down's view of biological 'degeneracy' and the racial non-specificity of racial differences (for Kingsley claims that despite appearances to the contrary trout and salmon are of the same 'race'); and the view of later Victorian social analysts that biological 'degeneration' can be caused by a poor environment and low self-esteem:

"Why do you dislike the trout so?" asked Tom.
"My dear, we do not even mention them, if we can help it; for I am sorry to say they are relations of ours who do us no credit. A great many years ago they were just like us: but they were so lazy, and cowardly, and greedy, that instead of going down to the sea every year to see the world and grow strong and fat, they chose to stay

and poke about in the little streams and eat worms and grubs: and they are very properly punished for it; for they have grown ugly and brown and spotted and small; and are actually so degraded in their tastes, that they will eat small children."

"And then they pretend to scrape acquaintance with us again," said the lady. "Why, I have actually known one of them propose to a lady salmon, the impudent little creature."

"I should hope," said the gentleman, "that there are very few ladies of our race who would degrade themselves by listening to such a creature for an instant. If I saw such a thing happen, I should consider it my duty to put them both to death upon the spot." So the old salmon said, like an old blue-blooded hidalgo of Spain; and what is more, he would have done it too. For you must know, no enemies are so bitter against each other as those who are of the same race; and a salmon looks on a trout as some great folks look on some little folks, as something just too much like himself to be tolerated."

Thomas Huxley ('Darwin's Bulldog') was famous among quite ordinary people for his opposition to any notion that the wonders of the natural world should be attributed to what 'an impatient individual' provoked Down into calling the 'great goodness of the Fountain of life and motion'.

John Williams, M.D., was a surgeon living in Sudbury's Stour Street.

Suffolk and Essex Free Press, 25 March 1869, p. 7.

SUDBURY.

• • •

MECHANICS AND LITERARY INSTITUTION. — The third lecture for the season in connection with this institution, was delivered at the Town Hall, last Thursday evening, by Dr. Langdon Down, of London, on "Movements in Organic Life."

The attendance, although not nearly so numerous as the committee had reason to expect considering the interest of the subject and the known eminent attainments of the lecturer, was larger than at previous lectures and more influential. Among the company we noticed the respected president of the society (Rev. E. Sidney); who, although he has suffered severely of late and is still suffering from influenza, faced the coldness of the weather, in order to hear his esteemed friend Dr. Down, the Mayor of Sudbury, W. R. Bevan, Esq., J. Alexander, Esq., G. Mumford, Esq., and party, Dr. Williams, (Vice-President of the Institution), &c. The Rev. E. Sidney, who presided, in introducing the lecturer explained the causes why he, Professor Owen, and another gentleman had all been obliged to disappoint the members and friends of the society by not delivering the lectures which earlier in the season had been announced. He himself had been too unwell; Professor Owen had been called away from England to attend the Prince and Princess of Wales in their foreign tour; and the third gentleman who had kindly intended to lecture had equally from unforeseen circumstances been prevented from doing so. He was quite sure they would all feel the more deeply indebted to their kind friend Dr. Down, who, at great trouble and inconvenience on account of his professional avocations elsewhere, had prepared them he believed, a lecture calculated to interest and instruct. — Dr. Down then delivered his lecture to which the greatest attention was paid, as it most fully merited. The language used, remembering the scientific nature of the subject, was most clear and lucid; the facts conveyed through that language were, besides probably new to most, interesting and impressive[;] they were given in the most pleasing and popular manner, with frequent anecdote and witty illustration, and the most technical portions of the address were illustrated by means of well-executed diagrams of animals (including man) birds and fishes. It would be hardly possible – and we are not sure that it would be interesting to the general reader – to give in a brief report any idea of the subject grasped by the lecturer in all its fullness and importance. He clearly showed how well and how closely subsisting is the connection between the nerves and muscles of animals and in what surprising and infinite proportion the great Maker of all things has adapted the motions of every animal, bird or fish to its necessities. In conclusion Dr Down was entering into a statement of Professor Huxley's opinions as to the organisation of species, especially man, when he was interrupted by an individual in the room who, with greater impatience than well became considerations of the occasion and the lecturer, interfered and requested an explanation. Dr Down, although apparently surprised at the intrusion, explained that he was not arguing the subject nor indeed stating his own views, but simply setting before his hearers the views and published statements of Professor Huxley. He then concluded his eloquent and happily delivered lecture by again reverting to the great goodness of the Fountain of all life and motion, and calling upon his hearers to adore the wonders of motion, and of creation. — The Chairman, in an exceedingly able manner, also spoke upon the subject, and strongly advised its further pursuit and study by all present, especially young men of the Institution, who, he wished, would provide microscopes to be kept at the Society's rooms. Those instruments could now be obtained at a very reasonable price, and would always afford pleasure and interest. Speaking of the two kinds of motion – voluntary and involuntary – the Chairman said he was quite sure their motion of approval would be quite voluntary when, in their name, he tendered to Dr. Down the warmest and most cordial thanks (much applause). — Dr. Down returned thanks, and advised the encouragement of microscopial investigations by the young, after which the proceedings terminated.

XXXIV UNAVOIDABLY PREVENTED: OR, CERTAIN CROTCHETY PEOPLE 1869

Auberies, at Bulmer, outside Sudbury, is best known as the residence in the eighteenth century of Mr and Mrs Andrews, whom Gainsborough painted amongst their fields. The portrait hangs in the National Gallery. The present (1998) occupant is Peter Burke, Esq. Oliver Raymond was rector of Middleton; David Rose Fearon was a former vicar of Assington.

Gainsborough Dupont ('Mr. G. Dupont') was the son of Sarah Dupont, sister of Thomas Gainsborough. Gainsborough Dupont was himself a competent artist, who repainted the figures of saints which appear in the lower panels of the rood screen in St Peter's Church, Sudbury. He lived in a property originally called *Wisteria Cottage*, which is now 6 Old Market Place, Sudbury, and occupied by the Victoria Wine Co. Ltd.

Suffolk and Essex Free Press, 14 October 1869, pp. 5, 8.

LITTLE CORNARD.

THE ACCIDENT TO THE REV. E. Sidney. — In our account of the Sudbury Agricultural Society's meeting at Sudbury will be found the particulars of the accident which occurred to the highly esteemed rector of this parish on Saturday last. We are glad to be able to state that the rev. gentleman is progressing well, his injuries were fortunately limited to severe bruises to his face. Mr. Sidney is announced to plead the cause of the Eastern Counties Asylum for Idiots, Colchester, at a public meeting to be held at Thetford, on 21st inst., when the Duke of Grafton was to take the chair. Mr. Sidney has almost a world wide reputation of aiding these noble institutions, for which his extraordinary activity and great talents have so long well befitted him, and we believe that everywhere the account of his accident will be read with sympathy and regret.

SUDBURY AGRICULTURAL ASSOCIATION.

The twenty-second anniversary of the above-named Society was held on Tuesday last, and the show in the Corn Exchange was well attended. Ploughing was, as usual, the first business to be done, and the ploughs, 42 in number, were assembled outside the Town-hall at seven o'clock in readiness to proceed to the field of Mr. Whybrew, jun., on the Melford-road, about three parts of a mile from the town, where the competitions were to take place. The conditions were the same as in former years, and the work was done satisfactorily, especially in the boys' class, considering the state of the ground ....

The vegetable show took place as in former years at the Corn Exchange, which from early in the morning was filled with anxious exhibitors, and skeps and baskets containing almost all varieties of allotment and garden produce. The Rev. E. Sidney, Rector of Little Cornard, and Secretary of the Society, has in previous years, as our readers know, taken great interest in this show, as well as indeed every department of the Society's operations; and he may be considered as the pivot upon which the whole working of the association depends. He it was who mainly founded it, he it was, coupled with Mr. Barnardiston and a few other friends, who watched over its infancy and nourished it into healthy existence, and if now in any degree interest in the association flags or falters it is not because of any lessening of exertion on the part of Mr. Sidney, Mr. Barnardiston, Mr. G. Mumford, and others of the old members, so much as because with every advancing and successive year changes have been introduced into agriculture and added to the old ways some that are new; and increased activity is needful to adapt that institution to the present wants and inclinations of agriculturalists. As well might men blame the world because it is every twelve-month growing older as to blame the pioneers and originators of the society because its rules change not nor do its advantages become more open and extended. On the other hand there is no doubt that as the system of farming has considerably changed of late years, so changes are in many respects absolutely required in the association if ever it is to be kept in vigorous existence, and we mistake the aged and venerable as well as most highly respected secretary, we mistake the no less earnest in desire for well-doing president, and we mistake also the equally well-minded coadjutors in office of those two gentlemen, if we are not correct in believing that they would willingly countenance and support any change in the constitution, objects, or working of the association that could be proved better for the agricultural interest generally, that of the labourer in particular. To say therefore that the society is in danger because it may be, or we will even say is, in some respects defective, is to say almost in as many words that those who thus complain and yet keep aloof from the society, are fault-finders without disposition or knowledge to mend. Let them become members, not by force of entreaty or compulsion so much as voluntarily, and with a clear and definite desire boldly expressed to make the society what it should be, and we believe could be made, a credit to the town and neighbourhood; let their objections to what is done and their arguments for what they may desire, be put upon the broad basis of fairness and equity, and they will deserve credit. Otherwise, if they are content to say we have a society which we know to be good in intention but defective in working, and we won't assist because certain people we call crotchety are upon it, and therefore it must go down; or, as was said at the annual dinner, we don't assist because we have not been asked to subscribe to a society that has been founded and worked amongst us for one and twenty years, then beyond doubt down must go the society in time, and other associations, such as the more enterprising and spirited one of Lavenham, must take its place. However, what we were about to say before we digressed somewhat for the good of the association, was this, that the Rev. E. Sidney, whose interest in the society and in the cottagers' show is so well known, was this year unavoidably prevented from attending by an accident, happily not of a very serious or permanent character, which befel [sic] him last Saturday evening at the Auberies. He was walking with his friend, Mr. Burke, in the latter gentleman's grounds, when his foot suddenly stumbled against a stone, throwing him down. Mr. Sidney fell with his face upon another stone, bruising his forehead and face, and rendering rest for a few days desirable. His duties on Sunday were performed, we understand, by the Revds. O. Raymond, and A. [sic] Fearon. His absence from the show and from the dinner was much regretted and unfeigned hopes for his speedy recovery were expressed. His duties devolved upon Mr. Mumford and Mr. T. Fitch, jun., who both are assistant secretaries, and who were assisted by Mr. G. Dupont and Mr. Canham. The judges were Messrs. C. Nightingale and — James, the latter of whom is gardener to Mr. Barnardiston, at the Ryes. The arrangements (including the charge for the first time of an admission fee of 6d. to the hall, preventing overcrowding and annoyance to visitors) were undoubtedly improvements upon last year and the show itself, in nearly all kinds of vegetables, was one of the best, if not the best, the society has held. Potatoes were especially numerous and fine, those from Bures particularly so, in fact that parish gained almost an utter monopoly of the prizes in all classes. ...

XXXV EDWIN SIDNEY 1872

Suffolk Chronicle, 26 October 1872, p. 8.

THE DEATH OF THE REV. E. SIDNEY, a gentleman well known in the district, took place on Tuesday. Mr. Sidney was rector of Little Cornard, near Sudbury, and had been some time ill. The rev. gentleman was an able lecturer, and getting on for 30 years ago had made his mark upon the district in which he lived. His scientific acquirements were far above the common, and he also devoted much time of an active life in aid of the poor idiot both at Red Hill and at Essex Hall, Colchester. In all respects he was an able and laborious man. The living is worth £509, with house and 50 acres of glebe, and will be taken by the Rev. J. Ambrose, of Stow-cum-Quy, Cambridge.

Essex Standard, 1 November 1872, p. 2.

FUNERAL OF THE REV. EDWIN SIDNEY. — On Tuesday afternoon the mortal remains of the Rev. Edwin Sidney, M.A., Rector of Little Cornard, whose lamented death we recorded last week, were deposited in their resting place, close to the tower, at the West end of the Church in which he has officiated for so many years. A large number of his parishioners and friends attended to witness the ceremony, which was conducted in the most unostentatious manner. The funeral *cortége* [*sic*] left the Rectory shortly after half-past 12 o'clock, and consisted of the hearse, two mourning coaches, and a private carriage. The chief mourners occupying the carriages were Mr. John Vaughan (London), Mr. Robert Gardner (London), and Mr. H. C. Canham (Sudbury), the trustees of the deceased's estate; Mr. J. Sikes (Sudbury), Rev. Henry Goodwin, Mr. Newman Sparrow (Cornard Parva), Mr. Maurice Mason (Sudbury), Mr. George Mumford (Little Cornard), and Mr. Charles Nightingale, his attached and confidential attendant for many years. Many Clergymen and other of the deceased's friends in the district, as a mark of their respect and appreciation for the late reverend gentleman, joined the procession at the Church, including the Revds. C. J. Martyn (Melford), J. W. H. Molyneux (Sudbury), C. Badham (Sudbury), H. B. Faulkner (Melford), T. L. Green (Sudbury), J. Sparrow (Great Cornard), J. Wilson (Sudbury), and J. Harding (Chilton); and G. Hollier, Minister at the Trinity Congregational Chapel, Sudbury; Messrs. N. C. Barnardiston, A. Mumford, jun., T. Fitch, J. J. Harding (Sudbury), J. Garrad, jun. (Bures), E. Baker (Great Cornard), the children of the Sunday School. A large number of the villagers were also in attendance, and the little Church was crowded to overflowing, many present being in mourning. The service was conducted in an impressive manner by the Rev. J. SPARROW, Vicar of Great [Cornard].

The author of the following splendid specimen of provincial Victorian funeral oration was vicar of All Saints, Sudbury, from 1847 until his death in 1874. His scholarly *History and Antiquities of All Saints Church, Sudbury, and the parish generally* was published in 1852; it contained (pp. 81–5) an eloquent expatiation upon the significance for the living of churchyards and funeral monuments. One may hope that his acquaintance with Sidney's 'calm, good temper' was an ultimate benefit to him, for in 1856 Sudbury magistrates had fined him £5 for assaulting one of his pupils.

Bury and Norwich Post, 5 November 1872, p. 7.

FUNERAL SERMON BY THE REV. G. [*sic*] BADHAM.

On Sunday morning the Vicar of All Saints, Sudbury, the Rev. Chas. Badham, preached a funeral sermon on the recent death of the Rev. E. Sidney, Rector of Cornard Parva, who had for over twenty years been a personal friend of the preacher, and a frequent preacher in his church, when he was listened to by large numbers of the parishioners and inhabitants generally. The Vicar paid a well merited tribute of respect and regard to the memory of the departed, and was much affected during the delivery of the sermon, so much so that in the passages where he spoke of his personal connection and friendship with Mr. Sidney his faltering voice betrayed his deep emotion, and for some seconds he could not continue his discourse. The text was taken from 2 Timothy ii.15 – "*A workman that needeth not to be ashamed.*" After a brief general exordium the preacher continued: – "The removal of the remarkable man and minister of Christ whose loss we deplore has produced so strong a sensation in this town and neighbourhood, that had there been no more than the general duty to turn such visitations to profitable account I should be justified in attending to it. But there are special reasons why, in this place, the death of my lamented friend should claim more than a passing allusion. To you, he has, at intervals, for twenty years, preached the truths of the Gospel. Before you he has, on very many occasions, pleaded the cause of this Church and of missions to the heathen world. When your Minister at intervals (few and far between) was able to obtain a Sunday's rest and absence, he not only rejoiced at it but cheerfully offered to supply his lack by undertaking an entire Sunday evening service. More than I need enumerate were the kind offices which he rendered, and I am very grateful to his memory. On the present occasion it is some satisfaction to me to know that you neither think me capable of offering the tribute of unmerited commendation, nor labour under that ignorance of his character which would induce the suspicion that undistinguishing partiality had drawn the portrait. You know both: you know the preacher: you knew his friend.

"The work of a minister of Christ does not necessarily demand the possession of high intellectual powers, for it is a matter of fact that the larger portion of the preachers of the Gospel have in all ages been men of ordinary talents. But if the Head of the Church has occasion for the use of minds of uncommon strength, he knows where to find and how to call them into his service. Such was the mind of our departed friend. Powerful in its grasp, comprehensive in its range, keen in its perceptions, and vigorous and quick in its actions, it possessed many of the qualities, had his early training been less imperfect, to constitute a master reasoner. His powers of thought were, as is common with men of mind, kept in constant activity. He loved thinking for its own sake; as the eagle delights in the exercise of its pinions, and cleaves the sky as it soars for the sole gratification arising from the use of its strength, so did he live in the habitual employment of his uncommon faculties. His love of truth was great; one of the rewards of this noble feeling was skill in the detection of errors. The calm, good temper – for he was never violent, and seldom severe – with which he would sometimes almost with a touch reduce to nothing the baseless fabric of some fond theorist, showed how little he had been perplexed by what to others seemed unanswerable. I have already observed that he loved truth – he promoted its interests with the zeal of a professed champion. He presented himself immoveable [*sic*] against all the assaults of his enemies; but he never used any weapons in its cause which candour and integrity would have disowned, nor stooped to the employment of artifice or concealment to obtain a temporary triumph. While firm to inflexibility in the maintenance of the great principles which he had espoused, he never indulged anything like uncharitable feeling towards those who differed from him.

"I must mention another quality of our departed friend, which is no ordinary advantage to the minister of Christ. He was naturally of a feeling heart, even to tenderness. No high abstractions ever removed him from the sphere of humanity. His relationship to the family of man was never forgotten. He had a good word for all with whom he came into contact. The law of kindness was on his tongue. He was the instructor, the friend, the helper, and father of his people. He pleaded in almost every large town in England the cause of the blind, the idiot, and the imbecile, and with such effect that it is not too much to say, as some one has already said, that many of those whose minds were blank, or worse, had some, at least, of the rational lineaments of manhood restored by his instrumentality. Not a few of such cases within his own neighbourhood he watched over from month to month, from year to year; and it rejoiced his heart to see the most desperate of human calamities capable of so much help. Always cheerful, often even to playfulness, in his most unbending hours he was guarded from unseemly levity, and was never unable, naturally and with grace, to enter upon religious conversation. In such conversation he was ever ready to engage, but the unaffected solemnity and deep feeling of his manner constantly indicated his conviction that the great realities of the spiritual life are to be treated with reverence and caution. It is almost unnecessary to say that, having once mastered the argument for the truth of Christianity as a Divine revelation, he held it with a firm and unyielding grasp. This was to be expected from the character of his mind; and the conclusions of his intellect were ever gaining strength from the exercise of his heart.

"The great doctrines of the Gospel, as a system of recovery and reconciliation, were ever in his thoughts. Upon them he built his own confidence, and invited others to reply. The fall of man, his moral impotency and contracted guilt, he regarded not as a matter of speculation, but as a fearful fact. The consequent necessity and adequate communication of spiritual influence, to enlighten, renew, and sanctify, occupied an equal place in his estimation. To the mighty principle of justification through faith his attachment was not inferior to that of Paul or Luther. And the atonement made by the blood of Christ was, in all its fulness and its freeness, the great centre of attraction to all his thoughts and all his affections. He was from conviction a member of the Church of England, and among all her sons there are few who loved her with more ardent affection, or who did her work with more unshaken fidelity; and he was her firmest unyielding champion against the attempts of the modern innovator [i.e., the Ritualists]. Attached to our Communion by the strongest ties, he resisted every endeavour to encumber her with foreign and meretricious decorations, and opposed every plan for unduly exalting her authority, as ultimately destructive of her real power. No pretence of antiquity consecrated, in his eyes, the superstitious puerilities of Rome; still more jealous was he over the purity of the doctrines of the English church. He applied from an early period the powers with which he was entrusted in the acquisition of knowledge, and trained them for its communication. If he was not 'enriched in all knowledge,' he possessed much general knowledge; and he was 'apt to teach.' Very many ministers of the Gospel have addressed themselves to their work with ampler stores of theological learning than he possessed, but few could turn the knowledge they had acquired to greater account. With the works of our great divines he had only a limited acquaintance. His mind was well saturated with Holy Scripture, and therefore, like Elihu, he was always 'full of matter.' That masculine understanding, that ponderous sense, the energy of that capacious heart, which were so conspicuous in his conversation, were visible in his preaching which, however, upon the whole was more luminous than searching, more remarkable for exhortation than for rebuke. He was not possessed of vehement and overpowering eloquence, but the earnestness of his delivery chained the attention of his hearers, and often produced a powerful impression. His addresses afforded no sentiments of surpassing grandeur or beauty which linger in the ear, as was the case in the sermons of one [?Rowland Hill] to whom he was nearly allied, and to whom, during his last days, he personally bore an increasingly striking resemblance. He embalmed no religious truths in immortal words. He had little imagination, and in pathos he was deficient. The peculiar charm of his public ministrations, besides their intrinsic excellence, was calmness and gravity. And though his voice was as powerful as it was melodious, nothing was violent. Like his own mind – all was equable and tranquil.

"Though our venerable friend had reached that period of life which constitutes old age, it was a fresh and green old age. Until the last two or three years age had impaired little or nothing of his vigour; its chief effect was that of imparting additional dignity to his countenance and of weight to his character. His span was prolonged beyond the common lot of man; his sun cannot seem to have gone down while it is still yet day who was permitted to number so many years. Life then seems to drop like the ripe and mellow fruit of autumn from the bending tree, and we reconcile ourselves the more easily to the event because it has taken place in its most natural season. The loss which the Church has sustained in his death is great; the loss to this town and neighbourhood probably will not be repaired. Severer still is their privation who had the claim which pastoral relationship gave them to his wise counsels and unfailing sympathy. As I have already said, the shepherd is taken from his flock, the sage adviser, the patron of the poor and destitute, whose countenance could not be beheld without tender veneration, is no more. The name of Edwin Sidney will long be associated with the parish of Cornard Parva, and the stranger will indulge a laudable curiosity in inspecting the place where he dwelt and the church where he exercised his ministry. Nearly two years have now elapsed since he addressed you from this place. Since then you have not seen him; but often and often has he expressed his regret that he had since been unable to do so.

Not four months past, in a letter I then received from him, he entertained a 'good hope' that he should yet again be permitted to ascend this pulpit; but his Heavenly Father, and ours, saw fit to disappoint that expectation, and to determine that he should instruct us from the tomb. That such would be the issue I felt assured, after a visit I paid him of nearly two hours' duration, some weeks ago. That day, or a day or two before, was 'the beginning of the end', and he felt it. From that time, in the largest significance of the phrase, I have reason to believe he shut out the world. Whatever interest he manifested in its concerns had a reference to those whom he loved and was leaving. He knew that he had done with it; that for him its 'fashion was passing away.' As was beautifully said of one under circumstances not unlike – he resembled a person embarked on a voyage to a distant country, and meeting at intervals with ships going home. What freights or passengers they carry affect him not; he employs them to send back letters and kind messages to his friends. He was outward-bound. His thoughts, during the intervals of ease from severe suffering, rested with anxious but humble curiosity upon the kingdom and people he was soon to live among. If ever Christianity appears in its power it is when it takes its votaries where the world leaves them, and fills the breast with immortal hopes in dying moments."

A suitable exhortation to the congregation concluded the sermon, which was listened to with the deepest interest, feeling and attention.

XXXVI JOHN SIKES 1874

Bury and Norwich Post, 28 April 1874, p. 8.

SUDBURY.

We have this week to record the death of one of the most respected inhabitants of this borough, John Sikes, who expired on Friday last at his residence in the Old Market-place, at the ripe age of three score years and ten. Mr. Sikes had been for many years a Justice of the Peace for the county of Suffolk, and he was also one of the oldest members of the Sudbury Lighting and Paving Commission, one of the Directors of the Suffolk Alliance Fire Office, &c.

For George Andrews see above, Introduction. W. W. Hodson was Sudbury's principal town historian in the nineteenth century.

Bury and Norwich Post, 5 May 1874, p. 8.

SUDBURY.

• • •

FUNERAL OF THE LATE MR. SIKES. – On Friday last the mortal remains of this respected gentleman were interred in the family vault near the south-east corner of the pleasantly situated churchyard of Little Cornard. The funeral procession arrived at the church at about one o'clock, and was met by a number of gentlemen and friends of the deceased, who stood on each side of the churchyard path as the mourners passed. These latter consisted of the Rev. T. Sikes (brother of the deceased), Rev. J. Sikes (nephew), Rev. G. Coldham, and Messrs. Carr, Churchill, Canham, Sicklemore, Yateman, Crabbe, G. W. Andrewes, Bevan and Lynch. The funeral service was read by the Rector, the Rev. J. Ambrose, and the coffin was placed above that of the deceased's first wife, who died in August, 1840. Amongst those who attended to pay a last tribute of respect to the memory of the deceased, were the Rev. J. B. Sparrow, Messrs. Grover, Harding, Westoby, G. Mumford, A. Mumford, J. Alexander, T. Fitch, N. Sparrow, H. W. Westropp, H. S. Adams, E. Baker, H. W. Welham, J. Ling, W. W. Hodson, Siggers, Griggs, Beaumont, &.c, and a number of parishioners of Great and Little Cornard. All the funeral arrangements were carried out by Mr. Geo. Bridgman, of Market-hill, Sudbury.

XXXVII ELIZA SIDNEY 1882

Bury and Norwich Post, 30 May 1882, p. 5.

DIED.

• • •

On the 27th inst, at Bulmer, near Sudbury, after a long illness borne with much patience, Mrs. SIDNEY, the beloved widow of the Rev. Edwin Sidney, so well known in Bury St. Edmund's [*sic*] and elsewhere as a genial lecturer on scientific subjects, and for his efforts in support of the Idiot Asylums of Earlswood and Essex Hall.

XXXVIIII *TERMINAT HORA OPUS* 1891

Suffolk and Essex Free Press, 1 July 1891, p. 5.

FUNERAL OF MR. GEO. MUMFORD, J.P., OF LITTLE CORNARD.

A quarter of a century back the primitive church of Cornard Parva, and the Rectory Barn, situate not far distant, were frequently visited by pilgrims from many a mile around. On Sunday afternoons the plain, unpretending village House of Prayer was frequently crowded with a deeply attentive congregation, largely made up of visitors from Sudbury, Bures, and neighbouring hamlets. And periodically the Rectory Barn was equally crowded with members of the Sudbury Agricultural Association and others to hear demonstrated lectures specially prepared for that association. At both places the main attraction was the well known popular and genial Rector, the Rev. Edwin Sidney, who, for the time lifted the retired village from obscurity, bringing to it such distinguished men as Professors Owen and Henslow, Lord Arthur Hervey, the Duke of Wellington, and other notabilities.

On these eventful occasions one prominent dignified form was invariably to be seen in near proximity to the beaming parson and lecturer, that of his churchwarden and personal friend, Mr. Geo. Mumford, who was usually accompanied by members of his family, as noticeable and affable as himself, and equally friends and workers for the parish, the church, and the schools. Rector and churchwarden have now passed away, and their place know[s] them no more. The one sleeps peacefully at the west end of the ancient, weather-worn tower of the church, where for so many years he faithfully preached the gospel of his Divine Master to "the rude forefathers of the hamlet," and the mortal remains of the other were deposited in sure and certain hope "of a joyful resurrection" at the east end of the same venerable building on Thursday last, in the family vault where some years ago, were buried his wife and one of his daughters. The scene was an unwonted one, for in this thinly populated parish, a funeral is of rare occurrence, and especially one so largely attended by friends and visitors desirous of doing honour to the memory of the departed.

The hearse and mourning coaches left Cawston [*sic*] Hall about half past one, passing through winding, narrow lanes, undulatory in character and bordered by the fresh foliage and bright field flowers of "leafy June," and by cottages embroidered with ivy, honeysuckle, and roses, whose little gardens were all aglow with the old-fashioned, sweet-scented flowers, that many of our poets love to describe in their most tuneful verse. There were four mourning coaches, the first containing Miss Mumford, daughter of the deceased; Mr. G. Edward Mumford, son; Miss Laura Mumford, daughter; and Dr. A. H. Mumford, son. In the second carriage were Mrs. Evans, daughter, and Messrs. Allan A. Sidney and Murray Mumford, sons. In the third coach were Mr. Wm. Garrad, son-in-law, and Mr. John Garrad, grandson, and in the fourth the servants and nurse. Passing past the drive past Peacock Hall, the residence of Mr. Allan Mumford, J.P., and the old high, cleanly shaven yew hedge, the procession halted at the churchyard gate, from whence the massive coffin was borne into the church and placed on high tressels in the chancel, by six workmen, who for years had been in the employ of the deceased. The corpse and mourners were met by the Rector, the Rev. J. C. Ambrose, who read the service in the church and at the grave. This was very plain and there was no singing of either psalm or hymn. There were plants in front of the stone reredos, and a white floral cross on the retable. The coffin was of polished oak, with brass furniture and bore the inscription:–

"George Mumford,
Died June 21st, 1891,
Aged 87 years."

The lid was completely covered with floral mementoes of affection from the sorrowing children, and sympathetic friends, among which were the following:–

"A loving remembrance from the children of Brook House;" "From Ada Mumford in affectionate remembrance;" "With deepest regret from W. T., and S. Springett and family;" "In most affectionate remembrance from Winifred, Guy, Nora, and Gerald Mumford." The shell and coffin were made, and the general arrangements excellently carried out by Messrs. Baker and Son, undertakers, Sudbury, under the personal direction of Mr. H. H. Baker.

Among the friends present were Rev. T. Lingard Green, Sudbury; Rev. J. Wilson Brown, Assington; (as representing the Committee of St. Leonard's Hospital, the deceased being for many years the Chairman) the Mayor of Sudbury, Mr. G. H. Grimwood; Mr. Alderman Whorlow, J.P., and Mr. G. Lancelot Andrewes, (as representatives of the Borough Justices); Mr. G. Coote, Mr. and Miss Lynch, Mr. W. Prigg, Mr. R. Taylor, Mr. and Mrs. N. Taylor, Mr. A. and Mrs. Segers, Mr. W. W. Hodson, Mr. J. Green, Wormingford, and a numbers [*sic*] of ladies and villagers. The day was fine and the weather very hot, but the breeze from the hill side and vale beneath, tempered the sultry heat and rustled the ancient venerable trees, which guard this secluded "God's acre."

APPENDIX I
Sermons and Offertories

For village and local historians brief details are offered below of some of Edwin Sidney's Suffolk and Essex occasional sermons – gala occasions in the histories of small communities.

Boxted (near Glemsford)

Essex Standard, 16 September 1853, 1st. ed., p. 4.

SUDBURY.

Tuesday, the 6th inst., being the re-opening of the parish Church, and the anniversary of the Sunday School, at Boxted, was quite a gala day in that pleasant village. There was a large attendance of the principal families in the neighbourhood at the hospitable mansion of J. G. W. Poley, Esq. A sermon in aid of the funds was preached by the Rev. Edwin Sidney, from 1 Chronicles xxix., 5 — *"Who then is willing to consecrate his service this day unto the Lord?"* The reverend gentleman's able and energetic appeal produced the liberal collection of £23.12.3½, and to this considerable addition was made by a fancy bazaar, and also by the sale of bouquets by the ladies, nominally priced at 6d. each, but which, from such attractive vendors and in so good a cause, were eagerly and gallantly purchased at 1s. The beautiful grounds of Boxted Hall afforded a delightful promenade to the company, and the day altogether was one of unmixed enjoyment. The children were plentifully regaled on the occasion, and a band of music still further enlivened the scene.

APPENDIX I

Bures

The distinguished firm of J. W. Walker & Sons Ltd, now of Brandon, Suffolk, was established in 1828.

Essex Standard, 9 July 1852, 1st. ed., p. 3.

> The Church of Bures St. Mary was densely crowded in the afternoon of Sunday last on the occasion of the opening of a new organ by Mr Walker, of London. ... [T]he sermon was preached by the Rev. Edwin Sidney, from 2 Chronicles xxix., 30 — *"Moreover Hezekiah the king and the princes commanded the Levites to sing praise unto the Lord with the words of David, and of Asaph the seer. And they sang praises with gladness, and [they] bowed their heads and worshipped."* [The sermon was four-part in structure, and contained a specific exhortation to contribute generously to the collection.] Never was a discourse heard with more intense attention; and the sum collected of £116.18.3½p., not by any one large donation, but by a uniform liberality according to the means of each, is the best proof of the effect it produced. We think the parish of Bures has done itself the highest credit; and the courtesy of the churchwardens and principal inhabitants, who quitted their own seats and stood in the aisles to accommodate the strangers who attended, was remarked by everyone. The organ was played by Miss Walker, daughter of the respectable builder, and supported by a choir from Colchester and the children of the parish schools.

Bury St Edmunds

'The nobleman, ever most forward' was the first marquess of Bristol (1767–1859), M.P. for Bury St Edmunds 1796–1803.

Bury and Norwich Post, 8 October 1851, p. 2.

> RESTORATION OF THE NORMAN TOWER. — The sermon preached by the Rev. Edwin Sidney, at St James's Church, on Thursday last, as a last appeal for the completion of this protracted and arduous work, was an impressive discourse upon

Hebrews ch. 3, v. 4 ['For every house is builded by some man: but he that built all is God']; and the appeal was so far successful as to produce the sum of 15*l*. 18*s*. 4*d*., of which sum we may be allowed to mention that 5*l*. was an offering of the nobleman, ever most forward in support of our local institutions and improvements, who on that same day completed his 82d [*sic*] year. There is still a deficiency in the funds to clear up the liabilities of the Committee.

Glemsford

Bury and Norwich Post, 25 October 1848, p. 3.

On Saturday last, a sermon, on occasion of the opening of a new organ, was preached in the parish Church of Glemsford, by the Rev. E. Sidney, from the 17th v. of the 28th c. of Ezekiel — *"Thou hast corrupted thy wisdom by reason of thy brightness,"* which he used to shew the worthlessness and the danger of education, if not founded upon religious instruction. The day was exceedingly unfavourable, but through the energetic and eloquent appeal of the reverend gentleman in behalf of the Sunday and National Schools, and that of a subsequent appeal by the Rev. G. Coldham, who placed the organ in the Church entirely at his own expence [*sic*], upwards of 14*l*. was collected — a large sum for the place. The organ was played by Mr. Ambrose [V], and the singing of the children reflected great credit upon their teachers. After divine service they (about 200 in number) repaired to the school-rooms, which were very prettily decorated for the occasion with dahlias and evergreens, where they were plentifully regaled with cake, wine, &c., their kind friends vieing with each other in contributing to their enjoyment.

Glemsford

Suffolk and Essex Free Press, 27 September 1860, p. 3.

LAYING THE FOUNDATION STONE OF THE TOWER OF GLEMSFORD CHURCH.

On Tuesday last the foundation stone of the tower of this ancient church, which had been pronounced in a dangerous condition and taken down, was laid amidst a large assemblage of the parishioners and a number of ladies and gentleman resident in the neighbourhood, as well as several who had come a considerable distance, arrangements having been made to render the occasion an edifying and solemn one, and to give due *éclât* to the interesting ceremony.

A laurel arch spanned the entrance gate, and crowns and other emblems composed of the same leafy material, were placed at conspicuous points, a number of boughs shading the spot where the stone hung poised in the air waiting to be lowered, laid, and then levelled by the fair hands of the lady [Mrs Starkie Bence, of Kentwell Hall, Long Melford] who had kindly undertaken the office. St. George's Ensign also floated from a staff, and the afternoon fortunately turning out fine after the copious showers of the morning, there was a very large number of people present.

Divine service was previously held in the church … the sermon preached by the Rev. Edwin Sidney, rector of Cornard Parva, who took his text from Nehemiah, chap. 2, part of the 20th verse, "The God of Heaven will prosper us; therefore we his servants will arise and build." The reverend gentleman preached a most excellent and suitable discourse with his accustomed eloquence and was listened to with devout attention. The church was very full, numbers sitting and standing in the aisles. Two appropriate hymns were sung, the committee at the conclusion taking up the collection, which amounted to the very handsome sum of £45.2s.4½d.

• • •

APPENDIX I

Great Cornard

'These useful schools' stood near the church, on the present site of Singleton Court.

Suffolk and Essex Free Press, 21 July 1864, p. 2.

DAY AND SUNDAY SCHOOLS. — A sermon in aid of the fund for carrying on these useful schools at Great Cornard was preached at Great Cornard Church, by the Rev. E. Sidney, on Sunday evening last. Prayers were read by the Rev. J. B. Sparrow, rector [*sic*]. The sermon was most appropriate for the occasion, and a collection amounting to 4*l*. 8*s*. 6*d*., in aid of the school funds was the response of the congregation. Mr. R. Ling, organist, of London, played the "Hallelujah Chorus" in an artistic style at the conclusion of the service.

Middleton

Essex Standard, 23 September 1853, 1st. ed., p. 2.

[Middleton church was reopened in September 1853, after extensive renovation and cleaning, and after the installation of a new organ. On Wednesday, 14 September, Sidney attended two services in the church, and preached at both. His first text was Psalm 96 viii, 'Bring an offering, and come into his courts'; his second, Psalm 93 v, 'Holiness becometh thine house, O Lord, for ever'.] The preacher on both occasions with his accustomed eloquence enforced the duty of maintaining suitable edifices for the worship of Almighty God. [The two collections totalled £28.12s.0d.]

APPENDIX I

Milden

Essex Standard, 6 August 1852, 1st. ed., p. 3.

OPENING OF THE ORGAN AT MILDEN. — The Rev. Edwin Sidney, whose powerful advocacy has during this summer twice before been exerted on a similar occasion, preached a sermon at the parish church of Milden, on Sunday evening, in aid of the fund for the erection of an organ. ... [His text was from] 12 v. of ii Hebrews, — *"In the midst of the church will I sing praise unto Thee."* The church, as well as the churchyard, was crowded, numbers being unable to obtain admission into the sacred edifice. [The collection was £11.]

Pentlow

Bury and Suffolk Herald, 8 September 1847, p. 2.

The Thirty-first Anniversary of the Pentlow Sunday School was held on Friday, the 27th ult. The Annual Sermon was preached by the Rev. Edwin Sidney, rector of Cornard Parva, from Proverbs 29th ch., 15th verse: — "A child left to himself bringeth his mother to shame." — The church was densely crowded, and the Sermon admirably adapted to the occasion. After divine service the children were regaled with cake and wine in the rectory grounds (which are of a very extensive character), and at the close of their repast, "Praise God from whom all blessings flow" having been sung, they received unlimited permission to amuse themselves in the grounds. The weather proved beautifully fine, and we doubt not but that the day will be long remembered as well by the children themselves as by those who were present on the occasion. The collection in aid of the funds amounted to £15.12s.

APPENDIX I

Essex Standard, 29 March 1854, p. 2.

PENTLOW. — The church of Pentlow, with its round tower and apse (chancel), is considered one of the most ancient and interesting in this county. Here it is that one of the first Sunday Schools in Essex was formed, and a carefully trained village choir has existed for fifty years. An old and imperfect organ was last week removed from the church, and a new one introduced, built by Mr. Robson, of the Apollonicon Rooms, in London. It contains nine stops, a general swell, an octave and half of German pedals, and an octave of Bourdon pedal pipes extending to CCC. This instrument was used for the first time on Friday last, and played very beautifully by Mr. William Ambrose [V], professor of music, of Sudbury. A considerable body of neighbouring clergy attended, and the church was filled. The prayers were read by the Rev. Charles Badham, Vicar of All Saints', Sudbury, when the sweet and powerful tones of the organ seemed most congenial to the solemnity of the service and the present season. The sermon was preached by the Rev. Edwin Sidney, Rector of Cornard [*sic*], from Psalm cl. 6 ['Let every thing that hath breath praise the Lord. Praise ye the Lord'], in which the spirituality of acceptable worship was duly inculcated. A collection was afterwards made, amounting to £14.18.1, in aid of the fund that had been previously raised in the parish.

APPENDIX II

Newspapers and the Reading Public

In 1812, Francis Jeffrey, editor of *The Edinburgh Review*, in praising Suffolk's poet George Crabbe for addressing his poems to the 'middling classes' of society said also that probably no fewer than 200,000 persons among those 'middling classes' then (1812) read for amusement or instruction, that in the 'higher classes' there were not as many as 20,000, and that 'a great part of the larger body are to the full as well educated and as high-minded as the smaller; and ... their sensibility is greater'. When in 1814 he republished these remarks, the former figure became 300,000, the latter 30,000. See Ian Jack, 'Tennyson, the poet and his audience', *The Times Higher Educational Supplement*, 11 June 1982, p. 16. Jeffrey surely offers us a clue as to why Edwin Sidney was often concerned that his lectures should be published in the newspapers.

In south-west Suffolk in early Victorian times a wide variety of local newspapers was available. Most were published weekly. Though their front pages generally contained little save advertisements, their other pages, closely printed, were replete with national and international as well as with local news. Frequently they reported in full the speeches and sermons of Church of England clergymen, and the speeches of other local worthies. Their extensive editorializing was often laden with apposite allusions to letters, philosophy, history, and the sciences.

In the 1840s probably the commonest local paper circulating in the Sudbury area (certainly it should be the first to be consulted by the historian of Sudbury for that period) was the moderately liberal

APPENDIX II

Bury and Norwich Post, which was founded in 1782, and which was published in Bury St Edmunds. The *Post* ran till Christmas day, 1931; thereafter it was incorporated with the *Bury Free Press* (founded 1855). Competing for some years with the *Post* was the conservative *Bury and Suffolk Herald* (1828), also published in Bury. On 2 January 1850 the *Herald* was devoured by its stronger rival. Also containing much news of Sudbury and district was the conservative *Essex Standard* (1831), published in Colchester. In 1892 the *Essex Standard* became the *Essex County Standard*, under which title it flourishes still. Published in Ipswich in the 1840s were the conservative *Ipswich Journal* (1720), the liberal *Suffolk Chronicle* (1810), and the liberal *Ipswich Express* (1839). The *Ipswich Journal* ceased publication in 1902. In 1899 the *Suffolk Chronicle* became the *Suffolk Chronicle and Mercury*, which in 1962 became the *Suffolk Mercury*. The *Ipswich Express* circulated chiefly in the east of Suffolk, but also in places near Sudbury, such as Hadleigh and Halstead; it was incorporated with the *East Anglian Daily Times* upon the latter's foundation in October 1874. The paper now (1998) running as the *Suffolk Free Press* has always been published in Sudbury, and since its foundation has always in a special sense been 'Sudbury's paper'. It first appeared on 5 July 1855 as the *Free Press and General Advertiser for West Suffolk and North Essex*. On 30 August 1855 it became the *West Suffolk and North Essex Free Press*, and remained so until on 19 June 1856 it appeared as the *Suffolk and Essex Free Press*. It became the *Suffolk Free Press* on 20 January 1949. From November 1857 to January 1859 there was also published in Sudbury the *Suffolk and Essex News*, a sister-paper to the *Suffolk and Essex Free Press;* it was published (still in Sudbury) as the *Essex and Suffolk News* from the latter date until its demise in December 1921.

It would be incautious to generalize too readily concerning which classes of early Victorian people in south-west Suffolk did or did not read which Suffolk and Essex newspapers. Certainly the poorest of the poor could hardly have afforded newspapers at all, priced as they were at four or five pence a copy, even after the abolition of the notorious newspaper stamp duty in 1855. In the *Suffolk and Essex Free Press* of 13 November 1862 (p. 2), it is recorded, however, that in that year the reading room of the Sudbury Literary and Mechanics' Institution supplied a most catholic assortment of twenty-one newspapers (national and local) and periodicals, including *The Times* (two copies), the *Morning Star*, the *Daily Telegraph*, the *Suffolk and Essex Free Press*, the *Essex Standard*, the *Bury and Norwich Post*, the *Suffolk Chronicle*, the *Ipswich Express*, the *Cambridge Chronicle*, the *Bury Free Press*, the *Illustrated News* (? the *Illustrated News of the World*), the *Illustrated Times*, *Punch*, and the *Launceston News* (?the *Launceston Weekly News*).

FURTHER READING

G. Kitson Clark, *Churchmen and the Condition of England, 1832–1885*, London 1973, concerns the social role of the Anglican clergy during the period covered by this book. But see also David Roberts, *Paternalism in Early Victorian England*, London 1979, especially ch. vi, 'The Shepherds and their Flocks'. For some impression of the Norfolk *milieu* of Edwin Sidney see Owen Chadwick, *Victorian Miniature*, London 1960.

The definitive contemporary account of Suffolk agricultural practice in the 1840s is William and Hugh Raynbird, *On the Agriculture of Suffolk*, London 1849.

For the scientific culture of the earlier part of the period see Morris Berman, *Social Change and Scientific Organisation: the Royal Institution, 1799–1844,* London 1978; and Jack Morrell and Arnold Thackray, *Gentlemen of Science: early years of the British Association for the Advancement of Science*, Oxford 1981. A succinct account of the relationship between science and religion in the early Victorian period is Owen Chadwick, *The Victorian Church*, part i, London, 2nd. ed. 1970, ch. viii, part 3, 'Genesis and Geology'. For the clergyman-scientist as victim of the advance of 'professionalized' science in later Victorian England, see Frank M. Turner, 'The Victorian conflict between Science and Religion: a professional dimension', *Isis*, vol. lxix, 1978, pp. 356-76. A well-illustrated survey of 'popular' natural history during the period is Lynn Barber, *The Heyday of Natural History, 1820-1870*, London 1980; but the text is not always reliable. A facsimile edition of the first edition (1844) of Robert Chambers' *Vestiges of the Natural History of Creation* was published by Leicester University Press in 1969, with an introduction by Sir Gavin de Beer. A notable modern contribution to 'catastrophist' theory is Michael Allaby and James Lovelock, *The Great Extinction*, London 1983 – a work severely criticised, however, at the 1983 annual meeting of the British Association for the Advancement of Science; see the *Daily Telegraph*, 25 August 1983, p. 7 and *The Times*, 25 August 1983, p. 1.

E. M. W. Tillyard, *The Elizabethan World Picture*, Harmondsworth 1972, discusses the Great Chain of Being and related matters. A good account of William Paley is M. L. Clarke, *Paley: evidences of the man*, London 1974. For Paley compared with Ray, see C. E. Raven, *Organic Design: a study of scientific thought from Ray to Paley*, London 1954. D. R. Oldroyd, *Darwinian Impacts: an introduction to the Darwinian revolution*, Milton Keynes 1980, places the achievements of Darwin in historical context. The only modern biography of Henslow is Jean Russell-Gebbett, *Henslow of Hitcham: botanist, educationalist and clergyman*, Lavenham 1977. But for Henslow as educator see David Layton, *Science for the People: the origins of the school science curriculum in England*, London 1973, ch. iii, 'John Stevens Henslow and Systematic Botany'.

Further Reading for Particular Items

III FIRE AT CAUSTONS HALL 1844

For the fate of Micklefield as a transportee see the Archives Office of Tasmania, CON 33/86. Norfolk Island as a penal colony is vividly described in Robert Hughes, *The Fatal Shore: a history of the transportation of convicts to Australia 1789–1868*, London ed. 1988, *passim*.

V ENLARGING A SACRED EDIFICE 1847, 1848

William Ambrose advertised in E. R. Kelly, ed., *The Post Office Directory of Suffolk,* London 1869, p. 914.

VI FOSSIL ELEPHANTS 1849

For fossil elephants and confused persons see Richard Owen, *A History of British Fossil Mammals and Birds,* London 1846, pp. 218ff. For Brown and the Felixstowe phosphates see *The London Geological Journal,* September 1846, pp. 17–20. The fullest account of the opening on 2 July 1849 of the railway from Marks Tey to Sudbury appears in the *Chelmsford Chronicle,* 6 July 1849, p. 2.

IX GEOLOGY AND FERTILISERS 1850, 1852

For the merits of farmyard manure relative to those of mineral fertilisers see John Bennet Lawes and J. H. Gilbert, 'On Agricultural Chemistry – especially in relation to the Mineral Theory of Baron Liebig', in *Journal of the Royal Agricultural Society of England,* vol. xii, 1851, pp. 1–9, reprinted in G. E. Mingay, ed., *The Agricultural Revolution: changes in agriculture 1650–1880,* London 1977, pp. 172–8. For guano see John Peter Olinger, 'The Guano Age in Peru', in *History Today,* June 1980, pp. 13–23. For the ruffled clergyman see Hugh Miller, *The Testimony of the Rocks,* Edinburgh 1857, ed. 1876, pp. 353-5. For Henslow, Owen, and the Felixstowe phosphates see Richard Owen, *History of British Fossil Mammals and Birds,* pp. 526, 535. Sidney's lecture to the Royal Institution is reported in the *Bury and Norwich Post,* 29 May 1844, p. 3. Erasmus Darwin's influence on Wordsworth is discussed in Desmond King-Hele, *Erasmus Darwin and the Romantic Poets,* Basingstoke 1986.

FURTHER READING

X   SILVER SALVER 1851

For Fulcher see C. G. Grimwood and S. A. Kay, *History of Sudbury, Suffolk*, Sudbury 1952, p. 119.

XVI   IN MEMORIAM 1857

Some account of Clutterbuck appears in Martin Harrison, *Victorian Stained Glass*, London 1980, pp. 14, 22, 35, 36.

XX   BRAMBLES AND CRINOLINES 1859

For the prince consort and the morals of the lower orders see Theodore Martin, *The Life of His Royal Highness the Prince Consort*, vol. iv, London 1879, p. 14. For crinolines see C. Willett Cunnington, *English Women's Clothing in the Nineteenth Century*, London 1937, pp. 170 ff.

XXII   FOR THE CHURCH MISSIONARY SOCIETY — FOUR LECTURES 1961, 1862, 1863, 1865

For Japan see *History Today*: C. R. Boxer, 'The Closing of Japan: 1636–1639', December 1956, pp. 830–9; C. R. Boxer, 'Sakoku, or the Closed Country: 1640–1854', February 1957, pp. 80–8; Carmen Blacker, 'The First Japanese Mission to England', December 1957, pp. 840–7; Henry McAleavy, 'The Meiji Restoration', September 1958, pp. 634–45; Henry McAleavy, 'The Making of Modern Japan', May 1959, pp. 297–307. For the colonial see of Victoria see *Crockford's Clerical Directory for 1860*, London 1860, p. 626; *The Clergy List for 1860*, London 1860, pp. 391, 392. For the Veitch family see James H. Veitch, *Hortus Veitchii: a history of the rise and progress of the nurseries of Messrs. James Veitch and Sons*, privately published, London 1906. For Victorian overseas plant-gathering in general see Tyler Whittle, *The Plant Hunters*, London 1970, and Peter Raby, *Bright*

Paradise: Victorian scientific travellers, London 1996, ch. v, 'The Plant-Hunters'. For missionary activity in the Pacific see K. L. P. Martin, *Missionaries and Annexations in the Pacific*, Oxford 1924. For summary histories of Tahiti, the Hawaiian Islands, and Madagascar see *Encyclopedia Britannica*, Chicago ed. 1970: vol. xxi, pp. 623, 624 (Tahiti); vol. xi, p. 177 (Hawaii); vol. xiv, p. 665 (Madagascar). For T. N. Staley, see T. N. Staley, *Five Years' Church Work in the Kingdom of Hawaii*, London 1868. For V. W. Ryan see V. W. Ryan, *Mauritius and Madagascar: journals of an eight years' residence in the diocese of Mauritius, and of a visit to Madagascar*, London 1864; W. M. Egglestone, *Bishop Ryan: a memorial sketch*, Stanhope 1889. For Ellis see John Ellis, *Life of William Ellis*, London 1873. For Hill on Ellis, see Edwin Sidney, *The Life of the Rev. Rowland Hill, A.M.*, London, 3rd. ed. 1835, pp. 165, 166.

XXIII   BURGLARS? 1852

For Arnold and the stuffed birds see G. W. E. Russell, ed., *Letters of Matthew Arnold 1848–1888*, 2 vols., London 1901, vol. i, pp. 31, 32, and the *Essex Standard*, 16 December 1870, p. 2.

XXV   WEDDING 1863

Queen Victoria's reproof to Archbishop Longley appears in Georgina Battiscombe, *Queen Alexandra*, London 1969, pp. 42, 43. Mr C. J. Simpson advertised in Kelly, *Directory of Suffolk*, 1969, p. 916; references to his singing and to his Conservatism appear in the *Suffolk and Essex Free Press, passim*.

XXVI   LECTURE TO JUVENILES 1863

For Pepper's Ghost see Geoffrey Lamb, *Victorian Magic*, London 1876, ch. iv.

FURTHER READING

XXVIII   HARVEST HOME 1860, 1864, 1865

Some useful discussion of the Victorian harvest festival appears in J. Obelkevich, *Religion and Rural Society: South Lindsey 1825–1875*, Oxford 1976, pp. 158–61. The question of who 'invented' the festival is considered in Owen Chadwick, *The Victorian Church*, part i, London 2nd. ed., 1970, p. 517. For medieval and Tudor agrarian jollifications see Thomas Tusser, *Five Hundred Points of Good Husbandry*, written in verse and originally published in 1573. (Tusser had once farmed at Cattawade, on the Suffolk side of the Stour estuary.) The harvest customs of Norfolk and Suffolk in the 1840s are described in graphic detail by the Raynbirds (see above, 'Further Reading'), pp. 305 ff. For John Impit Lushington see E. A. Goodwin and J. C. Baxter, eds., *East Anglian Verse*, Ipswich 1974, pp. 64, 65, 118, 119.

XXIX   VALUABLE PIONEERS AND COADJUTORS 1866

Thomas Prentice and Catherine Ridley are portrayed in Tim Jeal, *Livingstone*, Pimlico edition, London 1993, pp. 20, 21.

XXXII   MICHAEL FARADAY 1868

A notable biography of Faraday is L. Pearce Williams, *Michael Faraday*, London 1965. For the Royal Institution in the earlier nineteenth century see Morris Berman, *Social Change and Scientific Organization: the Royal Institution 1799–1844*, London 1978. 'Table-turning' is considered in Brian Inglis, *Natural and Supernatural: a history of the paranormal from earliest times to 1914*, London 1977, especially ch. xxiii. For Faraday's own account of his investigations into the matter see *The Times*, 30 June 1853, p. 8, and *The Athenaeum*, 2 July 1853, pp. 801–3. One renowned 'table-turner' who came to Faraday's attention was the acclaimed medium Daniel

Dunglas Home, for whom see Elizabeth Jenkins, *The Shadow and the Light: a defence of Daniel Dunglas Home, the medium*, London 1982.

XXXIII   MOVEMENTS IN ORGANIC LIFE 1869

A very short but very useful survey of the life and career of Langdon Down is Lord Brain, 'Chairman's Opening Remarks: historical introduction', in G. E. W. Wolstenholme and Ruth Porter, eds., *Mongolism: in commemoration of Dr John Langdon Haydon Down*, being papers delivered to the Ciba Foundation Study Group, no. 25, London 1967. For Down himself on mongolism see J. Langdon Down, *On Some of the Mental Affections of Childhood and Youth: being the Lettsomian Lectures delivered before the Medical Society of London in 1887, together with other papers*, London 1887.

XXXIV   UNAVOIDABLY PREVENTED: OR, CERTAIN CROTCHETY PEOPLE 1869

For Gainsborough Dupont see C. G. Grimwood and S. A. Kay, *History of Sudbury, Suffolk*, Sudbury 1952, pp. 50, 114, 126.

XXXV   EDWIN SIDNEY 1872

For Badham's fine see the *West Suffolk and North Essex Free Press*, 8 May 1856, p. 4.

XXXVI   JOHN SIKES 1874

For Andrewes and Hodson see C. G. Grimwood and S. A. Kay, *History of Sudbury, Suffolk*, Sudbury 1952, pp. 117, 119, 120.

INDEX

A

Abrey, W. 206
agrarian agitation and riots 32ff.
Addison, John 69–70
Albert, Prince, and schemes for museums 176
Alderson, Sir Edward Hall (Baron Alderson) 137, 142
Alexander, J. 235
Alexander, Mrs C. F. 17, 19–20, 31, 103
Almack, Mr 192, 193
Ambrose, William 146, 147
Anderson, Charles 227
Andrews, Mr & Mrs (Gainsborough painting) 236
Arabia and the Arabs 186–7
Archbold, John Frederick 188
Aristotle 43–5, 55
Arnold, Matthew 188
astronomers 56
Auberies 236

B

Badham, the Revd Charles 242
Bailey, the Revd J. 214
Baker, Hugh 25
Baldwin, Mary 174
Bane, Walter 23
Barnardiston, N. C. 159, 164, 226, 238
Bell, A. 206

Bell, Charles 206, 221
Bell, Frederick Charles 179
Bell, John 141, 168
Bell, jun., Charles 206
Bell, Maria 221
Berkeley, Miles 153
Berners, J. 159
Bevan, R. W., mayor of Sudbury 160
Bevan, W. R. 235
Bird, Mr (auctioneer) 135
Blair Warren, the Revd J. C. 160
Blake, William 17, 51, 155
Blythe, Ronald 18
Boileau, Sir John 13, 94, 100, 108
Borley, Frederick 142
Botwright, Edmund 142
Bridgman, Henry 25–6
Bridgewater Treatises 83ff.
Bright, John 33
British Association for the Advancement of Science 76, 79
British and Foreign Bible Society 185
Brock, William 211
Brontë, Emily 18–19
Brown, John, FGS 147
Brunel, 226
Buggs, James 206
Burke, Mr 227
Burke, Peter 237
Butler, Joseph 59–62, 68
Byng, the Revd Mr 160

INDEX

C

Carpenter and Westley, Messrs, opticians and suppliers of magic lanterns 157, 171, 205
Carrington, H. 206
Carter, Ellen 190, 200
catastrophism 81–2
Caustons Hall 27, 136–42; demolition of old Hall 29
'Cetotolites' 151
Chadwick, Owen 78, 156
Chambers, Robert 84, 86
Chantry, Sir Francis Legatt 177
Childs, Major Joseph 137
Christmas Juvenile Lectures, given by Michael Faraday 204
Church Missionary Society 110, 180
Church Missionary Society Lectures 180–7
Chuzzlewit, Anthony 18
Civil Registration Act 25
Clapham Sect 180
Clutterbuck, Charles 170
Cobbett, William 28
Coleridge, Samuel 155
Constable family 24
Constable, Nathan 24
Cook, James 226
Copley, John Singleton, 1st baron Lyndhurst 177
coprolites 151
Crabbe, George 42
crinoline petticoats 176–7
Cuvier, Georges 79, 81–3

D

Dante Alighieri 51–3
Darwin, Charles 12, 37ff., 62, 91, 93
Darwin, Erasmus, as poet 154–5

Darwinism 153; *see also* Darwin, Chas
Daubeny, Dr Charles 150
Davey, George 137
Davies, Peter 195, 198
Davy, Sir Humphry 76, 223
Dickens, Charles 17, 18, 19, 75, 83, 103, 109
Disraeli, Benjamin 209; D.'s *Coningsby* 209
Donne, John 42
Dowman, William 144
Down, John Langdon Haydon 13, 230–36; D. and 'degeneration' of human stock 232
'Down's syndrome' 230
Drain Tiles, auction of 220
Duffield, the Revd R. Dawson 148
Dupont, Gainsborough 164, 165, 237
Dupont, Sarah 237

E

Eastern Union railway 19
Eastern Counties railway 188
Edward Albert, prince of Wales (later Edward VII) 202
Edwick, Sarah 27
'electricians' 84–5
Ellis, the Revd William 185
Essex Hall, Colchester, Idiot Asylum 119–22; visit of 2nd duke of Wellington 169
Evans, George Ewart 22
Everett, Isaac 136–7, 142

F

Faraday, Michael 63, 75, 222–30
"Faraday's Saw" 228
Fearon, the Revd David Rose 160, 237

fertilisers, manufacture of 34, 150
Felixstowe phosphates 147, 150–52
Fitch family 186
Fitch, T. 203
Fitzroy, Capt. Robert, commander of HMS *Beagle*, 91
Flaubert's *Madame Bovary* 149
Forster, the Revd Mr 160
fossil elephant 147, 148
Foster, Catherine, hanging of 19
Fowke, the Revd Thorpe William 26
Francis, Emma Jane 28–9
Fulcher, George William 147, 155, 164

G

Gainsborough family 24
Gallant, Golding 28, 138
Game, Ambrose 205–7
Game, Arthur 206
Game, Henry 205–7
Gamp, Mrs 20
Garrad, J. 160, 186
General Medical Council 174
geology and fertilisers 149ff.
geological nomenclature 153
Geological Survey for England and Wales 147
Gibbs, Mr 165
Gillray, James 28
Gooday, Mr 190, 191, 192
Great Chain of Being 44–8, 68, 79–80, 233
Great Eastern railway 188
Great Exhibition (1851) 77, 176
Green, Joseph 194
Green, the Revd Mr 160
Greene, Mr (deputy coroner) 175

guano 151
Gunning, Mr 141
Gurdon, John 168
Gurdon, Mr (counsel) 138

H

Hale, Mr 197
Halifax family 160
Hallward, the Revd N. W. 187, 192
Hammond, Robert 142
Hanuš's astronomical clock in Prague 51
Harris, Norman 204
Harvest Home at Cornard 214
Henley, the Revd Mr 160
Henslow, John Stevens 86, 91–4, 99, 107–8, 150–51, 154, 158, 218; H.'s *Report on the Diseases of Wheat* 152
Herbert, George 31, 61
Hervey, Frederick Augustus 4th earl of Bristol 104–5
Hervey, the Revd Lord Arthur 106–7, 146, 159, 164
Higgs, S. 186
Hill family of Shropshire 98–9
Hill, Lord 167
Hill, the Revd Rowland 98, 185
Hills, J. 227
Hitchcock, John 144
Hitler, Adolf, and eugenics 232
Holiday, Henry, *Dante and Beatrice* 51–2
Holland, Charles 199
Holland, James 199
Howlet, Mr 139
Hum, John 143–4
Hume, Joseph 141
Huxley, Thomas Henry 96, 97, 234

INDEX

I
incendiarism in East Anglia 33–6
Ion, J. W. I. 206
Isaacson & Tattersall, auctioneers 135
Ipswich Museum 93–5
Islands of the Pacific 182–4

J
Jacob, Samuel 142
Jaggs, John 140
Japan 180, 182; J.'s isolation 180
Johnson family, of Lavenham 160
Jones, Jacob 206
Jonson, Ben 209

K
Keats, John 70, 155
Keeble, Daniel 189–94
Kilvert, the Revd Francis 11
King, William Doubleday 188
Kingsley, Charles 233; K.'s *The Water Babies*
Kirby, the Revd Mr 160
Kirby, William 154
Kirchhoff, Gustav 109

L
Ladd, 227
Lamarck, the Chevalier de 79–81
Lankester, James 142
Layzell, Sarah 24
Leffley, Robert John 190, 196, 198
Lefley & Sons, Ltd., fishmongers and greengrocers 187
Liebig, Justus von 151
Linnean Society 79
Livingstone, David 218–19
London Missionary Society, at Ongar, in Essex 218

Longley, Archbishop 202
Lorkin, *see* Lorking
Lorking family 24
Lorking, George 139, 174–5
Lorking, William 139, 140, 174
Lushington, John Impit (alias 'Quill') 210
Lyell, Sir Charles 79, 82–3, 93, 153
Lynch, John Cox (surgeon) 207

M
Macaulay, Thomas Babington, Lord 12
Madagascar 184–6
magic lantern 171
Mainard (Maynard), Frances, w. of Robert Gainsborough 24
Marcet, Mrs Jane 225, 227
Mason, W. 160
Meeking, Thomas 164
Micklefield, James 12, 28, 136–43
Mitchell, George 198
Molyneux, the Revd John 124, 202
Morse's Road 206
Mose, Alfred 207
Moss family 25
Moss, William and Kezia 25
'Mosses Road' 25
Mower, Isaac 219
Mumford family 27–8, 186, 217
Mumford, Allan 205–6
Mumford, George 13, 27, 137–41, 203, 206, 235, 238, 249
Mumford, Sidney Lugar 27
Mumford, the Revd H. 217–18
Mumford, W. L. 201
Murillo, Bartolomé Esteban 170–1

N

Negretti and Zambra, Messrs, manufacturers of cameras and scientific instruments 181
newspapers 260–2
Newton, Isaac 65
Newman, John Henry 96
Nightingale, Charles 102, 108, 133
Norman, Charles 189, 194–201

O

Oersted, Hans Christian 227
Opie, Amelia 102
Origen 50
Origin of Species, *see* Charles Darwin
Ottley, the Revd Lawrence 19
Owen, Sir Richard 86–91, 151
Oxford Movement 122

P, Q

Paley, William 72–4, 77
Parker, Sir William 187, 192
Partridge, G. A. 168
Peacock Hall 29, 36; sale of 135
Peacock Hall Estate, fire at 149
Pellew, the Hon. George, dean of Norwich 156, 159
Pepper, John H. 204
'Pepper's Ghost' 204–5
Perry, Commodore, visit to Tokyo 180
Pharmaceutical Society 230
philosophes 65–7
phosphate of lime used as agricultural fertiliser 150
Piper, Alfred 189–201
Piper, George 189, 195, 197
Plato 42ff, 57
Playle, Lydia 198

Pochin family 26
Pochin, William 26, 174
Poley, J. 159
Pomare II, king of Tahiti 183
Poor Law system 35
Pope, Alexander 68–9
Prentice, Thomas and Manning 218
Prospect House 29, 189
Ptolemy 44
'Puseyism' in Sudbury 123–6
Pythagoras 43
'Quill', *see* Lushington

R

Radàma I, king of Madagascar 184
Radàma II, king of Madagascar 185
Railway, Eastern Union 19
Rànavàlona, queen of Madagascar 184
Randall, Layzell Hicks 137, 142
Raven, Charles 37
Ray, John 57–9, 64–5, 75
Raymond, the Revd Oliver 237, 240
Rayner family 24
Rayner, William 23–4
rectory barn 156
Regulation of Railways Act 1844 168
Ridley, Anne, Catherine and Susanna 218
ritualism, *see* 'Puseyism'
Roberts, the Revd Mr 160
Robinson, the Revd Mr 160
Rogers, James 189, 200
Rolfe, W. R. 220
Rossetti, Dante Gabriel 51
Rowley, Lady 159
Royal Institution of Great Britain. 223, 229
Royal Polytechnic Institution 204

INDEX

Royal Society of London 223
Rudwick, J. S. 153
Ryan, Vincent William, bp of Mauritius 185

S

Sach, Superintendent 189
Sandalls, Mr 139
Sandeman, Robert, and Sandemanianism 223
Scholefield, Inspector 189
Scott family 24
Seagrave, Mr 204
Sedgwick, Adam 72, 75–6, 99
Segers family 29–30
Segers, Alfred 206
Segers, Henry 27, 206, 221
Segers, Samuel 206
Segers, Sarah 221
Shelley, Percy Bysshe 71, 155
Sidney, the Revd Edwin 96–133, 145, 148, 154; S.'s agricultural lectures 156; S. and geology 152; S.'s lecture on diseases of wheat to Royal Institution 152; S.'s 'Lectures to Juveniles' 204; S.'s death 240
Siggers (Segers?) 139
Sikes, John 19, 27, 160, 165, 170, 187, 203, 227, 247–8
Simpson, C. J. 202–3
Smith, Bestoe 168
Smith, George, bp of Hong Kong 181
Smith, W. B. 170
Society for the Propagation of the Gospel 110
Sparrow family 29
Sparrow, J. R. 217

Sparrow, John Newman 27, 29, 169, 175, 189
Sparrow, Newman 12, 135, 186, 203
Sparrow, the Revd J. B. 186
spiritualism ('table-turning') 225
Springett family 23
Staley, Thomas Nettleship, bp of Honolulu 183
Stanley, Edward, bp of Norwich 94, 100
Stark, A. R. 189
Starke, Celia 200
Stephenson, George 226
stetch 179
Strutt, R. 200
Sudbury Agricultural Association 27, 127, 129, 131–2, 176, 178, 238–9
Sudbury Literary and Mechanics' Institution 108, 126, 226
Sudbury Volunteer Rifle Corps 211
Swift, Jonathan 172
Sykes, *see* Sikes
Sylvester, Charles 199
Symmons, Mr (surgeon) 175

T

Tahiti 183
Taylor, Newman 206
Tennyson, Alfred Lord 78
Tovell, Mr 190
Trevelyan, G. M. 28
Turner, Martin 142
Turner, William 206

U

uniformitarianism 80, 153
Upson, Samuel 189

V

Valdes' *Rhetorica Christiana* 47
Vaughan, Eliza (Mrs Edwin Sidney) 102, 249
Veitch, James 181
Veitch, John Gould 181, 182

W

Wakelin, J. 206, 207
Wates, Percy John 189, 193
Weightman, the Revd Mr 160
Wellington, 2nd duke of 169
Wellington, Arthur Wellesley, 1st duke of 167
West Suffolk Society for the Improvement of the Condition of the Labourers 36
Whybrew, Mr 238
Whyett, Benjamin 25
Wilberforce, William 180
Williams, John, M.D. 230, 234
Williams, Sir John 136, 137, 142
Woodforde, 'Parson' 11
Woods, John 137
Wordsworth, Christopher, bp 53
Wordsworth, William 71–2, 155
Wyatts 25

Y

Yelloly, F. T. 160